SUBHASH CHANDRA BOSE AND FREEDOM

SUBHASH CHANDRA BOSE AND FREEDOM

Dharam C. Vyas

CYBER TECH PUBLICATIONS
4264/3, Ansari Road, Daryaganj, New Delhi-110002 (India)
Ph.: 011-23244078, 011-43559448 Fax: 011-23280028
E-Mail: cyberpublicationsdelhi@yahoo.com
Website: www.cybertechpublications.com

SUBHASH CHANDRA BOSE AND FREEDOM

Dharam C. Vyas

First Edition 2010

Published by : Asian Offset Printers

G.S. Rawat for **Cyber Tech Publications**
4264/3, Ansari Road, Daryaganj, New Delhi-110002 (India)
Ph.: 011-23244078, 011-43559448 Fax: 011-23280028
E-Mail: cyberpublicationsdelhi@yahoo.com
Website: www.cybertechpublications.com

Preface

Subhas Chandra Bose, popularly known as Netaji was an outstanding leader of the Indian National Movement. The life of Subhas reads like a thrilling saga of most dramatic events. Subhas was truly the greatest hero of India's struggle for freedom.

Subhas Chandra Bose was born on 23 January, 1897 at Cuttack in Orissa. Subhas was almost hypnotized by Swami Vivekananda's teachings "seek your salvation in the welfare of humanity." He had found his ideal to which he could devote his whole being. He graduated from the Calcutta University and qualified for the Indian Civil Service. This led to mental conflicts as to whether or not he should join the coveted heaven born service. At last he resigned his attractive career to serve the cause of India's freedom. Subhas Chandra Bose had joined the non-cooperation movement and since then had been a promising dynamic young man of the Congress organization. Yet he nurtured revolutionary ideas and was never really-fully happy with Gandhiji's philosophy and technique of political agitations. He was convinced that India could not achieve independence without foreign assistance. INA was the last major attempt made by Subhas Chandra Bose on a foreign soil in a bid to Free India from British Yoke. He could not adjust himself with the Congress High Command and formed a new party known as the forward bloc. In 1941 he was under strict surveillance of the government at his own house at Calcutta. From there he suddenly slipped away from India and through north-east frontier and Afghanistan reached Germany. There he launched himself on a new course of political career.

This outstanding book in two volumes studies the ideas, vision and struggle of Netaji Subhas Chandra Bose for India's freedom

— *Author*

CONTENTS

1

BOSE: INTRODUCTION TO EARLY LIFE

Subhash Chandra Bose, generally known as Netaji (lit. "Respected Leader"), was one of the most prominent and highly respected leaders of the Indian Independence Movement against the British Raj. Bose was elected president of the Indian National Congress for two consecutive terms but resigned from the post following ideological conflicts with Mahatma Gandhi. Bose believed that Mahatma Gandhi's tactics of nonviolence would never be sufficient to secure India's independence, and advocated violent resistance. He established a separate political party, the All India Forward Bloc and continued to call for the full and immediate independence of India from British rule. He was imprisoned by the British authorities eleven times.

His stance did not change with the outbreak of the second world war, which he saw as an opportunity to take advantage of British weakness. At the outset of the war, he fled India and travelled to the Soviet Union, Germany and Japan seeking an alliance with the aim of attacking the British in India.

With Japanese assistance he reorganised and later led the Indian National Army, formed from Indian prisoners-of-war and plantation workers from Malaya, Singapore and other parts of Southeast Asia, against British forces. With Japanese monetary, political, diplomatic and military assistance, he formed the Azad Hind Government in exile, regrouped and led the Indian National Army to battle against the allies in Imphal & Burma during the World War II.

His political views and the alliances he made with Nazi and other militarist regimes opposed to the British Empire have been the cause of arguments among historians and politicians, with some accusing him of Fascist sympathies and of Quislingist actions, while most others in India largely sympathetic towards his inculcation of realpolitik as a manifesto that guided his social and political choices. He is believed to have died on 18 August 1945 in a plane crash over Taiwan. However, contradictory evidence exists regarding his death in the accident.

EARLY LIFE

Subhash Chandra Bose was born in 1897 to an affluent Bengali family in Cuttack, Orissa in India. His father, Janakinath Bose, was a public prosecutor who believed in orthodox nationalism, and later became a member of the Bengal Legislative Council. Bose was educated at Ravenshaw Collegiate School, Cuttack, Scottish Church College, Calcutta and Fitzwilliam College at Cambridge University. In 1920, Bose took the Indian Civil Services entrance examination and was placed fourth with highest marks in English. However, he resigned from the prestigious Indian Civil Service in April 1921 despite his high ranking in the merit list, and went on to become an active member of India's independence movement. He joined the Indian National Congress, and was particularly active in its youth wing. Still, Bose's ideals did not match those of Mahatma Gandhi's single belief in nonviolence. He therefore returned to Calcutta to work under Chittaranjan Das, the Bengali freedom fighter and co-founder (with Motilal Nehru) of the Swaraj Party.

In 1921, Bose organised a boycott of the celebrations to mark the visit of the Prince of Wales to India, which led to his imprisonment. In April 1924, Bose was elected to the post of Chief Executive Officer of the newly constituted Calcutta Corporation, In October that year, Bose was arrested on suspicion of terrorism. At first, he was kept in Alipore Jail and later he was exiled to Mandalay in Burma (where earlier Bal Gangadhar Tilak had spent 6 years in prison). On January 23,

1930, Bose was once again arrested for leading an "independence procession", protesting against British rule in India. After his release from jail on September 25, he was elected as the Mayor of the City of Calcutta.

Over a span of 20 years, Bose was incarcerated eleven times by the British, either in India or in Rangoon. During the mid 1930s he was exiled by the British from India to Europe, where he championed India's cause and aspiration for self-rule before gatherings and conferences.

After his father's death, the British authorities allowed him to land at Calcutta's airport only for the religious rites, which would be followed by his swift departure. He travelled extensively in India and in Europe before stating his political opposition to Gandhi. During his stay in Europe from 1933 to 1936, he met several European leaders and thinkers. He came to believe that India could achieve political freedom only if it had political, military and diplomatic support from outside, and that an independent nation necessitated the creation of a national army to secure its sovereignty.

Subhash Chandra Bose married Emilie Schenkl, an Austrian born national, who was his secretary, in 1937. According to Schenkl, she and Bose were secretly married in Bad Gastein on 26 December 1937. They had one daughter, Anita, born in 1942. Bose wrote many letters to Schenkl during the period 1934–1942, of which many have been published in the book *Letters to Emilie Schenkl*, edited by Sisir Kumar Bose and Sugata Bose.

Bose became the president of the Haripura Indian National Congress in 1938, against Gandhi's wishes. Gandhi commented "Pattavi's defeat is my own defeat. Anyway, Subhash Bose is not an enemy of the country". Gandhi's continued opposition led to the latter's resignation from the Working Committee, and the possibility that the rest of the CWC would resign. In the face of this gesture of no-confidence, Bose himself resigned, and was left with no alternative but to form an independent party, the All India Forward Bloc. Bose also initiated the concept of the *National Planning Committee* in 1938.

ACTIONS DURING THE II WORLD WAR

Bose advocated the approach that the political instability of wartime Britain should be taken advantage of—rather than simply wait for the British to grant independence after the end of the war (which was the view of Gandhi, Nehru and a section of the Congress leadership at the time). In this, he was influenced by the examples of Italian statesmen Giuseppe Garibaldi and Giuseppe Mazzini. His correspondence reveals that despite his clear dislike ...for British subjugation, he was deeply impressed by their methodical and systematic approach and their steadfastly disciplinarian outlook towards life. In England, he exchanged ideas on the future of India with British Labour Party leaders and political thinkers like Lord Halifax, George Lansbury, Clement Attlee, Arthur Greenwood, Harold Laski, J.B.S. Haldane, Ivor Jennings, G.D.H. Cole, Gilbert Murray and Sir Stafford Cripps.

He came to believe that a free India needed Socialist authoritarianism, on the lines of Turkey's Kemal Atatürk, for at least two decades. Bose was refused permission by the British authorities to meet Mr. Ataturk at Ankara for political reasons. It should be noted that during his sojourn in England, only the Labour Party and Liberal politicians agreed to meet with Bose when he tried to schedule appointments. Conservative Party officials refused to meet Bose or show him the slightest courtesy due to the fact that he was a politician coming from a colony, but it may also be recalled that in the 1930s leading figures in the Conservative Party had opposed even Dominion status for India. It may also be observed here that it was during the regime of the Labour Party (1945-1951), with Attlee as the Prime Minister, that India gained independence.

THE ESCAPE

On the outbreak of war, Bose advocated a campaign of mass civil disobedience to protest against Viceroy Lord Linlithgow's decision to declare war on India's behalf without consulting the Congress leadership. Having failed to persuade Gandhi of the necessity of this, Bose organised mass protests in Calcutta calling for the 'Holwell Monument' commemorating the Black Hole of Calcutta, which then stood at the corner of Dalhousie Square, to be removed. A reasonable measure of the contrast between Gandhi and Bose is captured in a saying attributable to him: "If people slap you once, slap them twice". He was thrown in jail by the British, but was released following a seven-day hunger strike. Bose's house in Calcutta was kept under surveillance by the CBI, but their vigilance left a good deal to be desired. With two court cases pending, he felt the British would not let him leave the country before the end of the war. This set the scene for Bose's escape to Germany, via Afghanistan and the Soviet Union. Bose had never been to Afghanistan, and could not speak the local tribal language (Pashto).

Bose escaped from under British surveillance at his house in Calcutta. On January 19, 1941, accompanied by his nephew Sisir K. Bose, Bose gave his watchers the slip and journeyed to Peshawar. With the assistance of the Abwehr, he made his way to Peshawar where he was met at Peshawar Cantonment station by Akbar Shah, Mohammed Shah and Bhagat Ram Talwar. Bose was taken to the home of Abad Khan, a trusted friend of Akbar Shah's. On 26 January 1941, Bose began his journey to reach Russia through India's North West frontier with Afghanistan. For this reason, he enlisted the help of Mian Akbar Shah, then a Forward Bloc leader in the North West Frontier Province. Shah had been out of India *en route* to the Soviet Union, and suggested a novel disguise for Bose to assume. Since Bose could not speak one word of Pashto, it would make him an easy target of Pashto speakers working for the British. For this reason, Shah suggested that Bose act deaf and dumb, and let his beard grow to mimic those of the tribesmen.

Supporters of the Aga Khan helped him across the border into Afghanistan where he was met by an Abwehr unit posing as a party of road construction engineers from the Organization Todt who then aided his passage across Afghanistan via Kabul to the border with Soviet Russia. Once in Russia the NKVD transported Bose to Moscow where he hoped that Russia's traditional enmity to British rule in India would result in support for his plans for a popular rising in India. However,

Bose found the Soviets' response disappointing and was rapidly passed over to the German Ambassador in Moscow, Count vonder Schulenburg. He had Bose flown on to Berlin in a special courier aircraft at the beginning of April where he was to receive a more favourable hearing from Joachim von Ribbentrop and the Foreign Ministry officials at the Wilhelmstrasse.

ATTEMPTS OF ASSASSINATION

In 1941, when the British learned that Bose had sought the support of the Axis Powers, they ordered their agents to intercept and assassinate Bose before he reached Germany. A recently declassified intelligence document refers to a top-secret instruction to the Special Operations Executive (SOE) of British intelligence to murder Bose. In fact, the plan to liquidate Bose has few parallels, and appears to be a last desperate measure against a man who had thrown the British Empire into a panic.

In Germany

Having escaped incarceration at home by assuming the guise of a Pashtun insurance agent ("Ziaudddin") to reach Afghanistan, Bose travelled to Moscow on the passport of an Italian nobleman "Count Orlando Mazzotta". From Moscow, he reached Rome, and from there he travelled to Germany, where he instituted the Special Bureau for India under Adam von Trott zu Solz, broadcasting on the German-sponsored Azad Hind Radio. He founded the *Free India Centre* in Berlin, and created the Indian Legion (consisting of some 4500 soldiers) out of Indian prisoners of war who had previously fought for the British in North Africa prior to their capture by Axis forces. The Indian Legion was attached to the Wehrmacht, and later transferred to the Waffen SS; its members swore their allegiance to both Hitler and Bose to secure India's independence. He was also, however, prepared to envisage an invasion of India via the U.S.S.R. by Nazi troops, spearheaded by the Azad Hind Legion; many have questioned his judgment here, as it seems unlikely that the Germans could have been easily persuaded to leave after such an invasion, which might also have resulted in an Axis victory in the War.

The lack of interest shown by Hitler in the cause of Indian independence eventually caused Bose to become disillusioned with Hitler and he decided to leave Nazi Germany in 1943. Bose had been living together with his wife Schenkl in Berlin from 1941 until 1943, when he left for southeast Asia. He travelled by the German submarine *U-180* around the Cape of Good Hope to Imperial Japan (via Japanese submarine *I-29*). Thereafter the Japanese helped him raise his army in Singapore. This was the only civilian transfer across two submarines of two different navies in World War II.

SOUTH-EAST ASIA

Indian National Army

The Indian National Army (INA) was originally founded by Capt. Mohan Singh in Singapore in September 1942 with Japan's Indian POWs in the Far East. This was along the concept of-and with support of-what was then known as the Indian Independence League, headed by expatriate nationalist leader Rash Behari Bose.

The first INA was however disbanded in December 1942 after disagreements between the Hikari Kikan and Mohan Singh, who came to believe that the Japanese High Command was using the INA as a mere pawn and Propaganda tool. Mohan Singh was taken into custody and the troops returned to the Prisoner-of-War camp.

However, the idea of a liberation army was revived with the arrival of Subhash Chandra Bose in the Far East in 1943. In July, at a meeting in Singapore, Rash Behari Bose handed over control of the organisation to Subhash Chandra Bose. Bose was able to reorganise the fledging army and organise massive support among the expatriate Indian population in southeast Asia, who lent their support by both enlisting in the Indian National Army, as well as financially in response Bose's calls for sacrifice for the national cause. At its height it consisted of some 85,000 regular troops, including a separate women's unit, the Rani of Jhansi Regiment (named after Rani Lakshmi Bai), which is seen as a first of its kind in Asia.

Even when faced with military reverses, Bose was able to maintain support for the Azad Hind movement. Spoken as a part of a motivational speech for the Indian National Army at a rally of Indians in Burma on July 4, 1944, Bose's most famous quote was "Give me blood, and I shall give you freedom!". In this, he urged the people of India to join him in his fight against the British Raj. Spoken in Hindi, Bose's words are highly evocative. The troops of the INA were under the aegis of a provisional government, the Azad Hind Government, which came to produce its own currency, court and civil code, and was recognised by nine Axis states—Germany, Japan, Italy, the Independent State of Croatia, Wang Jingwei's Government in Nanjing, Thailand, a provisional government of Burma, Manchukuo and Japanese-controlled Philippines. Recent researches have shown that the USSR too had recognised the "Provisional Government of Free India". Of those countries, five were authorities established under Axis occupation. This government participated as a delegate or observer in the so-called Greater East Asia Co-Prosperity Sphere.

The INA's first commitment was in the Japanese thrust towards Eastern Indian frontiers of Manipur. INA's special forces, the Bahadur Group, were extensively involved in operations behind enemy lines both during the diversionary attacks in Arakan, as well as the Japanese thrust towards Imphal and Kohima, along with the Burmese National Army led by Ba Maw and Aung San. A year after the islands were taken by the Japanese, the Provisional Government and the INA were established in the Andaman and Nicobar Islands with Lt. Col. A.D Loganathan appointed its Governor General. The islands were renamed *Shaheed* (Martyr) and *Swaraj* (Self-rule). However, the Japanese Navy remained in essential control of the island's administration. During Bose's only visit to the islands in late in 1943, when he was carefully screened from the local population by the Japanese authorities, who at that time were torturing the leader of the Indian Independence League on the Islands, Dr. Diwan Singh (who later died of his injuries, in the Cellular Jail). The islanders made several attempts to alert Bose to their plight, but apparently without success. Enraged with the lack of administrative control, Lt. Col Loganathan later relinquished his authority to return to the Government's head quarters in Rangoon.

On the Indian mainland, an Indian Tricolour, modelled after that of the Indian National Congress, was raised for the first time in the town in Moirang, in Manipur, in northeastern India. The towns of Kohima and Imphal were placed under siege by divisions of the Japanese, Burmese and the *Gandhi* and *Nehru* Brigades of I.N.A. during the attempted invasion of India, also known as Operation U-GO. However, Commonwealth forces held both positions and then counter-attacked, in the process inflicting serious losses on the besieging forces, which were then forced to retreat back into Burma.

Bose had hoped that large numbers of soldiers would desert from the Indian Army when they would discover that INA soldiers were attacking British India from the outside. However, this did not materialise on a sufficient scale. Instead, as the war situation worsened for the Japanese, troops began to desert from the INA. At the same time Japanese funding for the army diminished, and Bose was forced to raise taxes on the Indian populations of Malaysia and Singapore, sometimes extracting money by force. When the Japanese were defeated at the battles of Kohima and Imphal, the Provisional Government's aim of establishing a base in mainland India was lost forever. The INA was forced to pull back, along with the retreating Japanese army, and fought in key battles against the British Indian Army in its Burma campaign, notable in Meiktilla, Mandalay, Pegu, Nyangyu and Mount Popa. However, with the fall of Rangoon, Bose's government ceased be an effective political entity. A large proportion of the INA troops surrendered under Lt. Col Loganathan when Rangoon fell. The remaining troops retreated with Bose towards Malaya or made for Thailand. Japan's surrender at the end of the war also led to the eventual surrender of the Indian National Army, when the troops of the British Indian Army were repatriated to India and some tried for treason... His other famous quote was, "Delhi chalo", meaning "On to Delhi!". This was the call he used to give the INA armies to motivate them. "Jai Hind", or, "Glory to India!" was another slogan used by him and later adopted by the Government of India and the Indian Armed Forces.

Disappearance and Alleged Death

Officially, Bose died in a plane crash over Taiwan, while flying to Tokyo on 18 August 1945. However, his body was never recovered, and many theories have been put forward concerning his possible survival. One such claim is that Bose actually died in Siberia, while in Soviet captivity. Several committees have been set up by the Government of India to probe into this matter. In May 1956, a four-man Indian team (known as the Shah Nawaz Committee) visited Japan to probe the circumstances of Bose's alleged death. The Indian government did not then request assistance from the government of Taiwan in the matter, citing their lack of diplomatic relations with Taiwan.

However, the Inquiry Commission under Justice Mukherjee, which investigated the Bose disappearance mystery in the period 1999-2005, did approach the Taiwanese government and obtained information from the Taiwan Government that no plane carrying Bose had ever crashed in Taipei. The Mukherjee Commission also received a report originating from the US State Department, supporting the claim of the Taiwan Government that no such air crash took place during that time frame. The Mukherjee Commission submitted its report to the Indian Government on November 8, 2005. The report was tabled in Parliament on May 17, 2006. The probe said in its report that Bose did not die in the plane crash and the ashes at Renkoji temple are not his. However, the Indian Government rejected the findings of the Commission.

Political Views

Bose's earlier correspondence (prior to 1939) also reflects his deep disapproval of the racist practices of, and annulment of democratic institutions in Nazi Germany. He also, however, expressed admiration for the authoritarian methods (though not the racial ideologies) which he saw in Italy and Germany during the 1930s, and thought they could be used in building an independent India.

Bose had clearly expressed his belief that democracy was the best option for India. The pro-Bose thinkers believe that his authoritarian control of the Azad Hind was based on political pragmatism and a post-colonial recovery doctrine rather than any anti-democratic belief.. However, during the war (and possibly as early as the 1930s) Bose seems to have decided that no democratic system could be adequate to overcome India's poverty and social inequalities, and he wrote that an authoritarian state, similar to that of Soviet Russia (which he had also seen and admired) would be needed for the process of national rebuilding. Accordingly some suggest that Bose's alliance with the Axis during the war was based on more than just pragmatism, and that Bose may have been a Fascist, though not a Nazi; alternatively, others consider he might have been using populist methods of mobilization common to many postcolonial leaders. After the Independence of India, Subhash Chandra Bose did not get much importance, as the Gandhi-influenced Congress Party came to rule.

ROLE IN INDIAN INDEPENDENCE

When one thinks of the Indian independence movement in the 1930s and early 1940s, two figures most readily come to mind: Mahatma Gandhi, the immensely popular and "saintly" frail pacifist, and his highly respected, Fabian Socialist acolyte, Jawaharlal Nehru. Less familiar to Westerners is Subhash Chandra Bose, a man of comparable stature who admired Gandhi but despaired at his aims and methods, and who became a bitter rival of Nehru. Bose played a very active and prominent role in India's political life during most of the 1930s. For example, he was twice (1938 and 1939) elected President of the Indian National Congress, the country's most important political force for freedom from the *Raj*, or British rule.

While his memory is still held in high esteem in India, in the West Bose is much less revered, largely because of his wartime collaboration with the Axis powers. Both before and during the Second World War, Bose worked tirelessly to secure German and Japanese support in freeing his beloved homeland of foreign rule. During the final two years of the war, Bose—

with considerable Japanese backing—led the forces of the Indian National Army into battle against the British.

IDEOLOGY OF FUSION

As early as 1930—in his inaugural speech as mayor of Calcutta—the fervent young Bose first expressed his support for a fusion of socialism and fascism:

> *"... I would say we have here in this policy and programme a synthesis of what modern Europe calls Socialism and Fascism. We have here the justice, the equality, the love, which is the basis of Socialism, and combined with that we have the efficiency and the discipline of Fascism as it stands in Europe today."*

In years that followed, the brilliant, eclectic Bengali would occasionally modify this radical doctrine, but would never abandon it entirely. For example, in late 1944—almost a decade-and-a-half later—in a speech to students at Tokyo University, he asserted that India must have a political system "of an authoritarian character... To repeat once again, our philosophy should be a synthesis between National Socialism and Communism." In the wake of the crushing defeat in 1945 of Hitler and Mussolini, "fascism" has arguably been the most despised of all political ideologies. Postwar western society recognizes no fascist heroics, and even considers "fascist" traits—particularly the authoritarian, charismatic, personal style of leadership, and the positive evaluation of violence and the willingness to use it for political purposes—to be decidedly unpalatable. In India, though, Bose is regarded as a national hero, in spite of his repeated praise (as will be shown) for autocratic leadership and authoritarian government, and admiration for the European fascist regimes with which he allied himself.

Like the leaders he admired in Italy and Germany, Bose was (and still is) popularly known as *Netaji*, or "revered leader." "His name," explains Mihir Bose (no relation), one of Subhas' many biographers, "is given [in India] to parks, roads, buildings, sports stadiums, artificial lakes; his statues stand in place of those of discarded British heroes and his photograph adorns thousands of calendars and millions of *pan* (betel-nut) shops." It is always the same portrait, continues the writer: Bose in his Indian National Army uniform, "exhorting his countrymen forward to one last glorious struggle."

No less a figure than Gandhi paid tribute to Bose's remarkable courage and devotion. Six months after his death in an airplane crash on August 18, 1945, Gandhi declared: "The hypnotism of the Indian National Army has cast its spell upon us. Netaji's name is one to conjure with. His patriotism is second to none... His bravery shines through all his actions. He aimed high and failed. But who has not failed." On another occasion Gandhi eulogized: "Netaji will remain immortal for all time to come for his service to India."

Many of Bose's admirers have been inclined to downplay or even ignore the fascist elements in his ideology, and even to pretend they never existed. For example, the text of Bose's inaugural speech as mayor of Calcutta, cited above, was reprinted in a laudatory 1970 "Netaji Birthday Supplement" of the *Calcutta Municipal Gazette*, but with all references to fascism, including his support for a synthesis of fascism and socialism, carefully deleted. Several admiring biographers have found it easier to ignore the fascist elements in his ideology than to explain them. Their subjective accounts do not even inform the reader that Bose spoke positively about some features of fascism, or else, in an attempt to remove from their hero any possible taint, they qualify his remarks in ways that he himself did not. 'Fascist'?

During his lifetime, Bose was frequently denounced as a fascist or even a Nazi, particularly in the wake of the radical, revolutionary (as opposed to reformist) views he expressed in radio addresses broadcast to India from National Socialist Germany and, later, from quasi-fascist Japan. For example, *The Statesman*, a highly influential Calcutta periodical, charged in November 1941: "Mr. Bose's views are those of the Nazis, and he makes no secret of it," while the BBC, Britain's worldwide radio voice, frequently accused him of "Fascism" and "Nazism." Additionally, historians and writers who do not admire Bose readily point up his "fascist" views. A.M. Nair, a historian who has written favourably of Indian revolutionary Rash Behari Bose (who had sought Japan's help during and after the First World War), found nothing to praise about Subhash Chandra Bose. After all, wrote Nair, he was clearly a fascist.

RECOGNIZED LEADERSHIP

Bose, a patriot of almost fanatical zeal, first joined the Indian national movement in 1921, working under, C.R. Das, whom he idolized. He was jailed for six months in 1921-1922 because of his political activities. Immediately upon his release, the 25-year-old Bose organized (and presided over) the All-Bengal Young Men's Conference. As a result of his remarkable leadership abilities and ambition, he advanced quickly through nationalist ranks. He was soon elected General Secretary of the Bengal Provincial Congress Committee (BPCC).

In 1924, at the age of 27, Bose was elected the Chief Executive Officer of the Calcutta Municipal Corporation, which effectively put him in charge of the second-largest city in the British empire. As a result of his close ties with nationalist terrorists, in late 1924 he was detained by British authorities and held, without trial, for three years in prison. In 1928, the 31-year-old Bose was elected president of the BPCC, and, at the Calcutta meeting of the Congress party held that December, he came to national prominence by pressing (unsuccessfully) for the adoption by his provincial committee of an independence resolution.

By 1930 Bose had formulated the broad strategy that he believed India must follow to throw off the yoke of British imperialism and assume its rightful place as a leader in Asia. During his years in Mandalay prison and another short term of imprisonment in Alipore jail in 1930, he read many works on political theory, including Francesco Nitti's *Bolshevism, Fascism and Democracy* and Ivanoe Bonomi's *From Socialism to Fascism*.

It is clear that these works on fascism influenced him, and caused an immediate modification of his long-held socialist views: as noted above, in his inaugural speech as mayor of

Calcutta, given a day after his release from Alipore jail, he revealed his support for a seemingly contradictory ideological synthesis of socialism and fascism.

Until his death 15 years later, Bose would continue publicly to praise certain aspects of fascism and express his hope for a synthesis of that ideology and socialism. His detailed comments on the matter in his book *The Indian Struggle: 1920-1934*, which was first published in 1935, accurately represent the views he held throughout most of his career. As such, the most important of them, along with Bose's own actions, will be analyzed here in some detail.

PROGRAM OUTLINED

Contending that the Indian National Congress was somewhat "out of date," and suffered from a lack of unity and strong leadership, Bose predicted in *The Indian Struggle* that out of a "Left-Wing revolt there will ultimately emerge a new full-fledged party with a clear ideology, programme and plan of action." The programme and plan of action of this new party would, wrote Bose, follow this basic outline:

1. The party will stand for the interests of the masses, that is, of the peasants, workers, etc., and not for the vested interests, that is, the landlords, capitalists and moneylending classes.
2. It will stand for the complete political and economic liberation of the Indian people.
3. It will stand for a Federal Government for India as the ultimate goal, but will believe in a strong Central Government with dictatorial powers for some years to come, in order to put India on her feet.
4. It will believe in a sound system of state-planning for the reorganization of the agricultural and industrial life of the country.
5. It will seek to build up a new social structure on the basis of the village communities of the past, that were ruled by the village "Panch" and will strive to break down the existing social barriers like caste.

6. It will seek to establish a new monetary and credit system in the light of the theories and the experiments that have been and are current in the modern world.
7. It will seek to abolish landlordism and introduce a uniform land-tenure system for the whole of India.
8. It will not stand for a democracy in the Mid-Victorian sense of the term, but will believe in government by a strong party bound together by military discipline, as the only means of holding India together and preventing a chaos, when Indians are free and are thrown entirely on their own resources.
9. It will not restrict itself to a campaign inside India but will resort to international propaganda also, in order to strengthen India's case for liberty, and will attempt to utilize the existing international organizations.
10. It will endeavour to unite all the radical organizations under a national executive so that whenever any action is taken, there will be simultaneous activity on many fronts.

Synthesis

Bose went on to note that Nehru had said in 1933: "I dislike Fascism intensely and indeed I do not think it is anything more than a crude and brutal effort of the present capitalist order to preserve itself at any cost." There is no middle road between Fascism and Communism, said Nehru, so one "had to choose between the two and I choose the Communist ideal." To this Bose responded:

> *"The view expressed here is, according to the writer, fundamentally wrong... One is inclined to hold that the next phase in world-history will produce a synthesis between Communism and Fascism. And will it be a surprise if that synthesis in produced in India?... In spite of the antithesis between Communism and Fascism, there are certain traits in common. Both Communism and Fascism believe in the supremacy of the State over the individual. Both denounce parliamentary democracy. Both believe in party rule. Both believe in the dictatorship*

of the party and in the ruthless suppression of all dissenting minorities. Both believe in a planned industrial reorganization of the country. These common traits will form the basis of the new synthesis. That synthesis is called by the writer "Samyavada"—an Indian word, which means literally "the doctrine of synthesis or equality." It will be India's task to work out this synthesis."

Before taking a closer look at these remarkable words, four points need to be made. First, Bose's fascist model was almost certainly Mussolini's Italy, not Hitler's Germany. In 1934 Bose made the first of several visits to Fascist Italy and found both the regime and its leader very agreeable. On that occasion he had a cordial (first) meeting with Mussolini—"a man who really counts in the politics of modern Europe." After *The Indian Struggle* appeared in print in 1935, Bose made a special stop in Rome personally to present a copy to the *Duce*.

Second, the book was completed a full year before the commencement of the Italian invasion of Ethiopia (Abyssinia), in October 1935. While Bose would, by the time he completed his book, have known about such violent incidents as "The Night of the Long Knives"—the SS killing of dozens of SA men on June 30, 1934—he had no real reason to consider the European fascist regimes unusually violent, murderous or bellicose. "I should like to point out that when I was writing the book," he later explained,

"Fascism had not started on its imperialistic expedition, and it appeared to me merely an aggressive form of nationalism. .. What I really meant was that we in India wanted our national freedom, and having won it, we wanted to move in the direction of Socialism. This is what I meant when I referred to a "synthesis between Communism and Fascism." Perhaps the expression I used was not a happy one."

Third, despite Bose's claim to represent the political left, and that a party supporting a fusion of fascism and socialism would be ushered in by a "Left-Wing revolt," the ideology he expounded might more appropriately be regarded as right wing. Bose's ideology was radical and contained socialist elements—such as the desire to abolish the traditional class structure and create a society of equal opportunity, and the claim to represent the peasants and workers. To that extent it can be considered left wing. It is worth noting that Hitler's "right wing" political movement—the National Socialist German Workers' Party—shared many of Bose's "socialist" goals. Nehru, a committed socialist, challenged Bose's characterization of himself and his followers as left wing: "It seems to me that many of the so-called Leftists are more Right than the so-called Rightists. Strong language and a capacity to attack the old Congress leadership is not a test of Leftism in politics."

Lastly, it should be noted that Bose was willing to tone down his more radical political beliefs on those occasions when he considered it advantageous or necessary to do so. For example, in his February 1938 inaugural speech as President of the Indian National Congress, Bose—probably in a sincere attempt to placate the Gandhian faction—made statements that appear to represent almost an about face from the political views he had expounded in *The Indian Struggle*. In a future independent India, he said,

> *"the party itself will have a democratic basis, unlike, for instance, the Nazi party which is based on the "leader principle." The existence of more than one party and the democratic basis of the Congress party will prevent the future Indian State becoming a totalitarian one. Further, the democratic basis of the party will ensure that leaders are not thrust upon the people from above, but are elected from below."*

It is possible that these statements reflect a temporary change of mind, but it is more likely that they reflect Bose's efforts during this period to gain further political respectability, to prove that he was more than just a radical and revolutionary Bengali. By doing so he apparently hoped to win wider acceptance of the policies he wanted to implement in his year as Congress President: policies which were not especially radical or revolutionary. According to Nirad Chaudhuri, his former personal secretary, Bose tried very hard during this period to seek agreement with the Gandhian faction over the direction the Congress party should move, and even "showed something like tender filial piety towards Gandhi," of whom he had been very critical in *The Indian Struggle*. It is against this political background that Bose's statements to the Congress party meeting in February 1938 should be seen.

A year later he successfully recontested the presidential election, but two months afterwards was forced to resign because of his inability to resolve his differences with Gandhi and the Gandhian faction. Probably believing that his earlier suspicions of democracy had been proven correct, and feeling that there was now no use in trying to win the favour or approval of more conservative elements in the Congress party, Bose once again proclaimed his belief in the efficacy of authoritarian government and a synthesis of fascism and socialism.

Many similar examples can be cited to show how Bose outwardly (but probably not inwardly) modified his views to suit changing political contexts.

A Life for India

Throughout his political career, India's liberation from British rule remained Bose's foremost political goal; indeed, it was a lifelong obsession. As he explained in his most important work, *The Indian Struggle*, the political party he envisioned "will stand for the complete political and economic liberation of the Indian people." Speaking of Bose a few days after his death in August 1945, Jawaharlal Nehru said:

> *"In the struggle for the cause of India's independence he has given his life and has escaped all those troubles which brave soldiers like him have to face in the end. He was not only brave but had deep love for freedom. He believed, rightly or wrongly, that whatever he did was for the independence of India... Although I personally did not agree with him in many respects, and he left us and formed the Forward Bloc, nobody can doubt his sincerity. He struggled throughout his life for the independence of India, in his own way."*

Along with his abiding love for his country, Bose held an equally passionate hatred of the imperial power that ruled it: Great Britain. In a radio address broadcast from Berlin on March 1, 1943, he exclaimed that Britain's demise was near, and predicted that it would be " India's privilege to end that Satanic empire." The fundamental principle of his foreign policy, Bose declared in a May 1945 speech in Bangkok, is that " Britain's enemy is India's friend." Although these two speeches are from his final years, they express views he had held since before his April 1921 resignation from the Indian Civil Service. It was this principle of making friends with Britain's enemies in the hope that they would assist him in liberating India that brought him in 1941 to Germany and then, in 1943, to Japan.

Violence or Non-Violence?

Bose envisaged that "the complete political and economic liberation of the Indian people" would inevitably require the use of force. Just before resigning from the Indian Civil Service, he discussed with Dilip Kumar Roy, his closest friend, the subject of anti-British terrorism. "I admit is it regrettable," he said, "even ugly if you will, though it also has a terrible beauty of its own. But maybe that beauty does not unveil her face except for her devotees." Violence was not new to Bose, even at that early stage of his career. In 1916 he had been expelled from Presidency College in Calcutta for his part in the violent assault on Professor Edward Oaten, who had allegedly insulted Indian students. Moreover, although he occasionally claimed to "detest" violence, and criticized isolated acts of terrorism (which he considered ineffective and counterproductive), he was never really committed to Gandhi's policy of nonviolence. He regarded the Gandhi-supported civil disobedience campaign as an effective means of paralyzing the administration, but regarded it as inadequate unless accompanied by a movement aimed at total revolution and prepared, if necessary, to use violence.

Militarism

Related to Bose's willingness to use violence to gain political objective was his belief—expressed in *The Indian Struggle*, for example—that a government by a strong party should be "bound together by military discipline." Indeed Bose was infatuated with military discipline, and later commented that his basic training in the University Unit of the India Defence Force (for which he volunteered in 1917, while a student at Scottish Church College in Calcutta) "gave me something which I needed or which I lacked. The feeling of strength and of self-confidence grew still further." Bose was able to give much grander expression to his "militarism" when, in 1930, he volunteered to form a guard of honour during the ceremonial functions at the Calcutta session of the Congress party. Such guards of honour were not uncommon, but the one Bose formed and commanded was unlike anything previously seen.

More than 2,000 volunteers were given military training and organized into battalions. About half wore uniforms, with specially designed steel-chain epaulettes for the officers. Bose, in full dress uniform (peaked cap, standing collar, ornamental breast cords, and jodhpurs) even carried a Field Marshal's baton when he reviewed his "troops." Photographs taken at the conference show him looking entirely out of place in a sea of *khadi* (traditional Indian clothing). Gandhi and several other champions of Nonviolence (*Ahimsa*) were uncomfortable with this display.

INA

A high point in Bose's "military career" came in July 1943 in Singapore. At a mass meeting there on July 4, Rash Behari Bose (no relation) handed over to him the leadership of the Indian Independence League. The next day, Subhash Bose reviewed for the first time the soldiers of the Indian National Army (INA), which then comprised 13,000 men. In his address to the troops, which is a good example of his speaking style, he cited George Washington and Giuseppi Garibaldi as examples of men who led armies that won independence for their respective countries. Bose went on:

"Soldiers of India's army of liberation!...

"Every Indian must feel proud that this Army—his own Army—has been organized entirely under Indian

leadership and that, when the historic moment arrives, under Indian leadership it will go to battle...

"Comrades! You have voluntarily accepted a mission that is the noblest that the human mind can conceive of. For the fulfilment of such a mission, no sacrifice is too great, not even the sacrifice of one's life...

"...Today is the proudest day of my life. For an enslaved people, there can be no greater pride, no higher honour, than to be the first soldier in the army of liberation. But this honour carries with it a corresponding responsibility, and I am deeply conscious of it. I assure you that I shall be with you in darkness and in sunshine, in sorrow and in joy, in suffering and in victory. For the present, I can offer you nothing except hunger, thirst, privation, forced marches and death. But if you follow me in life and in death, as I am confident you will, I shall lead you to victory and freedom. It does not matter who among us will live to see India free. It is enough that India shall be free, and that we shall give our all to make her free.

"May God now bless our Army and grant us victory in the coming fight!"

This "Free India Army" ("*Azad Hind Fauj*") would not only "emancipate India from the British yoke," he told the soldiers, but would, under his command, become the standing national army of the liberated nation.

Choreography for Impact

As his staging at the 1930 Calcutta session of the Congress party suggest, Bose understood early on the importance of political choreography and the aesthetics of mass meetings. After his visits to Fascist Italy and National Socialist Germany, he was even more mindful of the importance for any successful broad-based political movement of mass meetings, marches, visual symbols, and ceremonial or liturgical rituals. For example, at the 51st session of the Congress party at Haripura in 1938, Bose made sure that his entrance as the new Congress President would be spectacular. Escorted by 51 girls in saffron saris (the number corresponding with the number of the Congress session), he was seated in an ancient chariot drawn by 51 white bullocks, and taken on a two hour procession through 51 specially-constructed gates, accompanied by 51 brass bands. Political choreography of this type—although not to this extreme degree—was very evident at all mass rallies (which sometimes attracted crowds numbering as many as 200,000) of the Forward Bloc party that Bose formed in 1939. Carefully chosen symbols, slogans and songs, coupled with a flood of written propaganda, were used in an unsuccessful attempt to make the Forward Bloc into a mass party.

Even during the last years of the war, when he was in southeast Asia heading the Provisional Government of Free India and the INA, he continued to choreograph carefully all of his rallies, meetings and ceremonies, in order to maximize their impact. He also realized that his own role in this choreography was central. Even in the hottest tropical weather, for instance, he wore an imposing military uniform, including forage cap, khaki tunic and jodhpurs, and shiny, knee-length black boots. Moreover, whenever he travelled "he demanded all the rights and privileges of a head of state. On his road travels in Malaya, for example, he insisted on a full ceremonial escort; Japanese military jeeps mounted with sub-machine guns, a fleet of cars, and motorcycle outriders."

Historian Mihir Bose argues persuasively that such carefully planned actions were manifestations not of megalomania, but rather of Subhash Bose's effort to create a sense of unity transcending class, caste and origin among the large and diverse populations of Indians in Southeast Asia, to increase their political awareness, to arouse and inspire both them and his INA troops, and to show the world that he regarded himself as a political leader of substance and importance.

This naturally raises the question of Bose's leadership style. In the passage from *The Indian Struggle* quoted above at length, he expressed his belief in what he called "the dictatorship of the party" (the party being the governing body of a free India), but he did not specify the precise nature of the party's leadership, or whether it, too, would be dictatorial. Most importantly, he did not state whether he saw himself as the party leader, or comment directly on what role he intended for himself in a free India. Nonetheless, clues about these details can be gleaned from other sections of *The Indian Struggle* and from the speeches and statements Bose made at various times throughout his career.

DETERMINED LEADERSHIP

Bose clearly admired strong, vigorous, military-type leaders, and in *The Indian Struggle* he listed several whom he particularly respected. These included Hitler, Mussolini, Stalin and even a former British governor of Bengal, Sir Stanley Jackson. Nowhere in this book is there any criticism of these individuals (three of them dictators) for having too much power, yet another man is chastised for this: Mahatma Gandhi. Bose admired Gandhi for many things, not least his ability to "exploit the mass psychology of the people, just as Lenin did the same thing in Russia, Mussolini in Italy and Hitler in Germany." But he accused Gandhi of accepting too much power and responsibility, of becoming a "Dictator for the whole country" who issued "decrees" to the Congress.

According to Bose, Gandhi was a brilliant and gifted man, but, unlike Mussolini, Hitler and the others mentioned, a very ineffectual leader. Gandhi had failed to liberate India because of his frequent indecision and constant willingness to compromise with the Raj (something Bose said he would never do). It is clear that Bose—who believed from his youth that he was destined for greatness —saw himself as a "strong" leader in the mold of those named above. "I ask those who have any doubts or suspicions in their minds to rely on me," he told the Indian Independence League Conference in Singapore on July 4, 1943. He continued:

> *"I shall always be loyal to India alone. I will never deceive my motherland. I will live and die for India. .. The British could not bring me to submission by inflicting hardships on me. British statesmen could neither induce me nor deceive me. There is no one who can divert me from the right path."*

Bose was decisive, aggressive and ambitious, and even as a university student, these features of his personality attracted many devoted followers. Dilip Kumar Roy, his companion during his days as a student at Cambridge, referred to him as "strength-inspiring," and the absolute leader of the Indian student population. Bose's militarism, ambition and leadership traits do not necessarily indicate (contrary to popular opinion) that he was a leader in the fascist mold. If they did, one would have to consider all personalities with similar traits—Winston Churchill, for example—as "fascist."

In this regard, it is worth noting that during his many years as head of various councils, committees and offices, and during 15-month tenure as President of the Indian National Congress (February 1938 to May 1939), Bose never acted in an undemocratic manner, nor did he claim powers or responsibilities to which he was not constitutionally or customarily entitled. Neither did he attempt in any way to foster a cult of his own personality (as, it could be argued, Gandhi did).

However, after he assumed control of the INA in July-August 1943, Bose's leadership style underwent a transformation.

First, he allowed a cult of his personality to flourish among the two million or so Indians living in southeast Asia. Prayers were regularly said on his behalf, and his birthday celebrations were—like Gandhi's in India—major festivals. He was invincible, according to one Indian myth from this period, and could not be harmed by bombs or bullets.

An image of Bose that stressed his strength of character, military prowess, and willingness to sacrifice for a free India was intentionally promoted in propaganda broadcasts and printed material. With his approval, the title *Netaji* ("Revered Leader") was added to his name in all articles about him appearing in the newspapers of the Indian Independence League; even his staff officers were permitted to address him with this title. By the end of the war, few Indians in south Asia still referred to him by name; he was always respectfully called *Netaji*.

AUTHORITARIAN RULE

Second, in contrast to his statement at the 1938 Haripura session of the Congress party (quoted above)—that leaders would be elected from below—Bose proclaimed, on October 21, 1943, the formation of the Provisional Government of Azad Hind ("Free India"). While retaining his post as Supreme Commander of the Indian National Army, he announced that he was naming himself Head of State, Prime Minister, and Minister for War and Foreign Affairs. (The most important of these positions—Head of State—he anticipated retaining in a free India.) These appointments involved no democratic process or voting of any kind.

Further, the authority he exercised in these posts was dictatorial and often very harsh. He demanded total obedience and loyalty from the Indians in south Asia, and any who opposed him, his army or government faced imprisonment, torture, or even execution.

Additionally, if wealthy Indians did not contribute sufficient funds to Bose's efforts, they risked confiscation of their property. Bose's threats were taken very seriously, and had the desired effect: funds did pour in.

His INA troops were obliged to swear an oath of loyalty to both the Provisional Government and to him personally. He ordered the summary execution of all INA deserters, and also prepared (but was never able to implement) law codes for the entire population of India.

These laws, which stipulated the death penalty for a range of offences, were to come into force when the INA, together with the Japanese Army, entered India to fight against the British. With regard to his leadership style during this 1943-1945 period, in fairness to Bose is should be pointed out that the entire world was then engulfed in a horrendous war, and political and military leaders everywhere, on all sides, adapted extraordinarily authoritarian and repressive measures. Some of the measures and policies adapted by the wartime government of the United States, for instance, were as oppressive and as severe as any planned or implemented by Bose.

A NEW INDIA

Bose clearly anticipated that the British would be driven out of India in an armed struggle (under his leadership), and that a social and political revolution would begin the moment the Indian people saw British rule under attack in India itself. This revolution, he believed, would bring an end to the old caste system and traditional social hierarchy, which would be replaced by an egalitarian, casteless and classless society based on socialist models. This process would require very careful guidance, with a firm hand, to prevent anarchy and chaos. Bose had, in fact, held these beliefs since the early 1930s, as Mrs. Kitty Kurti, a close German friend of Bose, revealed in her anecdotal memoir. At a June 1933 meeting attended by Kurti, Bose explained that:

> *"Besides a plan of action which will lead up to the conquest of power, we shall require a programme for the new state when it comes into existence in India. Nothing can be left to chance. The group of men and women who will assume the leadership of the fight with Great Britain will also have to take up the task of controlling, guiding and developing the new state and, through the state, the entire Indian people. If our leaders are not trained for postwar leadership also there is every possibility that after the conquest of power a period of chaos will set in and incidents similar to those for the French Revolution of the 18th century may be repeated in India. ... The generals of the wartime period in India will have to carry through the whole programme of postwar reforms in order to justify to their countrymen the hopes and aspirations that they will have to rouse during the fight. The task of these leaders will not be over till a new generation of men and women are educated and trained after the establishment of the new state and this new generation are able to take complete charge of their country's affairs."*

This explains what Bose meant in *The Indian Struggle* when he wrote (as quoted above) of the need for a strong, single-party government, "bound together by military discipline" with "dictatorial powers for some years to come, in order to put India on her feet." Only an very strong government, strict discipline, and dictatorial rule would, according to Bose, prevent the anticipated revolution from falling into chaos and anarchy. That is why the government would not—"in the first years after liberation"—"stand for a democracy in the Mid-Victorian sense of the term." It would use whatever military force was necessary to maintain law and order, and would not relinquish authority or re-establish more regular forms of government until it felt confident that "the work of postwar social reconstruction" had been completed and "a new generation of men and women in India, fully trained and equipped for the battle of life" had emerged.

Bose clearly anticipated that authoritarian rule would not last beyond the period when social reconstruction was completed, and law and order were established—when India was "on its feet," as he often wrote. As he frequently stated, Bose aimed for nothing less than the formation of "a new India and a happy India on the basis of the eternal principles of liberty, democracy and socialism." He rejected Communism (at least as it was practiced in the Soviet Union) principally because of its internationalism, and because he believed that the theoretical ideal found in the writings of Marx could not be applied, without modification, to India. Still, he maintained socialist views throughout his adult life, and, on very many occasions, expressed his hope for an egalitarian (especially classless and casteless) industrialized society in which the state would control the basic means of production.

He was opposed to liberalism, believing that greater emphasis should be placed on social goals than on the needs or desires of individuals. Individual wishes, he reasoned, must be subordinated to the needs of the state, especially during the struggle for independence and the period of reconstruction immediately following liberation. Nonetheless, having himself been imprisoned eleven times and sent into exile three times, he was fully committed to upholding the rights of minority intellectual, religious, cultural and racial groups. He hoped for an "all-round freedom for the Indian people—that is, for social, economic and political freedom," and would, he said "wage a relentless war against bondage of every kind till the people can become really free." It could be argued that he was not as committed to the principle of democracy as he was to socialism and freedom (as he defined it). While he extolled democracy on numerous occasions, at other times his words suggest a belief that other parties would have a place, in a free India, only as long as they were "working towards the same end, in whole or in part," as his governing party. Political pluralism did not appeal to him at all. He seems to have envisioned a free India that was more authoritarian than democratic. His own actions as head of the Provisional Government of Azad Hind illustrate a lack of regard for the democratic process.

Mass Mobilization

Bose was, nonetheless, a consistent advocate of total mobilization: the mustering of national resources on a scale normally associated with military-like action. Realizing that manpower was easily India's greatest resource (and arguably the only one available to the independence movement), he proclaimed that all Indians—male and female, urban and rural, rich and poor—should actively participate in the fight for freedom. From his earliest days in politics to his death in 1945, he sought to rouse the great Indian masses, and involve them directly in the political struggle. Their support for representatives at the provincial or national levels was not enough; they must themselves rise up and win independence.

During the 1930s, however, his political position was never strong enough to call for other resources than manpower, nor was India—under British control—able to offer other resources. Additionally, total mobilization during peacetime, without an impending war or revolution in the awareness of the masses, had never been achieved (not even by the Nazis) and, arguably, never could be achieved. Bose, an astute man, no doubt realized this. With the formation of the Provisional Government of Azad Hind, he was at last in a position to appeal directly for total mobilization to the mass of Indians—at least in Southeast Asia, and, less directly to those in India itself. Along with his call for mass mobilization, he demanded that all available resources be provided for the cause of freedom. For example, he told a mass meeting in Singapore in July 9, 1943:

> *"Friends! You will now realize that the time has come for the three million Indians living in East Asia to mobilize all their available resources, including money and manpower. Half-hearted measures will not do. I want Total Mobilization and nothing less, for we have been told repeatedly, even by our enemies, that this is a total war... Out of this total mobilization I expect at least three hundred thousand soldiers and three crores of dollars [$30,000,000]. I want also a unit of brave women to form a death-defying regiment who will wield the sword which the brave Rani of Jhansi wielded..."*

Of course, Bose demanded not only the total mobilization of Indian resources in south Asia, but of Indian resources everywhere. He called for mass mobilization not only in support of his army, but also for his dynamic new government, the various branches of which required financing and manpower.

Women's Equality

As can be seen from the passage quoted above, Bose called on both men *and* women for total support. Unlike the German National Socialists and the Italian Fascists, who stressed the masculine in almost all spheres of social and political activity, Bose believed that women were the equals of men, and should therefore be likewise prepared to fight and sacrifice for India's liberation. Throughout the 1920s and 1930s he had campaigned in India to bring women more fully into the life of the nation. After his return to Asia in 1943, he called on women to serve as soldiers in the Indian National Army—at the time a most radical view. "When I express my confidence that you are today prepared to fight and suffer for the sake of your motherland," he told the women's section of the Independence League in July 1943,

"I do not mean only to cajole you with empty words. I know the capabilities of our womanhood well. I can, therefore, say with certainty that there is no task which our women cannot undertake and no sacrifice and suffering which our women cannot undergo... To those who say that it will not be proper for our women to carry guns, my only request is that they look into the pages of our history. What brave deeds the Rani of Jhansi performed during the First War of Independence in 1857... Indians—both common people and members of the British Indian army—who are on the border areas of India, will, on seeing you march with guns on your shoulders, voluntarily come forward to receive the guns from you and carry on the struggle started by you."

A women's regiment was formed in 1943, and came to number about 1,000 women. It was named, appropriately, the "Rani of Jhansi Regiment," after a heroine of the Indian rebellion of 1857-58 against British rule. While those less suited to combat duties were employed as nurses and in other support roles, the majority were trained as soldiers. When the INA attacked British forces from Burma in east India in mid-1944, the women of the Jhansi Regiment fought alongside the men, suffering equally heavy casualties. When the army was forced to withdraw, the women were given no privileges. Along with the men, they marched for more than a thousand kilometres.

Commitment to Youth

Lastly, Bose was also deeply committed to the youth movement, a devotion that featured prominently in his political ideology. Convinced that young people were by nature idealistic, restless and open to new ideas —such his own radical and militant outlook—Bose accordingly devoted a great deal of time and effort to the new Youth Leagues that were formed in a number of provinces during the 1920s. Throughout his career he presided over far more youth conferences than any other all-India political figure, and his speeches to younger people he steadfastly urged a spirit of activism that contrasted sharply with the passivism preached by Gandhi and many of the older politicians. "One of the most hopeful signs of the time," he claimed at the 1928 Maharashtra Provincial Conference, "is the awakening among the youth of this country... Friends! I would implore you to assist in the awakening of youth and in the organization of the youth movement. Self-conscious youth will not only act, but will also dream; will not only destroy, but will also build. It will succeed where even you may fail; it will create for you a new India—and a free India—out of the failures, trials and experiences of the past."

India's liberation would be achieved not by Gandhi and the leading politicians of his generation, whose conservative, reformist policies bred passivity and inactivity. It would, Bose believed, be achieved only through the efforts and sacrifices of the militant, revolutionary and politically-conscious younger generation.

Economic Views

In contrast to the copious record of Bose's political ideology and actions, much less is available about other important elements of his outlook, such as his economic views and policies. For example, while he condemned capitalism and extolled socialism in the pages of *The Indian Struggle*, Bose was very vague about just what monetary or credit systems he foresaw in a free India. They would be set up, he simply wrote, "in the light of the theories and the experiments that have been and are current in the modern world." Throughout his career he never wrote or said anything more specific about such matters. He appears to have had no precise ideas about political economy, save that economics was not important in itself but must be subordinated to national political considerations. Any discussion here of what economic systems he favoured, and when and how he intended to implement them, would thus be merely speculative.

Unique Political Ideology

While Bose's political ideology can reasonably be described as essentially "fascistic," two qualifying points need to be made here.

First, his ideology and actions were not the result of any extreme neurotic or pathological psychosocial impulses. He was not a megalomaniac, nor did he display any of the pathological traits often attributed (rightly or wrongly) to fascist leaders, such as hostile aggression, obsessive hatred or delusions.

Moreover, while he was an ardent patriot and nationalist, Bose's nationalism was cultural, not racialist.

Second, his radical political ideology was shaped by a consuming frustration with the unsuccessful efforts of others to gain independence for India. His "fascist" outlook did not come from a drive for personal power or social elevation. While he was ambitious, and clearly enjoyed the devotion of his followers, his obsession was not adulation or power, but rather freedom for his beloved Motherland—a goal for which he was willing to suffer and sacrifice, even at the cost of his life.

Bose was favourably impressed with the discipline and organizational strength of fascism as early as 1930, when he first expressed support for a synthesis of fascism and socialism. During his stays in Europe during the 1930s, he was deeply moved by the dynamism of the two major "fascist" powers, Italy and Germany.

After observing these regimes first-hand, he developed a political ideology of his own that, he was convinced, could bring about the liberation of India and the total reconstruction of Indian society along vaguely authoritarian-socialist lines. Bose's lack of success in his lifelong effort to liberate India from alien rule was certainly not due to any lack of effort. From 1921, when he became the first Indian to resign formally from the Indian Civil Service, until his death in 1945 as leader of an Indian government in exile, Subhash Chandra Bose struggled ceaselessly to achieve freedom and prosperity for his beloved homeland.

Tripuri Congress Redux

The purpose of this essay is not to belittle Mahatma Gandhi. The reader will notice that nowhere has Gandhi's campaign to oust Bose been termed as immoral or unethical. At the same time it is not possible to know the truth by imposing divinity on Gandhi. The Tripuri Congress session of 1939 is a crucial event in the history of the Indian National Congress. The united resistance and non-cooperation of the conservative leadership cleared the way for the removal of the recently re-elected Congress president Subhash Chandra Bose.

Bose was compelled to resign very soon. It won't be an exaggeration to say that the Tripuri session was the theatre of the demise of Bose's political career. Mahatma Gandhi was not present in the Tripuri session, but later when Bose repeatedly sought his intervention to end the stalemate, his stubborn refusal only hastened Bose's resignation. Even today Tripuri remains in the collective memory of Bengalis as a gross injustice done by Gandhi to Bose and Bengal. The consequent loss of Gandhi's image continues till today. On re-evaluating the incident after almost 65 years, certain questions arise which have never been answered squarely. This essay raises those little-discussed issues.

Was Gandhi Afraid of Bose?

Gandhi himself proposed Bose's name as the President of Congress in the Haripura Session of 1938. But within a year he literally became desperate to remove Bose and did not hesitate to take recourse to any sort of tactics to serve the purpose. His only objective at that time was Bose's removal by any means. No opinion regarding whether Gandhi's move was ethical or not can be objective, but at the same time it is pertinent to ask if he was afraid of Bose. Blind followers of Gandhi will of course laugh away such a question. They will argue that at that the national level Gandhi's status and influence was supreme, whereas the sphere of Bose's influence was limited. In that case, the question that begs answer is why was Gandhi so worried? It was clear as daylight to the whole country that he did not want Bose to continue. Despite such explicit opposition from Gandhi how did Bose get re-elected? Certainly not by rigging the election! Perhaps Gandhi was not perturbed even by the British government to the extent as he was by Bose. If he was confident of himself, what was the reason for Gandhi not to confront Bose directly rather than reverting to political trickery?

It is important to be clear about one thing regarding this issue. Many intellectuals, despite having high regards for Bose, cannot consider the Bose-Gandhi feud objectively. It almost amounts to sin for them even to think that Gandhi can do something unethical. They meticulously desist from associating Gandhi with any sort of Machiavellian politics since they consider him as much above petty politics. Furthermore, they present the accounts of many contemporary revolutionaries who could not see any wrong in Gandhi's actions in spite of being Bose's followers. It is now time to show clearly how both schools of arguments do not hold ground.

Firstly, overwhelming evidence has come to light showing Gandhi directly involved in the conspiracy to remove Bose. Gandhi's statements, letters etc. of those days are now available with the publication of his complete works. However, it was not possible for the revolutionaries during the Tripuri session to understand Gandhi's intentions, which he did not share even with his closest associates. Thus, it was virtually impossible for those revolutionaries, who despite being followers of Bose respected Gandhi, to assess Gandhi's true character. Therefore, even as they were pained by the anti-Bose actions of Gandhi, they failed to realize the Machiavellian tactics adopted by him.

Secondly, the question of right or wrong is in once sense irrelevant here since Machiavellian strategies are to some extent required in realpolitik. If Gandhi was determined to get rid of Bose for the sake of his own power and influence then his actions can be regarded as the most unethical. On the other hand, if he was moved by the consideration that removing Bose was necessary for the good of the country then his actions cannot be labelled unethical, since the interest of the country is always larger than the individual.

It is not easy to resolve this debate. It can however be resolved easily if Gandhi is seen as a clever politician instead of placing him in the high pedestal as a divine personality, without going into the question of right or wrong. It is abundantly evident that Gandhi was bothered by the rise of Bose and that he took recourse to a confrontation by proxy rather than facing him in a direct way. It was almost a nonviolent guerilla war. From Gandhi's point of view he was right. It is foolish to expect that he would give up to his biggest political challenger. Rather it is expected that he would resist fiercely with his entire prowess.

Even if Gandhians are upset, it will have to be admitted that only when one is pushed to the wall one becomes as desperate to fight back as Gandhi was. From that perspective Bose emerged victorious at Tripuri. Gandhi's statement that Sitaramayya's defeat was an indirect defeat for him was true in essence. To wash off the bitter taste of defeat, Gandhi threw away his principle of means being more important than the goal. It was possible to see such an astonishing U-turn of Gandhism only due to Bose's victory.

Tripuri and the subsequent flow of events prove beyond any doubt that Gandhi jettisoned his cherished ideals and instead adopted a totally un-Gandhian approach. It can be said that changing strategies or positions in politics is not unethical. Therefore it will suffice to say, without raising the issue of ethics, that Gandhi became desperate and broke out of his own value system since he acutely felt an existential crisis. From that perspective, Tripuri saw the defeat of the conventional Gandhiism and the emergence of a new Machiavellian Gandhiism. The events of Tripuri provide the burning proof that Gandhiism is not based on eternal ideals and values.

Gandhi as an Avatar of Machiavelli

The name of the famous Italian intellectual Nicolo Machiavelli has been associated with all sorts of unethical means for achieving political goals. Machiavelli laid more importance on the goal than on the means and advocated the dissociation of religion from politics. In the second sense Gandhi was not Machiavellian since he advocated just the opposite, which is, associating religion with politics. In the first sense he did follow the Machiavellian way to remove Bose out of his way. Bose was ready to follow any path for the attainment of independence for India, but never adopted Machiavellian ways in case of internal politics of Congress. This is where he is different from Gandhi.

Although Bose understood perfectly the nature of the British Raj, he dangerously failed to understand Gandhi. It has been rightly said by Amalesh Tripathi that Bose did not realize that his real conflict was with Gandhi himself. In his letter to

Jawaharlal Nehru on 28 August 1939 he complained, "If the old guard wanted to fight why did they not do so in a straightforward manner? Why did they bring Mahatma Gandhi between us?" On 4 April 1939 Sarat Chandra Bose, Bose's elder brother had written to Nehru along the same lines, "I believe I shall not be unjust if I say that the members of the Working Committee would have shown greater courage and straightforwardness if they had decided to act on their own and not used Mahatmaji as their cover. Their plain duty was to keep Mahatmaji above all controversy as he should be in our political life." Both put on the dock Gandhi's followers like Sardar Patel, Bhulabhai Desai etc.

Sarat Bose expressed his displeasure in a sharp letter written to Gandhi on 21 March 1939. He wrote, "Tripuri was an eye opener to me. The exhibition of truth and nonviolence of your chosen disciples stunk in my nostrils. The election of Subhash was not a defeat for yourself, but of the high command of which Sardar Patel is the shining light." In fact the conservative leadership comprising of Patel, Desai and others kicked up a vilification campaign against Bose at Tripuri after calling his illness a 'political fever.' Bose wrote about this painful experience in his essay "My strange Illness." Patel was the focus of his wrath in his letter of 28 March too. Bose wrote to Nehru, "Was there nothing wrong in Sardar Patel making full use of the name and authority of Mahatma Gandhi for electioneering purposes?" He failed to understand that his true opponent was Gandhi who was actually controlling the unfolding of events from behind the curtain. In that sense Patel and others did not take recourse to any trickery and confronted Bose openly. The allegations that Bose brought agains them should have been raised against Gandhi. Why was he fighting a proxy war instead of playing a frontal role?

Gandhi wrote to his secretary Mahadev Desai on 29 January 1939 that he might not attend the Tripuri session if Bose wins the election. On 3 February 1939 he wrote to Nehru that he will serve the country although he will not attend the Congress session. He left for Rajkot on 27 February and the infamous Pant resolution was proposed on 8 March 1939: a classic example of pure Machiavellian politics. Gandhi knew well that the Pant resolution will be proposed in his absence, but then he will be able to deny any responsibility for the proposal. At a time when Bose was repeatedly asking for Gandhi's opinion and seeking his intervention, all he could say was that he did not want to impose his choice on Bose. He wrote on 10 April 1939 that the more he read the Pant proposal the worse he feels, but he can't explain. Today many intellectuals who have high regard for both Gandhi and Bose can't see any dishonesty in Gandhi's action.

They however cannot be blamed since Bose himself failed to see any dishonesty in Gandhi. He even rebuked Narendra Narayan Chakrabarty when he suggested so. The question that now arises is whether Gandhi would have felt it necessary to carry on with his programme of fast at Rajkot if Bose was defeated. Secondly, if Gandhi was unhappy with the Pant proposal why did he not ask for an amendment? Thirdly, while advising Bose to constitute his cabinet of similar thinking leaders, was Gandhi not aware of its impossibility at that point of time? It would be over simplification to say that Gandhi was revengeful, but the fact remains that such a crafty politician has rarely been seen in this country. That was one area where Bose could not equal Gandhi as he was a staunch opponent of the trend of politicking in Congress. The British Raj however knew Gandhi as a clever Machiavellian politician. Although Bose opposed Gandhi's politics, he had high regards for him. Perhaps that is why he could not comprehend the true nature of Gandhi's politics. Now the question is, did Gandhi play this game of war by proxy to maintain his image? If that was the case, it was a terrible miscalculation because the Tripuri events pained even many of his followers. In general his image suffered a blow. His true intentions were clear as daylight.

When he described Bose's victory as his own defeat, there was no deception. Rather such straight talk is laudable. Had be provided the leadership to the conservative politicians in opposing Bose then surely his image would have gained a new high and he would have been praised. But instead he chose a path which was murky. He gained a victory which was but temporary. It was impossible for Gandhi to suppress Bose. The evidence of that has been written in golden letters in future history.

Did Bose have a Weakness for Gandhi?

Bose started making efforts to bring an end to his conflict with Gandhi after the Tripuri session. Manabendra Nath Roy rightly advised him in a letter written on 1 February 1939 to accept Gandhi's challenge and constitute a cabinet of his liking. However Bose did not accept the advice. This was one reason of losing the support of the leftists. Revolutionary of the Juagantar group told the writer that Bose's seeking of Gandhi's support, who had meted him such undignified treatment, also led to anger in certain sections of the revolutionary groups. Late Manohar Mukhopadhyay, another revolutionary of the Jugantar group, also told the writer that Bose was hesitant act against Gandhi.

Perhaps there is some truth in such opinion, but if Bose showed any soft attitude in certain situations towards Gandhi it was due to strategic reasons, not due to any weakness. The former Prime Morarji Desai has made a laughable statement in his autobiography that Gandhi accepted Bose as the President in the Haripura Congress only after Bose promised that he will go by Gandhi's directions. Those familiar with Bose's character know well that he was not one to submit to Gandhi in such a way, but might have just restrained his extreme revolutionary identity for the time being. Rajendra Prasad has written in his autobiography that if Bose had expressed his willingness to be re-elected to Gandhi perhaps the Tripuri conflict could have been avoided. How strange! Would Bose beg Gandhi for his democratic rights? He did not compromise on this issue because with all his respect for Gandhi he was not prepared to take his words as the final. And if he had withdrawn himself from the contest in accordance with Gandhi's wishes, he could not have held his head high in future. This would have not only set a bad precedent, but would have stifled democracy in Congress.

Of course democracy was ultimately stifled in Congress due to Gandhi and his followers, but Bose was not involved with that. He did not sign the death warrant of democracy in Congress. It can of course be asked that why did Bose allow Pant resolution to be raised knowing that it was unconstitutional and undemocratic? He explained to Gandhi in a letter written on 25 March 1939 that he could have vetoed this proposal but did not do so because his democratic outlook had the priority over the issue of constitutional validity. He also wrote, "I felt it would be unmanly to take shelter behind the constitution at a time when I felt that there was the possibility of an adverse vote."

This is where Bose committed a blunder since it made easy for Gandhi to write on 30 March 1939, "Since you think that Pant's resolution was out of order and the clause relating to the Working Committee is clearly unconstitutional, and were ultra vires your course is absolutely clear. Your choice of the committee should be unfettered." Even if this might appear to be transparent, so certain questions are bound to arise. Firstly, why didn't Gandhi clearly comment on the Pant resolution? Gandhi asked Bose to form the cabinet of his choice only because Bose thought that the proposal was unconstitutional.

In other words, Gandhi himself did not think that the proposal was unconstitutional. He told Bose on 10 April 1939, "The framers meant well. But it does not answer the present difficulty. You should therefore give it your own interpretation." By talking about the good intention of the proposal Gandhi supported it indirectly, but never spelt it out clearly. It would have been manly if he had stated his opinion clearly, but instead he created a situation where there was no other way for Bose than to resign. It is true that Bose sought Gandhi's intervention repeatedly at that time, but that was not from his weakness for him.

He hoped against hope that Gandhi will resolve the internal conflict of Congress in the larger interest of the country. He wrote to Gandhi on 31 March 1939, "We are not vindictive and we do not nurse grievances. There is no doubt that today there is a wide gulf between the two main blocs or parties in the Congress. But the gulf can be bridged – that by you." In another letter he wrote, "I am temperamentally not a vindictive person and I do not nurse grievances. I have the mentality of a boxer that is to shake hands smilingly when the boxing bout is over and take the revolt in a sporting spirit." Bose could never imagine that his sportsman spirit will have no impact on Gandhi's mind. Gandhi was so disturbed by him that he had already thought up his course of action. Usually action agenda in politics is determined according to time and expediency, but in this case it was determined much earlier in what can be called fait accompli. Gandhi can be asked if he had started considering himself as weak. His innovativeness shows through the methods he adopted to remove Bose from his position. It is unfortunate that instead of applying such political methods against the British Raj, he used it against a great son of India.

Bose was a staunch anti-imperialist, but due to irony of fate he became a victim to both imperialist oppression and subversive internal politics of Congress. He wanted a compromise with Gandhi in the interest of the larger interest of the country.

The British Raj always wanted to split India by its divide and rule policy. Bose wanted to rise above personal grievances realizing that the internal conflict will only strengthen the British policy of divide and rule. But Gandhi was immovable from his position and thus all efforts of Bose failed. It must be remembered that despite all this Bose kept the path of cooperation with Gandhi open. He also joined the special session of Congress on Gandhi's invitation at Wardha after being expelled from Congress. Bose-baiters might see an effort of appeasement in this but if Bose truly had any weakness for Gandhi he wouldn't have searched for an alternative to the Gandhian way.

Probably he had hoped that he would be able to convince Gandhi to accept the relevance and importance of his plan of action. When he realized that he was only chasing a mirage, he decided to leave the country. Whether the country gained or suffered a loss will be judged by history but the fact remains that Bose was the only leader who showed the courage of proposing an alternative to the Gandhian way. The main source of his conflict with Gandhi can be found in his unique nature.

Paradoxical Ethics

Many people have charged Gandhi for adopting unethical means to get rid of Bose. According to this writer, the whole issue needs to be judged from a different point of view. As Krishna advised the Pandavas to take recourse to action which apparently was Adharma to be able to ensure victory of truth, Gandhi wanted to achieve a larger ethical framework by going through apparently unethical means. This can be called paradox of morality. Concepts of right and wrong etc. are never absolute. These are relative and can vary according to the time, place, persons involved etc. Gandhi's stubborn attitude towards Bose actually proves the flexibility of his mental makeup because it clearly shows that he did not cling on to any particular idea about morality.

Many people have opined that the rigid attitude shown initially by Gandhi towards the issue of violence and nonviolence was much relaxed during his later years. According to this author, it was on the issue of morality that Gandhi showed the most flexibility. He surpassed even Machiavelli in political maneuvering. Yet many intellectuals are still skeptical about this. Actually they have accepted absolutely accepted whatever Gandhi said, that is, they think that whatever he propounded is equally applicable in all cases.

However, Gandhi himself changed his position on many occasions without being bound by the fetters of so-called traditional morality. Those who want to show Gandhi as an idealist by ignoring his practical nature, forget that he himself had said, "I am a practical idealist." The practical side of his character was exposed during his campaign to oust Bose. There is a need to remove the illusion of the learned scholars on this issue.

Let there be No Illusion

A few years back a learned argument through letters between two historians was published in the pages of Jayasree. Shri Sandip Das and Shri Girish Chandra Maiti expressed their opposing views about the role of Gandhi in the Tripuri Congress. Girish Chandra provided the evidence that Gandhi was aware of the Pant proposal well beforehand and it is clear from his statement given on 5 May 1939 at the Gandhi Seva Sangh in Vrindavan that he was told about this proposal while he was fasting at Rajkot. Gandhi said that he himself would have gone beyond, that is, he would have introduced a no-confidence motion against Bose. He dared his followers in Wardha to introduce a no-confidence motion. Sandip Das, ignoring this vital piece of evidence, said that he learnt from many revolutionaries that Gandhi was not dishonest in his behaviour.

It has already been said in this essay that it was not possible for the revolutionaries to know the real intention of Gandhi at that time. Secondly, the above evidence emanates directly from Gandhi. Therefore it is pointless (unless the evidence is disproved) to say that Gandhi was not aware of the Pant proposal. If there is any doubt regarding the veracity of Gandhi's statement, that should be stated clearly. Historians have to depend on two kinds of sources – primary and secondary. Although oral history has gained currency at present, still rigorous research should place more importance on primary evidence rather than hearsay. Gandhi's statement is without doubt a primary evidence. It would be contrary to convention of historical research to reject that based on hearsay. If any documentary evidence to the contrary cannot be presented then the reliability of the above mentioned source is definitely established beyond doubt.

A critic definitely has the right to interpret and analyse events, but it is desirable to be rational rather than be driven by emotions. Thirdly, Shri Das has cited the following quote from Gandhi, "No doubt I like politics too. But it is a different kind. There is no place for scheming in it." There is no doubt about the veracity of the quote, it should be interpreted with an open mind. To say that there was no place of scheming in Gandhi's political activities or in his thoughts is to belittle him. Although the appeared as a saint actually he was a shrewd politician. Otherwise he couldn't have bothered the British Raj to that extent. The saintly prophetic image covered his true identity of a political leader of unlimited intelligence. Nothing is unmixed right or wrong in politics, but depends on the situation. What Gandhi meant by the above quote is that he cannot accept scheming for fulfilling petty ambitions of individuals. That does not mean he was indifferent to use of political maneuvering for achieving political goals. The tendency to paint Gandhi as a superhuman or a saint has stemmed from the traditional concepts of morality. Any assessment of Gandhi will be one-sided, nebulous and irrational if this illusion of traditionalism is not transcended.

The purpose of this essay is not to belittle Gandhi. The reader will notice that nowhere has Gandhi's campaign to oust Bose been termed as immoral or unethical. At the same time it is not possible to know the truth by imposing divinity on Gandhi. It is not possible to stay above conflicts after entering the world of politics. It is also a fact that once inside the political whirlpool, even great men show self-contradicting attributes. It is not desirable to ignore such attributes due to blind devotion. The centre space of politics is focused towards human beings and not divinities. Therefore any search for political values should be focused on human nature and not divine ones. The spiritual politics that Gandhi refers to is primarily morality-based politics but such morality is dynamic and ever changing. It is not bound by any ideological limits. It is the humble submission of this writer that many problems will be solved more easily if neither Gandhi nor Bose is treated as superhuman or divine beings, but as humans of flesh and blood.

2

POLITICAL WORKS AND VIEWS

Subhash Chandra Bose advocated complete freedom for India at the earliest, whereas most of the Congress Committee wanted it in phases, through a Dominion status. Even though Bose and Gandhi had differing ideologies, the latter called Bose the *"Prince among the Patriots"* in 1942.

Bose admired Gandhi, recognising his importance as a symbol of Indian Nationalism; he called him "The Father of Our Nation" in a radio broadcast from Rangoon in 1944, in which he stated that "I am convinced that if we do desire freedom we must be prepared to wade through blood", a statement somewhat at odds with Gandhi's philosophy of nonviolence. Thus, although they shared the goal of an Independent India, by 1939 the two had become divided over the strategy which should be used to achieve Indian Independence, and to some degree the form which the post-Independence state should take: Gandhi was hostile to industrialisation, whilst Bose saw it as the only route to making India strong and self-sufficient (in this he may have been influenced, like many other Indian intellectuals of the time, by reports of the success of the Soviet five-year plans). Nehru disagreed with Gandhi on this point as well, though not over the tactics of protest.

At the time the Second World War began, great divisions existed in the Indian independence movement about whether to exploit the weakness of the British to achieve independence. Some felt that any distinctions between the political allegiances and ideologies of the warring factions of Europe were inconsequential in the face of the possibility of Indian independence, given the fact that the British themselves showed so little respect for democracy or democratic reforms in India. Others felt that it was inappropriate to seek concessions when Britain itself was in peril, or else that pressure was better applied within India and in peaceful fashion, and found that their distaste for Nazi Germany and Japan outweighed any possibility that an alliance with them would bring India's independence closer.

Bose, in particular, was accused of 'collaborating' with the Axis, after he fled to Germany in 1941 and offered Hitler an alliance. He criticized the British during World War II, saying that while Britain was allegedly fighting for the freedom of the European nations under Nazi control, it would not grant independence to its own colonies, including India. It may be observed that along with Nehru, Bose had organized and led protest marches against the Japanese invasion of Manchuria in 1931, and of China itself in 1938, when he was Congress president. In 1937 he published an article attacking Japanese Imperialism in the Far East, although he betrayed some admiration for other aspects of the Japanese regime. Bose's earlier correspondence (prior to 1939) also reflects his deep disapproval of the racist practices of, and annulment of democratic institutions in Nazi Germany. He also, however, expressed admiration for the authoritarian methods (though not the racial ideologies) which he saw in Italy and Germany during the 1930s, and thought they could be used in building an independent India. Nevertheless, Bose's tenure as Congress Party President (1938-39) did not reflect any particular anti-democratic or authoritarian attributes. Nirad C. Chaudhuri, Anton Pelinka and Leonard Gordon have remarked that Bose's skills were best illustrated at the negotiating table, rather than on the battlefield.

That Bose eventually changed his political stance reflects his deep discontent with the nature of the British rule, and a growing belief that the formation of an Indian free state was too far into the future on the British political roadmap to be acceptable. At the Tripura Congress session of 1939, he made his views quite explicit-he demanded for a programme of immediately giving the British Government a six-months ultimatum to grant the national demand of independence and of launching a mass civil disobedience movement if it failed to do so. He believed that "... the country was internally more ripe for a revolution than ever before and that the coming international crisis would give India an opportunity for achieving her emancipation, which is rare in human history.". Bose's judgment in allying with the Japanese has been questioned, as many argue that he would have been unable to ensure an independent India had he ridden to power on Japanese bayonets, and was in danger of being turned into a puppet ruler like Pu-yi, the last Chinese Emperor in Manchukuo. In 1943 Rash Behari Bose had urged this on him during his last visit to Subhash Bose in Singapore, pointing out that the Japanese had claimed right of conquest in Manchuria and would do so in India, whilst Quit India had shown that this would not be accepted by the Indian Nation.

Nevertheless, given the INA's overwhelming dependence on Japanese military support, he would have been in a very weak position. Bose also seems to have ignored the appalling treatment meted out by the Japanese to the Asian inhabitants of the lands they conquered as part of the Greater East Asian Co-prosperity sphere, which included the forcible recruitment of labour from the overseas Indian population to build projects such as the Burma Railway, and massacres of Malayan Chinese in Singapore where he spent most of the War.

Bose has been branded as a fascist in some quarters. Others believe that Bose had clearly expressed his belief that democracy was the best option for India. The pro-Bose thinkers believe that his authoritarian control of the Indian National Army was based on political pragmatism and a post-colonial recovery doctrine rather than any anti-democratic belief.. However, during the war (and possibly as early as the 1930s) Bose seems to have decided that no democratic system could be adequate to overcome India's poverty and social inequalities, and he wrote that an authoritarian state, similar to that of Soviet Russia (which he had also seen and admired) would be needed for the process of national rebuilding. Accordingly some suggest that Bose's alliance with the Axis during the war was based on more than just pragmatism, and that Bose may have been a Fascist, though not a Nazi; alternatively, others consider he might have been using populist methods of mobilization common to many postcolonial leaders.

Had either of the alliances he forged during the war resulted in Indian independence in the manner he envisaged, it would have been at the cost of an Allied defeat in the Second World War, a price that some Indians would argue is too high: Gandhi himself, in the immediate aftermath of the war, said that Bose had been "foolish in imagining, that by allying himself with the Japanese and the Germans, who were not only aggressive Powers, but also dangerous Powers, he could get Indian freedom". The alternative of nonviolent protest within India espoused by Gandhi and the rest of Congress ultimately led to British withdrawal, albeit at the expense of the partition of the country along communal lines. Even before 1939, Congress had secured political concessions from the British in the form of elected Provincial Assemblies, and an agreement that the British taxpayer would foot the bill for Indian re-armament. Although it was rejected by Congress at the time, the 1942 Cripps mission's offer of full independence after the war could be considered the point at which the British departure became inevitable. Britain's weakness after the war, and domestic political pressure on the Labour Government also made British withdrawal more likely. Publicly at least, Bose never believed that this would happen unless they were driven out by force: as late as 1944, three years prior to Independence, he announced that "I am honestly convinced that the British Government will never recognise India's demand for independence".. Nirad Chaudhuri considered it a backhanded tribute to Bose that the Congress tricolor and the Muslim League green flag flew together for the last time during the mutiny of the Indian navy in Bombay unleashed in 1946 partly at anger within the Navy at the trial of INA officers by the British.

Judith Brown argues that the Mutiny of the Indian Navy was a minor factor in the British decision to leave compared to domestic political pressure, American hostility to any continuation of the *Raj*, and the breakdown of almost all networks of support and collaboration brought about by thirty years of Congress agitation. By 1946 over 50% of the members of the Indian Civil Service were Indians, and even Churchill recognised that the offer of independence made by the Cripps Mission in 1942 could not now be withdrawn. In this interpretation concerns over the loyalty of the military were only one factor amongst many amidst the general breakdown in authority: nor, it could be argued, did all this necessarily stem from the activities of Bose and the INA. The prospect of communalism infecting the armed forces worried the British just as much.

There is no doubt that Bose was considered a great patriot, and was considered as such even by his rivals in the Congress. Gandhi himself wrote that Bose's "... patriotism is second to none", and he was moved to proclaim after Bose's disappearance that he was a "prince among patriots"-a reference, in particular, to Bose's achievement in integrating women and men from all the regions and religions of India in the Indian National Army. Bose wanted freedom for India at the earliest opportunity, and to some extent, he didn't care who he had to approach for assistance. It is thus quite understandable that he remains a controversial figure to this day.

MODERN POPULAR VIEWS

The INA is fondly remembered by some Japanese rightwingers, who see the Japanese efforts to support Bose as proof of their view that Japan really was fighting on behalf of the oppressed peoples of Asia. In addition, the INA is seen by some as an organisation devoid of the divisive energies of parochialism that have since plagued Indian politics. Bose's portrait hangs in the Indian Parliament, and a statue has been erected in front of the West Bengal Legislative Assembly.

Bose was posthumously awarded the Bharat Ratna, India's highest civilian award in 1992, but it was later withdrawn in response to a Supreme Court directive following a Public Interest Litigation filed in the Court against the "posthumous" nature of the award. The Award Committee could not give conclusive evidence of Bose's death and thus it invalidated the "posthumous" award. Kolkata's civil airport and a university have been named after him.

In the period between the two world wars, Gandhi was the most powerful force within the Congress, and, it's probably fair to say, in nationalist politics. By this I mean not only that Gandhi was able to make the big decisions, or at least influence those decisions, but also that Gandhian methods had become the primary tactics of the nationalist movement. These tactics involved an emphasis on nonviolence, and a vacillation between non-cooperation and active participation. In other wards, the Gandhi and the Congress would go for years quietly coexisting with British rule, then launch a non-cooperation campaign, gain some concessions from the British, and then go back to another period of relative quiet. For the most part, there were few challenges to this approach outside the Congress. The terrorists carried on in certain areas of the country, especially Bengal, but they were, at the most, a nuisance. By the time of WW II, it had long become evident that elite terrorism was not going to inspire a popular revolution. After Gandhi came along and demonstrated how a popular movement might be generated, the terrorists became even less relevant.

The challenge to the predominance of Gandhi and Gandhian tactics in Indian nationalism came from within the Congress. It came from a man named Subhash Chandra Bose, who, at the height of his political influence, was one of the two or three most powerful leaders in the Congress. Gandhi certainly saw Bose as a rival and a dangerous upstart, and did his best to destroy him politically. I want to focus on Bose today not because I think his battles with Gandhi are particularly fascinating, but because Bose held up an alternative vision, not only of political tactics, but also of political objectives. Whereas Gandhi sought compromises with the British, Bose sought absolute victories. Gandhi was willing to wait a long time for independence, Bose wanted immediate action, if not immediate results. Gandhi was anti-materialistic and hostile to modern technology, Bose saw technology and mass production as essential to survival and dignity. Gandhi wanted a decentralized society and disliked the modern state; Bose wanted a strong central government and saw the modern state as the only solution to India's problems. And finally, Bose did not share Gandhi's dedication to nonviolence.

Bose came from a upper-class Bengali family. His father was a well-known lawyer in Cuttack. He was the ninth child in a big, busy family; but his parents were aloof, and Bose grew up as a loner. He was a voracious reader, and he was especially attracted to the writings of the 19th~century Hindu social reformer, Swami Vivekananda. From Vivekananda he picked up a desire to take India, especially Hindu India, back to an idealized past in which Indians had been strong, moral and free. As he grew older, and became interested in socialism, he lost this interest in mythical golden ages and his overtly Hindu outlook. But he kept his determination to do something about what he saw as social injustice towards low-caste groups, the poor, and women.

He was a brilliant student, and became active in student politics at Calcutta's Presidency College. In those wartime years, the university offered military training to students who were interested (sort of like the ROTC today), and Bose eagerly signed up. But unlike Gandhi, who also had military experience, Bose did not join because he saw it as his duty to the Empire. He joined because he believed military training was an important part of a nationalist's education. He fervently believed that India, and especially Hindus, had become politically subjugated because of their military weakness. If the nation was to be free and worthy of respect, Bose felt, its citizens must know how to fight.

Also at Presidency College, he had one of his first direct encounters with the British. He became involved in an assault by students on a British professor, and was kicked out of school. This incident has since become one of the major myths of Indian nationalism, with Bose presented as the hero and Edward Oaten, the professor, presented as a racist villain. The truth is probably not so clear-cut. What is more likely is that Oaten was tactless, and Bose was hot-headed. A sense of humour was not one of Bose's strong points; he tended to be touchy and took everything very seriously. He eventually graduated from Scottish Church college in Calcutta (after his father pulled a few strings to get him admitted), and was then packed off to England by his family to prepare for the ICS (Indian Civil Service) exams. He arrived in England in 1919, when he was 23 years old.

It's interesting to compare Bose's English experience with Gandhi's. Bose was probably a bit less socially isolated than Gandhi had been when he had first arrived; there were more Indians around for him to spend time with. As with Gandhi, the time Bose spent in England made a deep impression on his thinking. Like Gandhi, Bose became something of a dandy in England, always wearing expensive, perfectly pressed clothes. Like Gandhi, Bose was terrified of sex, and put all his guards up when he was around English women. And like Gandhi, Bose became more conscious of his Indian identity when he was in England.

But there were some very significant differences, as well. Gandhi did not become a nationalist while he was in England. That came later. Gandhi's nationalism developed slowly over the decades, and if we had to look for pivotal movements we would have to find them in South Africa and later in Jallianwalla Bagh. Bose arrived in England as a budding nationalist, and as somebody who was very conscious, and very resentful, of the racial basis of British rule in India. In England, he wrote one of his friends: "Nothing makes me happier than to be served by the whites and to watch them clean my shoes. In England, Bose's nationalism became more clearly defined, and more militant, than it had been before.

At the same time, Bose liked England. He enjoyed the openness of English society, the freedom of expression, the debates in Parliament and at the university, the fact that students weren't shadowed by the police. It made him acutely aware of how different life was in colonial India. Also, there was a lot that Bose admired about the British in England. He found them efficient and energetic, he appreciated their sense of a national interest, and what he saw as their can-do attitude.

These qualities-efficiency, energy, discipline, a sense of punctuality-are all central to modern industrial society, and they became central to Bose's vision of what India should be like.

He did very well in the ICS exams, and then faced a dilemma that had, by the 1920's, become common for Indian nationalists. Should he join the lAS, and participate in the administration of India, or should he keep his distance from the colonial government? Would participation constitute collaboration? Eventually Bose decided to stay away from the IAS.

Quite apart from his qualms about the Indian Civil Service, there was another major factor that influenced his decision. Bose was one of those people who desperately needed a father-figure in his life. Ever since he had been a child, he had attached himself to his teachers and to various swamis, hoping to find somebody who could be a combination of spiritual advisor, political mentor, and intellectual guide. For Bose, who was already leaning towards a career in nationalist politics, one possible choice might have been Gandhi, who served those functions for Nehru. But Bose never developed this intimacy with Gandhi. He admired Gandhi, but the philosophical differences were too great.

As he resigned from the Indian Civil Service, Bose finally found his father-figure. This was C.R. Das, who was another one of those nationalist lawyer-politicians active in the Congress. In some ways, Das was a curious choice of mentor for a hot-headed extremist like Bose. Das was the ultimate machine politician. He believed in building an administrative organization within the framework of the colonial government, and then running that organization as independently as possible. He did not look for revolution; rather like Gandhi, he believed in a gradual process of piecemeal concessions. Like Gandhi, he had responded to the Rowlatt Acts by throwing himself into the non-cooperation movement. He had abandoned his legal practice and his western suits, and adopting khadi and frugality, although he was never quite as frugal as Gandhi. Bose was drawn to C.R. Das primarily because he admired the latter's personal sacrifices. The fact that both men were Bengalis was also a factor. And perhaps, at a psychological level, Das-with his social, cultural and professional background-was sufficiently like Bose's own father.

So Bose wrote to C.R. Das, offering his services, and rather boldly outlining his own ideas of how to build a nationalist organization. Congress, he wrote, should have a permanent house. It should come up with a set of policies for all of India, including the princely states, It should have policies for improving the conditions of low-caste groups, It should have its own research and intelligence wing, and a well-organized public relations machine.

These ideas are important for several reasons, For one thing, they tell us a lot about how Bose was thinking about the present and the future. Already, in 1921, he wanted the Congress to function as a parallel government, This is something that very few people inside the Congress, including Gandhi, had given much thought to, or were comfortable contemplating, For another, these ideas highlight the emphasis Bose would place on efficient organization. They reflect his conviction that society's problems could be solved not through moral persuasion-which was the Gandhian line-but through pressure exerted by powerful organizations, such as a parallel government, or an independent nation-state.

Das was impressed by Bose's ideas, and invited Bose to work with him in Calcutta. So he went, and in 1921 he plunged immediately into hectic political activity mat fully utilized his talents as an organizer. Seeing a need to develop alternatives to the colonial educational system, Bose threw himself into creating a nationalist college. He set himself up as the principal, found professors who were willing to lecture, invented courses, developed course schedules, and even planned on taking some courses himself. All this was typical of the man: he wanted to be the leader, he wanted to plan and to organize, and at the same time he wanted to learn.

When he was not working on the nationalist college, Bose was organizing strikes and demonstrations in Calcutta as part of the non-cooperation movement. The British threw him in jail, along with C.R. Das and thousands of other activists, but this was pretty much what the non-cooperation movement aimed to achieve. He was released after six months, and was immediately back at work, doing what he did best: organizing large-scale operations. There had serious flooding in parts of Bengal. Bose, working with Congress volunteers, set up relief operations that were bigger and more effective than anything the Congress had done along those lines until then. Since the colonial government didn't do much to help the flood victims, Bose's reputation as an effective political leader grew larger.

At around this time, Bose began to have his first open disagreements with Gandhi. Actually, it was Das who had the disagreement with Gandhi, and initially Bose was involved only as Das' right-hand man, Das wanted the Congress to contest elections to local councils under the Montagu-Chelmsford Act of 1919, and to become actively involved in local government. Gandhi felt this would undermine non-cooperation, and refused. But Das had support within the Congress on this issue, particularly from the two Nehrus. They got together and formed the Swaraj Party. This was not really a separate party, but a group that remained within the overall Congress organization. Faced with this tension within the Congress, Gandhi compromised and allowed the Swaraj Party to participate in the elections.

In the 1924 elections to the Calcutta Municipal Corporation-*i.e.*, the city government of Calcutta-the Swaraj Party won a two-thirds majority. Bose became the Chief Executive Officer. In other words, at the age of 27, he was one of the most powerful men in the second-largest city of the British Empire. He loved the job: it allowed him to use his talent for developing and running big operations, to be innovative, and to be the boss. He took charge of all kinds of details, from designing city employees' uniforms, to creating new municipal programmes for education and public health.

In the meantime, the colonial secret service kept a close watch on him, and tried to come up with evidence that would bring him down. The colonial government had first noticed Bose during Oaten episode, and now he was seen as a particularly dangerous nationalist politician, who was becoming too powerful too fast. Eventually, in the fall of 1924, Bose was arrested on vague charges of conspiring with terrorists to kill the police commissioner of Calcutta. The charges were almost certainly false. Bose probably sympathized with the terrorists, and may have helped them find jobs, etc., but it's totally implausible that he would have jeopardized his career at that stage by trying to kill his own police chief.

In any event, the British wanted to get him out of the country, and he was sent off to jail in Burma. His health broke down in prison, and he was eventually released in 1927. He came back to India and found that a lot had changed in his political fortunes. For one thing, C.R. Das had died, and the leadership of the Swaraj Party had been taken over by Gandhi loyalists. This left Bose without a secure foothold in the political establishment. He remained active in the Congress, but his moment at the center of power had passed. He went back to being the permanent outsider. In sonic ways, this freed him up, especially when it came to being able to criticize Gandhi. Now he had less to lose.

He spoke out strongly on two issues. Firstly, he criticized Gandhi's hostility to modern technology and mass He declared: "We have to live in the present and to adapt ourselves to modern conditions. The days of the bullock cart are gone forever." And, for those of you who have been following the recent controversy over the Indian nuclear programme, he added: "Free India must arm herself for any eventuality as long as the whole world does not accept wholeheartedly the policy of disarmament."

His second point of disagreement with Gandhi was over the pace and the objectives of the nationalist movement. Gandhi tended to give the British a lot of time to respond to Congress demands, and there were long gaps between the periods of active agitation. Bose wanted immediate agitation, and could not understand why Gandhi always waited for the right moment. A true revolutionary, he felt, created the moment, rather than wait for it to arrive. Also, Gandhi and his allies within the Congress were not, in 1928, ready to come out and demand complete independence. They preferred to define the nationalist goal as dominion status, *i.e.*, as autonomy within the British Empire. Bose found this unacceptable, and he did not hesitate to say so.

Nevertheless, he was still working closely with the Congress. During the Congress' convention in Calcutta in 1928, Bose organized the ceremonies. In the process, he allowed his imagination to run wild: he put Congress volunteers in military-style uniforms, named himself General Officer Commanding, and held a military-style honour guard for Nehru senior. Once again, this was his childish delight in uniforms and smart salutes coming to the forefront. Most people didn't know whether to laugh or to cry. Gandhi, most likely, was not amused.

In 1929, Bose was elected president of the Bengal branch of the Congress, defeating Gandhi's candidate. Not long after that, he was jailed for protesting the government's treatment of revolutionaries and political prisoners. In 1930 Gandhi finally gave the call for complete independence, and launched a new campaign of civil disobedience.

Bose watched the campaign from prison. While in prison, he was elected mayor of Calcutta. When he was released in the fall of 1930, he immediately went back to being the organizer of massive nationalist demonstrations. After a confrontation with the police in which he was violently assaulted, he was sent back to jail. For the time being, his career as an active politician in India came to an end.

Bose's health failed again in prison, and he went to Europe to recover. He spent most of the 1930's in Europe, shadowed by the British secret service. Nevertheless, he travelled extensively in Switzerland, Germany, Austria, Italy, Ireland and eastern Europe. He developed extensive contacts with the European left as well as with the right, both of which had reasons to be anti-Britain, and to welcome Bose as a man who was fighting the British in India. He met Mussolini, discussed his revolutionary plans with him, and Mussolini was suitably impressed. This period in Europe had a profound effect on Bose's politics. For one thing, his exposure to the left sharpened his faith in revolutionary socialism, and his determination to lead a socialist revolution in India. For another, his exposure to the right gave him an admiration for the techniques of organization and administration that the Nazis were trying out in Germany, and that Mussolini's fascists had been trying out in Italy.

We now have to deal with the question of Bose's political ideology at this point, especially the question of whether or not he was a fascist. Well, in a word: yes, Bose was now a fascist. He had no problems with openly admiring fascism. At the same time, he was not a Nazi, in the sense that he was not a racist, and he had no interest in theories of national purity and cultural supremacy. Bose did not seek a Hindu India, or some pure version of Indian culture. He had long outgrown his old politics of Hindu nostalgia. He welcomed Muslim participation in Indian nationalism, and he did not hesitate when it came to forming alliances with Muslim politicians.

For Bose, fascism was a technique of political organization, and a diagram for relations between government and society. Bose was not a democrat. He may have been one in the 1920's, but by the late 1930's he was quite certain that parliamentary democracy was not suitable for India. In his mind, India needed firm control by a single party, which would direct every aspect of social, political, economic and even personal life.

He believed that India's problems-such as caste discrimination, class injustice, the need for economic modernization, etc.-were so deep-rooted that mey could only be weeded out through massive state intervention. For this, Bose believed, the machinery of the state had to be in the hands of a single, powerful, reforming party organization, such as the Nazi Party in Germany or the Communist Party in the Soviet Union. At this point, he still believed that this party would be the Congress. Bose finally returned to India in January of 1937. He was now much more radical than he had been when he had left. He was quick to reject the Government of India Act of 1935, which had allowed for greater Indian participation in the provincial governments.

For Bose, the law was too little too late. He was unhappy that the Congress had agreed to participate in the government under the Act, but this did not keep him away from Congress politics. The years in Europe had not diminished his popularity in India, and he had no trouble getting elected as the president of the Congress. He remained president for only a year, before Gandhi schemed to bring him down.

But for that one year, Bose was king, and he enjoyed himself thoroughly. As in the past, he threw himself into building Congress up as a practical parallel government. In keeping with his faith in modern technology, he set up a committee of prominent scientists to develop a viable industrial policy. He raised funds, and he campaigned tirelessly all over India. He emphasized his socialist ideals, and along with Nehru, became the recognized leader of the Congress left.

But Bose and Nehru did not become political allies. There are several reasons. There were the philosophical differences: Nehru was a democrat, Bose was authoritarian. Also Nehru, at heart, was something of an Anglophile, in the sense that he had a soft spot for India's connection with England. Bose had no such sentimental attachment. Then there were differences in temperament that played out in the way they each approached socialism and policy-making. Nehru was a visionary without much interest in the details of implementing his visions. But details mattered to Bose. And finally, there was the Gandhi factor.

In spite of his philosophical differences with Gandhi, Nehru was Gandhi's protege, and everybody knew it. Nehru would disagree with Gandhi on specific issues, but when push came to shove and a decision had to be made, he would give in and let Gandhi have his way. This was partly Out of a genuine respect for Gandhi's leadership, and partly because Nehru understood very well that his own political fortunes were linked to Gandhi's. As long as Nehru was Gandhi's boy, his own future within the Congress organization was insured. This reluctance to go up against Gandhi meant that when Gandhi turned on Bose, Nehru made no real effort to defend his fellow-socialist.

When Bose had been elected Congress president, Gandhi had accepted it. The break came in the fall of 1938, when war in Europe became a distinct possibility. Bose and the left saw the possibility of war as a tremendous political opportunity, and wanted to use this opportunity to pressure the colonial government for immediate concessions. Gandhi and the Congress right, on the other hand, wanted to issue a much weaker resolution, hoping that the British would simply do the right thing if war broke out. Bose and the left refused to give in, and Gandhi was furious. Even though Bose was the Congress president at this time, Gandhi had long enjoyed the status of the unofficial super-president of the Congress, and he did not like Bose's disobedience.

Bose was up for re-election in January of 1939, and Gandhi decided to block him. Quite apart from his personal animosity, there were real issues involved. Bose wanted the Congress to walk away from implementing the Government of India Act of 1935. He also wanted to give the colonial government an ultimatum demanding immediate independence, and to begin all-out civil disobedience if the government refused. Gandhi and the Congress right felt otherwise. In any event, Bose won his re-election, narrowly defeating P. Sitaramayya, who was Gandhi's chosen candidate.

Gandhi now worked actively to bring Bose down. The Congress constitution provided only two ways for getting rid of the president: he could be voted Out of office, or he could resign. Since Gandhi was unwilling to wait for the next election, he decided to force Bose to resign. Even though Bose was the Congress president, Gandhi's supporters controlled the party's Working Committee. Without their cooperation, the president could not operate effectively; it was a system of checks and balances similar to what we have in the US government.

Gandhi's supporters now resigned, and Bose found himself unable to form a new Working Committee against Gandhi's opposition. He tried hard to work out a compromise with Gandhi. He even offered to let Gandhi nominate the entire Working Committee, if Gandhi would only accept Bose's plan to launch an agitation for immediate independence. Gandhi politely refused, and Bose had no option except to resign, four months into his second term as president. One of the interesting things about this whole episode is that Bose blamed Nehru more than he blamed Gandhi. He never completely cut his ties with Gandhi, and continued to try to rebuild his bridges. But he never forgave Nehru for not helping him during this crisis.

On September 3 of 1939, war finally broke out in Europe. And not just in Europe, because the Viceroy Lord Linlithgow declared war on India's behalf, without consulting a single Indian. This was a major embarrassment for the Congress, which was now faced with two choices. It could either get some significant concessions from the colonial government. Or it could resign from the ministries it controlled under the Government of India Act. So the Congress went to the government, and asked for a clear statement of its military objectives.

The government stonewalled, saying that it was too early in the war to talk about military objectives. It also refused to talk about Indian independence, saying that any such discussion would have to wait until after the war. Since there was no clearly defined military objective, it meant that the government would decide when the war was over, and when Indian independence could be discussed. Congress now resigned from its ministries. It's been suggested that the British deliberately maneuvered Congress into resigning, to have a free hand in running the government during the war. Whatever the case may be, the Congress now found itself out of office, and with nothing but moral outrage to show for it. Still Gandhi refused to launch an agitation.

Bose, meanwhile, had been busy organizing his own party, called the Forward Bloc. This was initially within the structure of the Congress. But by 1940 it had become an independent political party, mainly because the Congress had refused to tolerate its allegiance to Bose instead of to Gandhi, and had kicked its officers out of office. Things were happening very fast for Bose, as usual. In July of 1940, he was arrested and sent to prison again for planning to lead a march demanding the removal of a memorial to the victims of the Black Hole of Calcutta. He went on a hunger-strike, and in December he was released. Then began his great adventure. Even before his last arrest, Bose had begun to think about getting himself Out of

India. He felt that there was little that he could achieve in India under the circumstances. His career in the Congress had stalled, and besides, the Congress was unwilling to do what he wanted it to do. The war, he felt, was too important an opportunity to waste. So he came up with a plan. He would escape from India, get to the Soviet Union, and then go on to Germany. When he got to Germany, he would persuade the Germans to help him in his fight against the British in India.

Bose now contacted a communist organization in Punjab. He asked if they might be able to smuggle him across the border into Afghanistan, and through Afghanistan into the USSR. They told him it was possible. In the winter of 1940-41 his journey began. Disguised as a Muslim life-insurance agent, Bose escaped from his family home in Calcutta in the middle of the night. He boarded a train at a remote rural station, and travelled to Peshawar on the border between Punjab and Afghanistan. From there, in a new disguise as a deaf-mute Pathan, and accompanied by his communist contact, he trekked across the desert to Kabul. His plan to travel across the border directly into the Soviet Union had been discarded as impractical. His current plan was to contact the Soviet embassy in Kabul.

Kabul in the 1940's was basically a truck-stop village with embassies. Bose, still posing as a deaf-mute, stayed at truck-drivers' hotel for weeks, trying to contact the Russians. He had no luck, the Russians suspected that he was a British agent trying to infiltrate the Soviet Union. Next Bose contacted the Germans. They heard him out, and were intrigued by his ideas, but dragged their feet. Eventually it was the Italians who rescued him. The Italian diplomat in Kabul was fascinated by Bose's plans. He gave Bose an Italian passport and the name Orlando Mazzotta, and persuaded the Germans and the Soviets to help him. Finally, in March of 1941, Bose travelled to the Soviet border in a diplomatic car, took a train to Moscow, and then flew to Berlin.

Bose remained in Germany for the next two years. He offered the Germans a deal. If they helped him, he said, he could trigger a revolution in India. Having to deal with a revolutionary situation in India would distract British forces from the war against Germany. In the process, Britain would lose the war with Germany, and lose India simultaneously. This was the big picture. To bring all this about, Bose put forward several ideas. Some of these he accomplished; in others areas he was frustrated. Let's look at his political objectives first.

Bose wanted facilities for broadcasting radio messages into India. This the Germans readily provided, and he made regular speeches directed at the Indian public. In his broadcasts, Bose urged people to use the war as an opportunity to break free. Germany would win the war, and the British should not be allowed to hang on in India. The first broadcasts created a sensation in India, largely because Bose's disappearance had generated a lot of public interest. But it didn't go much further than that. This was because in spite of Bose's presence in Berlin, to most Indians the war with Germany was still far away, and people couldn't really visualize the German army sweeping through the Caucasus to liberate India. Also, by this time, Gandhi and the Congress had finally launched the Quit India movement, and a violent revolutionary situation already existed in India.

Bose's other major accomplishment in Germany was organizing the Indian Legion. In the course of the fighting in north Africa, the Germans had taken thousands of Indian POWs. Bose went to the POW camps, and asked the Indian soldiers to join him to fight against the British. This idea was not entirely new. An expatriate Indian named Mohammed Iqbal Shedai had already made a start organizing Indian POWs captured by the Italians. For a while, Bose and Shedai ran parallel efforts with the POWs. Then the Indian soldiers in Shedai's camp mutinied, This discredited Shedai, and left Bose as the only Indian organizing an army to fight on the side of the Axis.

Ultimately, the Indian Legion that Bose organized in Germany numbered about 3000 soldiers. It was not easy putting this force together. Initially, when Bose visited the POW camps to talk to the soldiers, he got a hostile reception. The British Indian Army may have been an army without a nationalist ideology, but it would be a mistake to think of it as a purely mercenary force. The colonial army had its own ideology, which was a combination of loyalty to the British throne, loyalty to the commanding officer, loyalty to the regiment, and a tradition of service in which the same family or same village sent many generations of soldiers into the Army.

But Bose persisted. He had the men separated from their officers, and talked to them one on one. Eventually, he got through. He promised them proper treatment from the Germans, appropriate rank, pay and benefits, and he promised them victory. The British, he told them, were certain to lose the war; they were like a dead snake that people continue to fear. If only they shook off this fear, Bose said, victory and freedom would be theirs.

Bose had planned that when the German swing through the southern USSR and the Middle East reached India, the Indian Legion would spearhead the attack on India. He anticipated that this would have two results. One was that when the soldiers of the colonial Indian Army faced the Indian Legion, they would refuse to continue to fight for the British and desert en masse to Bose's side. The other was that an invasion of India by Indian Legion would galvanize the Indian population into rising up against the British, and make Bose's task easier.

As things turned out, however, the Indian Legion came to a rather sad end. First, the Russians stopped the German advance at the battle of Stalingrad. This, combined with the defeat at El Alamein, meant that the Germans would be unlikely to get anywhere near India. Second, after Bose left Germany in 1943, the Legion was left without an effective leader to look Out for them. They were absorbed into the German army and deployed in France. Now they knew they weren't going to be fighting for India's freedom, and their morale and discipline disintegrated. Many deserted, some joined the French resistance, and the rest disappeared in the chaos of the German retreat.

Bose's biggest frustration in Germany had to do with diplomatic recognition. He wanted Germany to officially recognize India as independent, and him as the leader of a government in exile. This the Germans refused to give him. The reasons lay partly in apathy, partly in the Master Race mentality, and partly in the peculiarities of Hitler's vision of the postwar world.

Hitler was not entirely comfortable with the idea of helping Indians-whom he saw as racially inferior-to defeat the British. The British were Aryans, after all. In his own way, Hitler admired the English, and through much of the war he continued to hope that he could come to some kind of an understanding with Britain: essentially, that Germany would get a free hand in Europe, and England would get to keep most of its empire. He was perfectly willing to use Bose to make trouble for the British, but he had no long-term interest in India's future, one way or another. Bose knew this, of course. He wanted to use the Germans for his own purposes. But eventually, as things turned out, neither was able to do very much for the other side.

,But by the middle of 1942, Bose was already looking beyond Germany, to Japan. The string of Japanese victories after Pearl Harbor had achieved two things. One was that Singapore, which was a major British military stronghold, had fallen to the Japanese. This placed tens of thousands of Indian soldiers in Japanese hands. What Bose had tried to do with the Indian Legion in Germany, he could try in Southeast Asia on a much larger scale. The other thing that encouraged Bose was the fact that Japanese forces had come all the way to the Indian border with Burma. In other words, if he could organize an army in Japanese-occupied territory, and attack on India would be a relatively practical idea.

So, in February of 1943, the Germans did Bose one last favour: they helped him get to Japan. He travelled in a German submarine to the coast of Mozambique, where he transferred to a Japanese submarine. This submarine took him to southeast Asia.

The former British colonies of southeast Asia-Burma, Malaya, and Singapore-had large Indian populations, and Bose was welcomed as a conquering hero. In a sense, they had been waiting for him; in spite of all efforts to keep his plans secret, rumours had been circulating that he would come. The Japanese welcomed him also, and were far more enthusiastic about working with him than the Germans had been.

I'll give you an example of the difference in attitude: when Bose was on the German sub, he ate bread that tasted like it had been dipped in diesel. On the Japanese sub, the crew had brought along Indian spices especially for him, and cooked him Indian curries until he protested about the frequent meals. After he reached Asia, Bose travelled widely in the Japanese-help territories: to Burma, Malaya, Singapore, the Philippines, Vietnam, occupied China, and of course Japan. Unlike his uneasy relationship with Hitler, he quickly developed an excellent relationship with Tojo.

The Japanese gave Bose two things which he had wanted very badly: diplomatic recognition as the premier of free India, and a real army. Let's talk about his political status first. He didn't have a territory, but he had a people: the Indian population of southeast Asia was placed under his jurisdiction. Bose got all the privileges and trappings of a head of state: the motorcade, the official aircraft, the honour guards, the works, He enjoyed it. In part, this was sheer megalomania: his old love of playing the great leader was resurfacing with a vengeance. In part, however, Bose recognized that it was necessary for him to play this role if was to deal effectively with the Japanese. He did not have any illusions about how the Japanese treated subject peoples. He knew that if he, and the Indians of southeast Asia, were to be taken seriously as allies, he had to insist upon his own status as an important political leader.

Bose did in fact run a real government in southeast Asia. I'm referring not to his status as leader of the government-in-exile of India, but to his status as leader of the local Indians. The regime Bose put together in Singapore, with the help of people who came forward to work with him, had the power to make and enforce laws, to collect taxes, and to recruit soldiers for the army. This people who paid the taxes and obeyed the laws did so willingly at first. Towards the end of the war, this cooperation became strained. As the Japanese collapsed and Tokyo's funding for Bose's army dried up, Bose pressed the local Indians for higher war taxes, and punished people who tried to hold back. This cost him some of his local popularity. The army, to some extent, already existed when Bose arrived in Asia. After the fall of Singapore, an Indian officer named Mohan Singh had created the Indian National Army, or the INA as it came to be known, from Indian POWs. This force was much larger than the Indian Legion in Germany. As such, it was a viable military and political resource. Mohan Singh himself had rather an unhappy career with the INA. Soldiers had joined the INA on the understanding that they would fight only on the Indian front. When the Japanese tried to send the INA to fight in other parts of southeast Asia, several units mutinied. These units were disbanded, and Mohan Singh ended up in a Japanese prison.

This was, in a way, a parallel of what had happened in Europe with Shedai's army. When Bose came to Asia, he quickly assumed command of what was left of Mohan Singh's old INA. At this time, this force had only 13,000 soldiers. But Bose had big plans. He wanted to expand the INA in two phases, first to 50,000 soldiers, and then to a force of 3 million. The men would come from the colonial Indian Army as well as from the southeast Asian Indian community.

The Japanese were shocked at such an ambitious plan, and told Bose that they would be able to arm a much smaller force, of about 30,000. Eventually, the INA reached a peak strength of around 50,000. It was an interesting social experiment in more ways than one. The colonial Indian Army had organized its units around ethnicity and religion, so that the British could play off one group of Indians against another if necessary. In contrast, the INA had fully integrated units. It also had a regiment of female troops: this was the Rani of Jhansi Brigade, named after the queen who had died fighting the British in the Rebellion of 1857.

For Bose, the big numbers were necessary for their political effect. It didn't matter if most of the 3 million weren't equipped with adequate weapons. He saw the INA as a psychological force as well as a military asset. He knew that if people in India became aware that a nationalist army of 3 million was waiting just across the border, ready to invade, it would have a tremendous effect on the way Indians related to the British. It would inspire pride and confidence, it would take away the fear of British power, and it would make it impossible for the British to maintain control.

In fact, Bose's whole strategy for using the INA depended upon this psychological factor. He wanted the force to spearhead a Japanese invasion, expecting that this would totally demoralize and dissolve the colonial Indian army, ,,,drawing its soldiers into the INA. He expected also that the general public would respond with overwhelming support.

It turned out that he was half right. The INA lost the war, but won the peace. In the summer of 1944, the Japanese were finally ready to begin their invasion of India. They attacked from Burma in a two-pronged approach, hoping to capture the town of Imphal. This would then become the base for the rest of the invasion. But, at this critical point in Bose's plan, everything that could go wrong went wrong, The monsoon came early, and the Japanese assault became bogged down in the rain and the mud.

Also, by this point, the war in the Pacific was going very badly for the Japanese. Therefore the Japanese had allocated most of their air power to the Pacific theatre, leaving their forces in the Burma-India theatre without any air cover. This gave the British a crucial advantage.

Then there were other factors. Food rations became exhausted. Allied air strikes cut the supply lines. Japanese and INA units found themselves eating grass and jungle flowers to stay alive. Japanese commanders on the ground made some serious tactical errors. Normally, when things are going well, a few mistakes don't have to be fatal. But by 1944 the Japanese had overreached their capabilities. The attack on Imphal failed, and the counterattack was devastatingly effective. The INA became caught up in this disaster, and never recovered. The INA's coordination with Japanese units was poor to begin with. Once things began to go badly for the Japanese, INA units became stranded. Some units fought well and there were plenty of individual heroics to go around, but it made no difference to the overall failure.

The biggest failure was the INA's inability to break up the morale of the colonial Indian Army, which did most of the fighting at Imphal, and which played a major role in the Allied counterattack. Bose had expected that when the INA met the British Indian Army, colonial troops would immediately desert to the nationalist side. This did not happen. Bose had seriously underestimated the ideological strength of the colonial military. In fact, what often happened was the reverse. Starving and out of ammunition in the jungle, shocked by the failure of the Japanese offensive, many INA troops were eager to return to their old units and their old comrades in the colonial army. There were over 700 desertions, and eventually Bose had to give orders that deserters would be shot on suspicion.

After the Imphal defeat, the Japanese retreated steadily through Burma and into Malaya, pursued by British and colonial Indian troops. The INA retreated with them. This retreat, ironically, brought Out Bose's best qualities as a leader. On the long trek from Burma to Bankok, followed closely by British tanks and under frequent attack from the air, he marched for days on end, refusing the offer of a car while his men had to walk. Throughout the march, he made sure that INA troops had proper food and medical care. In the chaos of the retreat, Bose was their best protection, and everybody knew it. Without him, the Japanese would have been only too eager to abandon the INA.

Bose returned to Singapore and tried for a while to rebuild the INA. This was the period when he demanded ten percent of the value of peoples assets to pay for military expenses, and made himself unpopular with the wealthier Indians in Malaya. But for Japan, the war was almost over. After the nuclear bombing of Hiroshima and Nagasaki, there was nothing left for Bose in working with Tokyo. He now made a political gamble. The Soviets had been an ally of the British during the war, and an enemy of his allies, the Germans and the Japanese. But Bose correctly foresaw that the Soviet alliance with the west would not last. He decided to travel to Manchuria, which had just been overrun by the USSR. He planned to continue his fight against the British, but from Russia this time.

On 16th August, a day after the Japanese surrendered, Bose boarded a Japanese bomber in Saigon, on his way to Darien, in China. On the 18th of August, after a refueling stop in Taipei, the bomber crashed. Bose was still alive, but badly burned. He died in a Japanese military hospital in Taipei, soon afterwards. The story didn't end there, During the war, the British had carefully suppressed all news about the INA. This news now finally broke in India. Bose immediately became a hero of mythical proportions. People refused to believe he was dead; in fact, people refused to believe it for decades.

Also, Bose's predictions about the psychological value of his army were finally vindicated. The British played into his hands by making a series of miscalculations about how to deal with 25,000 captured INA soldiers. Misreading the public mood, the British decided to stage a series of highly publicized trials of INA officers in New Delhi. Incredibly, they believed that since the INA had taken up arms against Indians in the colonial army, the Indian public would want them to be severely punished.

Exactly the opposite happened. When three INA officers-Shah Nawaz Khan, G.S. Dhillon and Prem Kumar Sahgal-were put on trial for treason and murder in the Red Fort, the public quickly grasped the symbolism of the affair. The three officers included a Hindu, a Muslim and a Sikh. In other words, all three of India's major religious communities were seen as being on trial for having come together to fight for their country. The fact that the trials were being held at the Red Fort, where the last independent Indian regime had been based, was seen as an added insult. Even before the trials began, celebrations honouring the INA were held all over India. When the trials did begin, anti-British crowds besieged the Red Fort, and more than a hundred people were killed or injured by police firing. In Calcutta, Hindus and Muslims, flying the flags of the Congress as well as the Muslim League, attacked British and American military bases. Scores of military vehicles were damaged or destroyed. Over 200 military personnel were injured, and 32 Indians were killed. The violence soon spread across much of northern India, all the way to Bombay and Karachi.

Congress leaders like Gandhi and Nehru, who had been uncomfortable with Bose while he was alive, now eagerly jumped on the INA bandwagon. Nehru put on his old lawyer's robes and participated in the defense of the officers on trial. Gandhi made speeches praising Bose. Confronted by this public hostility, the British found themselves unable to punish the INA prisoners as severely as they would have liked. Most got commuted sentences, or short prison terms. Nevertheless, the British persisted with the trials, and the violence continued to grow. Early in 1946, martial law had to be declared in Calcutta. At around the same time, Indian troops in the colonial navy and air force mutinied, citing sympathy for the INA as well as unhappiness about their conditions of service. Within days, 78 warships had pulled down the Union Jack. Fierce battles erupted in the streets of Karachi and Bombay, in which tanks and machine-guns were used. In Bombay, the mutineers were supported by the working class. 600,000 textile workers went on strike, and joined the sailors in street battles against British forces.

The rebels eventually failed, in part because they didn't have the firepower that the British were able to call in, and in part because the Congress panicked and told them to stop fighting. The mutineers had looked to the Congress and the Muslim League to lead them. By the spring of 1946, however, the Congress and the League were too deeply implicated in the government of the country to see any good in this kind of unrest. Leaders like Nehru and Jinnah knew that independence was now at the most only a couple of years away.

As such, they did not want to encourage something as messy, as volatile and as dangerous as an armed rebellion. They had no experience and no stomach for leading this kind of movement, and they quietly supported the British efforts to crush the rebels.

But Bose's predictions about what would happen when the INA entered India had, to a considerable degree, come true, He had predicted a public uprising and sympathy from colonial troops, and now he was proved right. This is what I meant when I said that the INA lost the war but won the peace. But if Bose was right, where did he go wrong? Well, as I've argued, that Bose misread the nature of the colonial army. On the battlefield, when everything was at stake, the colonial army retained its loyalties. It was only after the war that sections of it mutinied.

It can also be argued that Bose misread the political situation in India in the 1940's. Being away in Germany and southeast Asia had isolated him from the political realities of wartime India, and he had missed some crucial changes in the way the wind was blowing. By 1942, the British were willing to discuss independence for India when the war ended. By 1945, there was no doubt that negotiations would soon begin. Yet Bose continued to fight a military battle, instead of rejoining the political process.

Was this unnecessary, and a mistake? Not if you were in Bose's shoes. He had taken up arms against the British, and his relations with the Congress had collapsed. He had reason to believe that if he returned to India while it was controlled by the British or the Congress, he would be treated as a war criminal. Also, although India was clearly on its way to independence by the mid-40's, this was not the kind of independence that Bose had wanted. For Bose, the revolution at home was as important as throwing out the British, and for this he needed to be completely in charge. He did not believe that the replacement of British rule by a conservative parliamentary democracy would not bring about fundamental changes in the structure of Indian society.

This brings us some of the most basic questions about Bose, the nationalist and the politician. What are we to make of the fact that he wanted to invite the Germans and the Japanese to invade India? And how do we reconcile his heroic status with the fact that he aligned himself with Nazi Germany, and that he openly advocated dictatorship as the best form of government for India?

Perhaps the biggest weakness in Bose's plan was his belief that even after bringing the Japanese into India, he could maintain effective control of the country. At a diplomatic level, he had grounds for believing he could pull this off. He refused to take India into the Japanese Co-Prosperity Sphere, which was the euphemism the Japanese used for their new empire in Asia, The Japanese accepted Bose's decision on this. Still, if the invasion of India had succeeded, it is difficult to see how he could have remained fully independent of Japanese control.

Bose felt that since the people of India would be with him, he would be able to resist Japanese demands. He knew that India was a long way from Japan, and that the Japanese were already at the limits of their capabilities. He also pointed out that the American revolutionaries had accepted assistance from France, and this didn't make the US a French colony. He may have had a point. But this analogy has its limits. Given the fact the INA was completely dependent on Japan for arms and ammunition, and that it would take time to develop an industrial infrastructure in India, Japan would probably have had a lot of leverage.

There is no getting away from the fact that Bose deliberately ignored the moral evil that Nazi Germany represented. He had lived in Germany for much of the 1930s and the early 40s. He must have known something of what was going on. He had the courage to speak out against some of the racist aspects of the Nazi ideology, and even speak his mind to Hitler himself. But he was not sufficiently disturbed by Nazism to reject Hitler's help. Similarly, his alliance with Japan ignored the atrocities that the Japanese had perpetrated against people in the countries they had occupied. Unlike Gandhi and Nehru, Bose believed that the end justified the means. He wanted freedom for India, and to some extent, he didn't care who he had to approach for assistance. But this explanation, I think, is too kind to Bose. At some basic level, Bose had an ideological affinity for fascism, and he was a little too comfortable with using the state to crush dissent and ideological diversity.

Indians who refused to believe that Bose was dead, and who continued to believe for decades that he was alive somewhere in the Soviet Union, hoped he would just surface again some day like a messiah, and solve all of India's problems. Yet these people misunderstand Bose, and what he stood for. Had the INA and Bose succeeded on the battlefield, a free India would have been a totalitarian society. Bose was passionate in his patriotism, and genuinely well-intentioned. He was genuine in his desire to help the disadvantaged segments of Indian society.

But good intentions are not enough. Some of the greatest tyrants of the 20th century had good intentions: Lenin, Mao, Pol Pot. (You'll notice that these are all tyrants of the left. Tyrants of the right like Hitler, Franco, or the Shah of Iran, don't get credit for good intentions.) Bose didn't seem to realize that the methods you choose do matter in the final analysis. Totalitarian institutions inevitably corrupt even the best-intentioned people. Even if it hadn't corrupted Bose himself, even if he had remained a so-called benevolent dictator, there would have been no guarantees that his successor would have been benevolent. Ultimately, dying at the end of the war was the best thing Bose could have done for India.

British 'Attempted to Kill Bose'

The British told their agents to assassinate India's independence war leader Subhash Chandra Bose in 1941, an Irish historian has claimed. Eunan O'Halpin, who has written several books on British intelligence, says the order came after Bose sought support of the Axis powers in World War II. British agents were told to intercept and kill Bose before he reached Germany via the Middle East, Mr O'Halpin says. Bose is believed to have died in a plane crash in Taiwan in 1945.

Puzzled

Mr O'Halpin says that once they found Bose was planning to oust the British with active support of the Axis powers, British intelligence was given "clear orders" to assassinate him in 1941.

"It appears to be a last desperate measure against someone who had thrown the Empire in complete panic" Eunan O'Halpin

In a lecture in Calcutta, Mr O'Halpin cited a recently declassified intelligence document referring to a top-secret instruction to the Special Operations Executive (SOE) of British intelligence to murder Bose.

Mr O'Halpin says the British were initially puzzled about the whereabouts of Bose after his escape from Calcutta in January 1941.

"They thought he had gone to the Far East, but they soon intercepted Italian diplomatic communication and came to know Bose was in Kabul, planning to reach Germany through the Middle East," said Mr O'Halpin.

"Two SOE operatives in Turkey were instructed by their headquarters in London to intercept Bose and kill him before he reached Germany," the Irish professor, who teaches at Trinity College, Dublin, said.

Mr O'Halpin said the SOE operatives in Turkey failed to because Bose reached Germany through Central Asia and the Soviet Union. "Every time [the operatives] checked back, headquarters told them the orders were intact and Bose must be killed if found."

Mystique

Describing the decision as "extraordinary, unusual and rare", Mr O'Halpin said the British took Bose "much more seriously than many thought".

He added: "Historians working on the subject tell me the plan to liquidate Bose has few parallels. It appears to be a last desperate measure against someone who had thrown the Empire in complete panic." Other historians who have worked on Bose say this will add to the mystique of India's most charismatic independence war figure.

"Bose would have reasons to compliment himself if he knew that the British were desperate enough to plan his assassination. That's a measure of how seriously they took him," says Calcutta historian, Lipi Ghosh. In retrospect, she says, the British had correctly assessed the potential of Bose.

Sugata Bose, Gardiner professor of history at Harvard University and a grand-nephew of Bose. said: "Since he ultimately managed to swing the loyalty of the Indian soldiers to the national cause from the King Emperor, they had all the reasons to contemplate the worst."

After 20 years in the Indian National Congress, Bose was elected its president but quit in disgust at Gandhi's plans for nonviolent struggle.

After reaching Germany he travelled to East Asia in a 90-day submarine journey to set up the Indian National Army from soldiers who had surrendered to Japan. Bose's army fought with the Japanese in the Imphal-Kohima campaign in 1944-1945.

The Strategy

"The time has come when I can openly tell the whole world, including our enemies, as to how it is proposed to bring about national liberation. Indians outside India, particularly Indians in East Asia, are going to organise a fighting force which will be powerful enough to attack the British Army in India. When we do so, a revolution will break out, not only among the civil population at home, but also among the Indian Army which is now standing under the British flag. When the British government is thus attacked from both sides-from inside India and from outside-it will collapse, and the Indian people will then regain their liberty. According to my plan, it is not even necessary to bother about the attitude of the Axis powers towards India. If Indians outside and inside India will do their duty, it is possible for the Indian people to throw the British out of India and liberate 388 millions of their countrymen."-*Speech by Netaji Subhash Chandra Bose at a mass rally, Singapore, 9 July 1943*

The Alternative Hero of the India's Struggle for Freedom....
It is 23 January 1981, and crowds all over India are celebrating the birthday of Subhash Bose. Politicians who have never known him, and many who fought him when he was alive, garland his statues, invoke his name and urge their audiences to follow his example. More than thirty years after his death Bose has become a myth: the alternative hero of the Indian struggle for freedom. And the banners at these meetings tell their own story. 'Subhash Bose 1897-1981'. Subhash Bose is not dead. One day he will return and rescue India.

The legends and the myths have been a long time in the making, and they express a deeper Indian unease: had he lived and returned to India after the war, he would have shaped a country far more successful than the one wrought by his rivals and successors: an India united, strong and fearless. Bose became a legend in his own lifetime, but his transformation into a myth fit to rank with ancient Hindu classics came after his death, through forces he had himself tried to harness for his cause. They were catalysed through the British decision to hold a symbolic trial of certain I.N.A. men in the Red Fort of Delhi.

The Decision to try the I.N.A....

The end of the war saw the I.N.A. (Indian National Army) scattered all over east Asia and in deep depression. As its personnel were finally shipped back to India they found the country ignorant of their existence and firmly under British control. 'Not a dog barked as they flew us back,' was how one officer recalled the journey home.

But within days of Japan's defeat the British had begun to think about the I.N.A. problem. London had left it for Delhi to decide, but Delhi was deeply divided and had yet to be convinced that Bose was in fact dead. On 24 August, the day the Japanese government announced the death, Wavell recorded in his diary:

'I wonder if the Japanese announcement of Subhash Chandra Bose's death in an air-crash is true, I suspect it very much, it is just what would be given out if he meant to go underground.'

He asked his Home Member, Sir R. F. Mudie, to prepare a note for the trial of Bose and the I.N.A.

Mudie could find nothing even in the extended definition of 'war criminal' that could be said to include Bose. His advisers were deeply worried about the consequences of a trial and the Home Department note he sent to Wavell acknowledged the difficulties of handling Bose. British interrogation of the I.N.A. and the other Indians in east Asia had established that, contrary to their own propaganda, Bose was regarded not as a puppet of the Japanese but as a great hero. He had dealt with the Japanese as an equal and had succeeded in creating India's first national army. Then there was his undoubted prestige and status in India, particularly in Bengal, where he 'ranks little, if anything, below Gandhi as an all-India figure'. After listing the various measures that could be taken to deal with Bose, the report went on to discuss their drawbacks. Public pressure would not allow him to be hanged in India; the Burma government was unlikely to want to try him there; trials in Singapore or elsewhere would create just as many problems. A quick military execution was a solution, but that could hardly be defended, and the military might read it as a subterfuge to avoid the independence issue which would figure in a civil trial. Imprisoning him would only lead to agitation for his release. The report concluded:

> *"In many ways the easiest course would be to leave him where he is and not ask for his release. He might, of course, in certain circumstances be welcomed by the Russians. This course would raise fewest immediate political difficulties but the security authorities consider that in certain circumstances his presence in Russia would be so dangerous as to rule it out altogether."*

After several investigations, the British had concluded by March 1946 that Bose might still be alive; but there was not much else they could do about it. The 25,000 I.N.A. prisoners being repatriated to India presented very different problems. Senior British Army commanders were convinced that the I.N.A. were traitors, and that, if the integrity and the discipline of the British Indian Army were to be maintained, they should be severely punished. Some would have preferred kangaroo courts and quick executions.

But the higher echelons of the Raj were not entirely convinced that this was the right policy; in any case, it was not possible to execute 25,000 men secretly. A few were executed, but for the great majority a more selective policy was implemented. They were classified into 'whites'-those who had joined the I.N.A. with the intention of re-joining the British; 'greys'-those who had been misled by Bose and the Japanese;

and 'blacks'-those who had fervently believed in the cause. The whites were to be restored to their former positions in the army, the greys were to be tried, dismissed and released; only the blacks were to bear the full brunt of British revenge. They were beyond redemption, and Auchinleck was convinced that when their full story emerged the Indian public would be horrified.

The I.N.A. was already housed in camps set up in Delhi's lied Fort, and this, it was decided, would be an excellent place for a trial. The Fort was ideally situated for press and media coverage. On 5 November 1945 the trial of Shah Nawaz Khan, Prem Kumar Salgal and Gurbaksh Singh Dhillon began. Dhillon was charged with murder, Shah Nawaz and Sahgal with abetting murder. All three were charged with 'waging war against His Majesty the King Emperor of India'. The trials lasted till 31 December, and proved to be a sensation-though not in the way Claude Auchinleck wished. The Trial & the Revolutionary Response of the Indian People....

> *The war had not brought Indian independence any nearer, and the British mistook the political quiet for approval. But almost nine months after the end of the war, when the British in Delhi held their victory celebrations, the Indians went wild with fury: the old Delhi town hall was partly gutted, Indians dressed in European clothes were attacked, parading troops were booed and the police had to open fire in order to restore order.*

The I.N.A. and Bose had created a potentially revolutionary situation: one on which the political parties were eager to build for their own ends-none more so than the Congress. The Congress had suffered a double defeat during the war: it had gained little through either negotiations or mass struggle, and now it was a case of 'the Congress proposes, the Muslim League disposes'. In these circumstances the Congress soon realised the potential of the fervour behind the I.N.A., and it quickly adopted resolutions both approving of their actions and pledging itself to defend them at the trial. A party dedicated to nonviolence was at last beginning to realise the usefulness of violence. Even

Jinnah urged the government to treat the I.N.A. prisoners with 'leniency'. By now the Indian press-freed from wartime censorship-was full of stories and legends of the I.N.A. and Bose. 'Jai Hind' had replaced all other greetings between Indians, and Bose's photographs-invariably in I.N.A. uniform-now graced a million pan shops.

The defence was led by Bhulabhai Desai, who in the past had been a bitter critic of Bose. By the time of his death, a few months after the trial, he was as great a champion of Netaji as any. The trial became, as Nehru said, a dramatic version of that old contest, England versus India: the legal niceties vanished and even the personalities of defendants were obscured.

For Indians it was not only illegal but a slur on Indian nationalism; the victors were disposing of the vanquished in the very place where the latter had planned to hold their victory parade. Besides, the three accused Shah Nawaz was a Muslim, Sahgal a Hindu and Dhillon a Sikh-represented all the major communities of India. Auchinleck may have hoped that would stress the communal nature of Indian politics-always Britain's strongest point; but for Indians it demonstrated that the I.N.A. was indeed a national army that Bose had indeed succeeded in getting Muslims, Hindus and Sikhs to unite for a common cause.

BRITISH COMMUTE SENTENCE TO AVOID MUTINY IN THE BRITISH INDIAN ARMY

The defence based its argument on the host of precedents, old and new, which supported the right of subject countries to fight for their freedom. But, for all Desai's eloquence, as far as the court-martial was concerned he was arguing a lost cause-one they were incapable of appreciating, let alone accepting. The predictable verdict was that all three of officers were guilty of waging war against the King. Dhillon and Salgal were acquitted of the charge of murder and abetment of murder; Shah Nawaz was found guilty of abetting murder. All three were sentenced to transportation for life, cashiering and forfeiture of arrears of pay and allowances.

However, the British military authorities had become painfully aware of the consequences of the trial. Even before it had opened, I. N. A. days had been organised in various parts of the country. The day the proceedings got under way the police had to open fire on a protesting crowd at Madura in south India.

Then, as the trial proceeded, the Red Fort itself was besieged; more than a hundred were killed or injured by police firing. Between 21 and 26 November Calcutta was strike-bound. In a rare gesture of communal amity, Hindus and Muslims-their trucks flying both Congress and Muslim League flags—jointly took over the city, attacking American and British military establishments and shouting the slogans of freedom and nationalism coined by Bose.

Some forty-nine military vehicles were destroyed and ninety-seven damaged, and about 200 military personnel injured: thirty-two Indians lost their lives and 200 were wounded. The violence soon spread along the Gangetic plain to Patna, Allahabad and Benares, and eventually places as far apart as Karachi and Bombay were affected. Claude Auchinleck was no longer the confident Commander-in-Chief who had ordered the trial, and even as it was proceeding he wrote to the Viceroy expressing his doubts:

> *"I know from my long experience of Indian troops how hard it is even for the best and most sympathetic British officer to gauge the inner feelings of the Indian soldier, and history supports me in this view. I do not think any senior British officer today knows what is the real feeling among the Indian ranks regarding the 'INA'. I myself feel, from my own instinct largely, but also from the information I have had from various sources, that there is a growing feeling of sympathy for the 'INA' and an increasing tendency to disregard the brutalities committed by some of its members as well as the forswearing by all of them of their original allegiance. It is impossible to apply our standards of ethics to this problem or to shape our policy as we would, had the 'INA' been of our own race.*

Not wishing to be caught napping again, Auchinleck set up a special organisation in his military headquarters 'to find out the real feelings of Indian ranks on this subject'. He also decided that no more I.N.A. personnel would be tried on the major charge of waging war against the King, and that only those who had committed 'acts of gross brutality' would be brought before the courts-at most between twenty and fifty men. Later Mason, joint secretary in the War Department of the government of India, declared that the I.N.A.'s 'patriotic motive would be taken at its face value and its members would be treated as though prisoners of war'.

A week before the trial ended the Viceroy empowered Auchinleck to commute sentences of death or transportation for life, and when, as required, Auchinleck came to confirm the sentences of the three men, he only agreed to the verdict of cashiering and forfeiture of pay: the transportation decision was quashed and, taking into account 'the prevailing circumstances', the men were set free.

I.N.A. Accused Released & Welcomed as Heroes

Shah Nawaz, Sahgal and Dhillon were welcomed like the heroes of a conquering army and their tales were carried back to the remotest villages of India to be told, retold and eventually mythologised. For a time the I.N.A. seemed to have become India-even for Gandhi. Now, in his weekly Harijan column, he invariably referred to Bose as 'Netaji', and conceded that 'the hypnotism of the INA has cast its spell upon us. Netaji's name is one to conjure with. His patriotism is second to none (I use the present tense intentionally). His bravery shines through all his actions.'

He, too, believed Netaji was alive. The British, however, continued with the selective trials, and on 4 February 1946 Captain Abdul Rashid was sentenced to seven years, imprisonment for certain acts of brutality. Rashid was a Muslim, and now the Muslim League came into the picture. For four days between 11 and 14 February the streets of Calcutta Bombay and Delhi witnessed unique political demonstrations in which Hindus and Muslims forgot their differences and came together to fight the I.N.A.'s battles. Four days of strict martial law were required to bring Calcutta back to normal; by then nearly fifty were dead and over five hundred injured.

In January, too, some 5,200 Royal Indian Air Force personnel had gone on strike to protest over their conditions and as an expression of sympathy for the I.N.A. cause. And on 18 February a revolt began on HMS Talwar, a training ship of the Indian navy moored off Bombay. By nightfall on the 20th virtually the whole of the Royal Indian Navy was in open rebellion: seventy eight ships in the various ports of India—Bombay, Karachi, Madras, Vizagapatanan, Calcutta and Cochin, and even in the Andamans-and nearly all the shore establishments had hauled down the Union Jack. Only ten ships and two shore establishments still remained with the British.

Other units of the armed forces were quickly affected. Between 22 and 25 February the R. I. A. F. in Bombay and Madras went on strike and on the 27th Indian soldiers in Jabalpur followed. In Bombay and Karachi, the main naval centres, ratings were able to generate impressive mass support. In Karachi gun battles had ensued which continued for two days before heavy British reinforcements finally defeated the men. In Bombay there had been what even the British owned Times of India was forced to call 'mass uprising. .. in sympathy with the naval mutiny. .. unparalleled in the city's history'. The communists and the Congress Left had called for sympathy strikes and over 600,000 workers from the textile mills of Bombay had responded. For almost three days they had fought running, unequal battles with British troops in the streets and lanes of Bombay.

The British had tanks and machine-guns, the workers had improvised weapons and even at times stones from dug-up roads. But for a few days some of Bombay's teeming working class slums had become 'no-go areas', and the British had to call in white troops to quell the uprising. In the end 270 had died and 1,300 had been injured (the government's official figures were lower: 187 and 1,002). Attlee quick to understand implications & negotiate 'independence'...

Undoubtedly a revolutionary situation had been created. But now, suddenly, the ratings found there were no leaders. They knew their navy but they had been horribly wrong about the Indian political parties. The naval ratings had virtually given the politicians a whole unit of the British Indian armed forces; they had even started calling it the Indian National Navy. For the politicians, however, this was too alarming a prospect.

Jinnah advised the men to go back and assured them that, if they did so, he would use constitutional means to remedy their complaints of bad food and service conditions. The Congress leaders were plainly frightened by the prospect of leading a revolution; Nehru came to Bombay and deplored the revolt. And as the ratings wondered what might have happened if there had been a leader prepared to lead them-Bose perhaps-the British re-took their ships. But if the Indian politicians had no use for revolutionary situations, the Labour government had been quick to understand the implications.

On 4 December 1945 Herbert Morrison announced in the House of Commons that a ten-member parliamentary delegation would visit India to study the situation. The five-week visit took place in January and February 1946 and by the end of it nearly all the visiting MPs were convinced that India was in a dangerous state. The February disturbances convinced Attlee that the imperial tide had at last ebbed. India could be held by force of arms for a few years more, but the cost for a Britain devastated by war would be too high.

The British government announced in February 1946 that a Cabinet mission of three ministers would visit India. That mission, in fact, failed in its purpose, the situation required another intervention by Attlee; it was his speech in the House of Commons on 20 February 1947-when he pledged the British government to transfer power to Indian hands, if necessary as two separate nations, 'not later than June 1948'-that finally led to the emergence of the two nations of India and Pakistan on 15 August 1947.

That such a situation existed in 1945 owed a great deal to Subhash Bose. He did not precisely visualise the extent of the post war turmoil; his wildest dreams could not have matched the fervour the I.N.A. trials produced. But he had told his men in Burma to fraternise with the Indians in the British Indian Army, and till the end he was confident that if Indians kept up their resolve, Britain-in an increasingly hostile postwar world-would have to concede independence.

True, his army did not parade as victors in the Red Fort; but their trial as vanquished had proved that his belief in a revolutionary consciousness that was grounded in a deeper understanding of the Indian people than his enemies credited him with, or even his most fervent friends believed in. The vision had been genuine: he just did not have the means, while alive, to translate it into a reality. Even Dilip, so sceptical of worldly struggles, recognised that the romance of Subhas' army had finally breached the dyke that separated Indians from the other army maintained to enslave them.

Through 1946 and 1947, as Indian leaders bartered with the British and among themselves to produce a divided India, they appeared to be constantly looking over their shoulders to reassure themselves that Bose's ghost was not like Hamlet's father, turning into flesh and blood. The years of struggle had wearied them, they did not have the stomach for another fight and they were relieved to get what crumbs they could from the imperial table. When the Congress finally accepted the partition plan Nehru had only this consolation to offer for the sudden abandonment of a lifetime's principles:

> *"But of one thing I am convinced, that ultimately there will be a united and strong India. We have often to go through the valley of the shadow before we reach the sunlit mountain-tops."*

It was poor comfort for the holocaust that partition produced, and even today, for many Indians, the sunlit mountain-tops are still obscured by the shadows. Had Bose returned to India....

> *Had Bose returned to India after the war he might well have prevented the tragedy. He was not a tired politician ready to accept office under any terms. Although his*

uncompromising hostility to Jinnah and Pakistan might have led to a civil war, the cost of that could not have been greater than the senseless waste of partition.

Certainly Bose's often repeated warning that the Congress would pay dearly for the acceptance of 'office mentality' was historically acute. It came when in the late thirties the Congress was struggling to cope with the consequences of the 1935 Government of India Act, and the blandishments it offered. In the 1936 elections, the Congress reaped the rewards of nearly two decades of unceasing mass struggle against the British and totally vanquished the Muslim League. But by 1945, after a decade of negotiations and some power-sharing with the British, the Congress was reduced to the level of the Muslim League; just another group, albeit powerful, seeking the rewards of office. And by placing such faith in the negotiating chamber the Congress had played into the hands of Jinnah, the master lawyer and negotiator. As Bose had foreseen, the Congress had thrown away the trump card of its power-mass struggle-for the dubious delights of the round table.

But could Indians have lived with Bose? An extreme man, he produced extreme reactions: total adulation or permanent rejection. Certainly the India of Bose would have been very different from the India of Nehru. Bose had often said that India needed at least twenty years of iron dictatorial rule, and he would most certainly have rejected the type of parliamentary democracy that has developed.

This opens up the whole question of whether it is better for people to have food or to have freedom to change their political rulers every five years. The argument can never be resolved-though, given the recent adulation of the West for China, some of the oldest democracies in the world seem to think food is more important.

Surely Bose's rule would have degenerated into autocracy, like that of Mrs. Gandhi between 1975 and 1977? Though the analogy is not quite accurate (Mrs. Gandhi's rule degenerated long before the events of June 1975), for conclusive evidence Bose's critics point to his behaviour in Germany and with the

Japanese during the war. In a climate that brooked no dissent and where the leader was always right, he too came to believe that he could do no wrong. Part of the possible reason for this change of personality-if there was a change-may lie in the fact that at that stage, particularly in southeast Asia, he found himself a king without any worthwhile courtiers. The people who surrounded him there were political innocents, thrust into the wider world by events beyond their control: they could only applaud, never interject. Bose was, as the official Japanese history puts it, 'a bright morning star amidst them'. There is also evidence to suggest that Subhash Bose was not quite the dictator a simple reading of his speeches makes him out to be.

No doubt there was an authoritarian streak in him, but his actions often belied his dictatorial postures in 1939, as Congress president, he behaved-against Gandhi's wishes-less like an autocrat and more like a negotiator who had won one round and expected to reap some benefit from it. Throughout his political career he was always loyal to colleagues even at the risk of damaging his own chances: hardly the mark of a man of iron.

Almost alone among Indian leaders, Bose offered solutions that were both visionary and practical. Nehru's socialism may have been more rounded; rigorously logical and free of Bose's celebrated eclecticism. But its strain of romanticism divorced it from the realities of India, and the Nehru years resulted, almost inevitably, in a country with the most progressive socialist legislation outside the Soviet bloc which happily allowed the most unbridled capitalism to grow and flourish on a feudal structure that had changed little, if at all, since the British days. The cynicism this produced has bitten so deep that every government since has had to struggle against it and no combination in Indian politics looks likely to counteract the years of wasted opportunities and lost hopes.

This may seem hard, given the undoubted economic progress India has made in the last thirty years. When the British left, India had little or no industrial capacity; now she is the tenth industrial power in the world, exporting machinery to the West and capable of producing her own nuclear weapons.

But the rapid industrialisation has been uneven and ill-directed, with the beneficiaries limited to a small, if growing, sector of the country.

Bose had the capacity to inspire total love and dedication, and produce gold from dross. He was hated by many, but those he 'touched' loved him with an almost overpowering sense of completeness. And this, combined with his rigorous, matter-of-fact manner and an instinctive feel for ancient Indian loyalties, might well have produced the revolution that India needed-and still lacks. The ideological development that Bose sought has never materialised...

Like Turkey's Kemal Ataturk-a man he admired-Bose might well have produced a nation at once new, yet full of old virtues. This is best illustrated in his approach to women: he was not one for making strident feminist statements but, even on that submarine bringing him from Germany to Japan, he was busily telling Abid Hasan of the need to get Indian women to join the I.N.A., and how they would have to abandon their beloved sarees in order to do so. In south Asia he did get many immigrant women to join the I.N.A.-demonstrating that Indian feminism could be happily blended with the exigency of war.

The ideological development that Bose sought has never materialised. Like all national-liberation movements, the independent Congress was a coalition: of business seeking to oust British capital, of rural kulaks confident that native rulers would do more for them than alien ones, of various interest groups and of socialists aware that the Congress was the only party capable of furthering their ideas. Gandhi did suggest that the Congress should disband after independence, but this was clearly impossible: self-interest, if nothing else, ruled it out. Today almost all the major political groups in India-communists, socialists, free-enterprise capitalists, Gandhian socialists-trace their ancestry to the Congress: only the right-wing Hindu Jan Sangh can claim a different parentage.

The absence of ideological development has meant the politics of banter, with interest groups perpetually feuding amongst themselves, extraordinary alliances-as between

Marxists and religious obscurantists-and, above all, comical political defections. Once, in a northern state, a single individual's change of support from Congress to opposition parties led to the fall of two state governments in a single day. The most valid criticism of Bose is related to the nature of the nationalist movement itself. For Bose's faults-and there were many-were inevitable in a nationalist fighting a colonial-imperial power that both fanned nationalism, and denied it legitimate expression. The Raj, as Marx penetratingly observed, did unwittingly bring modern ideas into India-but the nationalist reaction it produced in India was distorted by the British presence.

Pre-British India was seen as a land of milk and honey in which there had been no problems, no caste system and no evils, only Indian harmony and peace. And it is a measure of the failure of Indian nationalism that what in most countries would be dismissed as delicious nonsense is still taken seriously.

Today P.N. Oak, ADC to Major-General Bhonsle of the I.N.A., can claim respectable reviews in Indian papers by writing books asserting that 5,000 years ago India had an empire which included Britain. If the world has not appreciated this, it is, argues Oak, because the relevant chapters of world history have been 'lost'. Bose was aware of India's ills, but he often came close to endorsing the delicious nonsense of pre-British bliss, if only for rhetorical purposes.

Though he bravely maintained his independence from both the Germans and the Japanese-no mean feat-he deliberately avoided the wider implications of their awful philosophies. However, his argument that foreign help was required in order to drive the British out was justified by the events of 1945-6, and has been the bedrock of nearly all successful national-liberation movements since the war. In this, at least, Bose was probably far ahead of his time. In our age, when a national-liberation movement's accepting foreign help from all and sundry is a common fact of life, the idea may seem of no great significance. In the early forties, for a subject non-white race even to think of any such thing was revolutionary indeed.

> *....'It is our duty,' Bose told his I.N.A., 'to pay for our liberty with our own blood. The freedom that we shall win through our sacrifice and exertions, we shall be able to preserve with our own strength.' ....."*
>
> *Subhash Chandra Bose, the Indian National Army, and the War of India's Liberation- Ranjan Borra, Journal of Historical Review, no. 3, 4 (Winter 1982)*

"The arrival of Subhash Chandra Bose in Germany in 1941 (during the turbulent period of World War II) and his anti-British activities in that country in cooperation with the German government, culminated in the formation of an Indian legion. This marks perhaps the most significant event in the annals of India's fight for independence. This event not only can be regarded as a historical link-up with what Bose himself chose to describe as "The Great Revolution of 1857," and which (in his words) "has been incorrectly called by English historians 'the Sepoy Mutiny,' but which is regarded by the Indian people as the First War of Independence."

It also represents the historical fact that, by that time persuasive methods conducted through a nonviolent struggle under the leadership of Gandhi, had failed. An armed assault on the citadel of the British Empire in India was the only alternative left to deliver the country from bondage. While other leaders of the Indian National Congress fell short of realizing this fact and thus betrayed a lack of pragmatic approach to the turn of world events that provided India with a golden opportunity to strike at the British by a force of arms, Bose rose to the needs of the hour and was quick to seize that opportunity.

While Bose's compatriots in India remained totally wedded to an ideological creed (nonviolence), which at that time could only serve the British and postpone the advent of independence, and while their ideological interpretations of the new revolutionary regimes in Europe-again largely influenced by British propaganda-prevented them from even harboring any thought of seeking their alliance and cooperation in the struggle against a common enemy, Subhash Chandra Bose alone had the courage to take the great plunge, thus risking his own life and reputation, solely in the interest and cause of his country. In January 1941, while under both house arrest, and strict British surveillance, he escaped. After an arduous trek through the rugged terrains of several countries, with an Italian passport under the assumed name of Orlando Mazzota-(in which he was aided by underground revolutionaries and foreign diplomatic agents)—Bose appeared in Berlin, via Moscow, on 28 March 1941.

Bose was welcome in Germany, although the news of his arrival there was kept a secret for some time for political reasons. The German Foreign Office, which was assigned the primary responsibility of dealing with Bose and taking care of him, had been well informed of the background and political status of the Indian leader through its pre-war Consulate-General at Calcutta and also by its representative in Kabul. Bose himself, naturally some what impatient for getting into action soon after his arrival in Berlin, submitted a memorandum to the German government on 9 April 1941 which outlined a plan for cooperation between the Axis powers and India.

Among other things, it called for the setting up of a "Free India Government" in Europe, preferably in Berlin; establishment of a Free India broadcasting station calling upon the Indian people to assert their independence and rise up in revolt against the British authorities; underground work in Afghanistan (Kabul) involving independent tribal territories lying between Afghanistan and India and within India itself for fostering and aiding the revolution; provision of finances by Germany in the form of a loan to the Free India government-in-exile; and deployment of German military contingents to smash the British army in India.

In a supplementary memorandum bearing the same date, Bose requested that an early pronouncement be made regarding the freedom of India and the Arab countries. It is significant to note that the memorandum did not mention the need for formation of an Indian legion. Evidently the idea of recruiting the Indian prisoners of war for the purpose of establishing a nucleus of an Indian national army did not occur to him during his early days in Berlin. At that time the German government was in the process of formulating its own plan for dealing with Subhash Chandra Bose in the best possible manner. The Foreign Office felt itself inadequate to discharge this awesome responsibility without referring the whole matter to Hitler. While this issue was being considered at the highest level of the government, Bose's own requests as set forth in the submitted memorandum, made it far too complicated and involved to be resolved at an early date.

There was a long wait for Bose, during which period he often tended to become frustrated. Nevertheless, through several sympathetic officers of the Foreign Office, he continued to press his requests and put forth new ideas. Finally, after months of waiting and many moments of disappointment often bordering on despair for Bose, Germany agreed to give him unconditional and all-out help.

The two immediate results of this decision were the establishment of a Free India Center and inauguration of a Free India Radio, both beginning their operations in November 1941.

These two organizations played vital and significant roles in projecting Bose's increasing activities in Germany, but a detailed account of their operation lies outside the purview of this paper. It should suffice to say that the German government put at Bose's disposal adequate funds to run these two organizations, and he was allowed complete freedom to run them the way he liked at his own discretion.

In its first official meeting on 2 November 1941, the Free India Center adopted four historical resolutions that would serve as guidelines for the entire movement in subsequent months and years in Europe and Asia.

First, Jai Hind or Victory to India, would be the official form of salutation; secondly, Nobel laureate poet Rabindranath Tagore's famous patriotic song Jana Gana Mona was to be the national anthem for the free India Bose was fighting for; thirdly, in a multilingual state like India, the most widely-spoken language, Hindustani, was to be the national language; and fourthly, Subhash Chandra Bose would hereafter be known and addressed as Netaji, the Indian equivalent of the "leader" or the "Führer."

In November 1941, Azad Hind Radio (or the Free India Radio) opened its programme with an announcing speech by Netaji himself, which, in fact, was a disclosure of his identity that had been kept officially secret for so long. The radio programmes were broadcast in several Indian languages on a regular basis.

During this long period of "hibernation," the period between Netaji's arrival in Berlin and the beginning of operations of the two organizations, it can be reasonably assumed that the idea of forming an Indian legion that could be developed into an Indian Army of Liberation in the West, crossed Bose's mind. He might even have discussed this matter with his colleagues-the Indian compatriots in Germany who had joined him-as to how best to implement the idea. However, as mentioned earlier, his first memorandum submitted to the German Government did not include any such plan.

According to N.G. Ganpuley, who was his associate in Berlin, Netaji himself, when he left India, could not have, by any stretch of imagination, thought of forming a national army unit outside the country, and therefore he had no definite plans chalked out for its realization. Even while in Berlin, he could not think of it during the first few months of his stay there. When and how, therefore, did he come to conceive such a plan? Mr. Ganpuley relates an interesting episode in this regard. To quote again from his book:

> *It was all due to a brain wave of Netaji which started working by a simple incident. He read one day about some half a dozen Indian prisoners-of-war who were brought to Berlin by the Radio Department to listen to the BBC and other stations which sent out their programmes in Hindustani. He saw them there going about, not as free Indians, but as prisoners-of-war. They were brought to the Radio Office every day to listen to and translate the Hindustani programmes, and were sent back to their quarters escorted by a sentry ... After*

he had a talk with them about war, about their captivity and their present life, his active mind started working... He pondered over it for some time and decided to form a small national military unit ... No sooner was this decision taken by him ... he started negotiating with that section of the German Foreign Office with which he was in constant touch. He put before them his plans for training Indian youths from the prisoners' camps for a national militia.

Although somewhat skeptical and hesitant at the beginning, the German response to the plans was encouraging. It was a time psychologically well-chosen by Netaji. The allied forces had been defeated on the Continent, and the Wehrmacht was marching ahead successfully in the Soviet Union. It was also a historical coincidence that a large number of British Indian prisoners-of war, captured during Rommel's blitzkrieg in North Africa, lay in German hands.

Netaji's first idea was to form small parachute parties to spread propaganda in, and transmit intelligence from, the North-West Frontier in India. The reaction of some selected prisoners who were brought to Berlin from the camp of Lamsdorf in Germany and Cyrenaica was so encouraging that he asked for all Indian prisoners held in North Africa to be brought over to Germany at once.

The Germans complied with this request, and the prisoners began to be concentrated at Annaburg camp near Dresden. The recruitment efforts, however, at the onset met with some opposition from the prisoners, who evidently had misgivings about Netaji's intentions and motivations. In this regard Hugh Toye writes:

When Bose himself visited the camp in December there was still marked hostility. His speech was interrupted, and much of what he had to say went unheard. But private interviews were more encouraging; the men's questions showed interest-what rank would they receive? What credit would be given for Indian Army seniority? How would the Legionary stand in relation to the German soldier? Bose refused to bargain, and some who might have been influential recruits were turned away. On the other hand, many of the men paid him homage as a distinguished Indian, several professed themselves ready to join the Legion unconditionally.

Netaji sought and got agreement from the Germans that the Wehrmacht would train the Indians in the strictest military discipline, and they were to be trained in all branches of infantry in using weapons and motorized units the same way a German formation is trained; the Indian legionaries were not to be mixed up with any of the German formations; that they were not to be sent to any front other than in India for fighting against the British, but would be allowed to fight in self defense at any other place if surprised by any enemy formation; that in all other respects the Legion members would enjoy the same facilities and amenities regarding pay, clothing, food, leave, etc., as a German unit. By December 1941 all arrangements were complete and the next important task was to persuade men to come forward and form the nucleus. It appeared that the POWs needed to be convinced that there were civilian Indian youth as well, studying, well placed in life and responsible to their families at home, who were ready to give up everything to join the Legion. Ten of the forty young Indians then residing in Berlin, came forward. They were quickly joined by five POWs who were already in Berlin in connection with the German radio propaganda, and the first group of fifteen people was thus formed.

On 25 December 1941 a meeting of Indian residents in Berlin was called in the office of the Free India Center, to give a send-off to the first fifteen who were to leave the following day for Frankenburg, the first training camp and headquarters for the Legion. The brief ceremony was simple and solemn. Netaji blessed the Legion, the first of its kind in the history of the struggle for Indian independence. He christened it Azad Hind Fauj (Indian National Army). The Indian Army of Liberation in the West thus had a humble and modest birth.

The strength of the Legion grew steadily, as the task of recruitment continued unabated. Once trained to a certain level and discipline, the members of the first batch were assigned the additional responsibility of visiting the Annaberg camp and aiding in the recruitment process. While the Legion was sent to Frankenburg in Saxony, another group was taken to Meseritz in Brandenburg to be trained in tactical warfare. Abid Hasan and N.G. Swamy, the two original recruiters whom Netaji had sent to the Annaberg camp in 1941, had become de-facto foundermembers of the Legion at Frankenburg and the irregular Company at Meseritz respectively.

At Meseritz, the Indians were placed under the command of Hauptmarm Harbig, whose first object was to make them forget that they had been prisoners. There were Tajiks, Uzbeks and Persians as well under training for operational roles similar to that envisaged for the Indians. In due course the trainees went on to tactical operational training, such as wireless operating, demolitions and riding, and also undertook special mountain and parachute courses. According to Toye, "Morale, discipline and Indo-German relations were excellent, the German officers first-rate."

Netaji visited the camps from time to time and watched progress of the trainees. Since he himself was inclined toward military training and discipline, he followed the German training methods with great interest. It is understood that while in Germany Netaji himself underwent the rigours of such training, although authoritative documents on this subject are yet to be located by this writer.

While in India, he was a member of the University Training Corps at school and commanded the volunteers at an annual session of the Indian National Congress, but he never had a formal military education prior to his arrival in Germany in 1941. As Joyce Lebra writes: "Though Bose was without any previous military experience, he got his training and discipline German-style, along with the soldiers of the Indian Legion."

To him, formation of a legion was more positive, more nationalistic and more gratifying than mere radio propaganda. Unlike his ex-compatriots in the Indian National Congress, including Gandhi, Nehru and Patel, he would rather seek confrontation with the British-with an army-than to work out a compromise with them on a conference table, on the issue of

India's freedom. A firm believer in discipline and organization, nothing perhaps could be more satisfying to him than to see his men being trained by the German Command, with officers of the highest calibre. In four months, the number of trainees rose to three hundred. In another six months a further three hundred were added. By December 1942, exactly a year after the recruitment of the Legion was inaugurated, it attained the strength of four battalions. At the beginning of 1943 the Legion would be 2000 strong, well on its way up to the culminating point of 3500 men. But let us step back to early 1942, almost a year after Netaji's arrival in Berlin. After the inauguration of the Free India Center, Free India Radio, and the sending of the first fifteen legionaries to the Frankenburg training camp, Netaji's activities in Germany began in full swing. His presence in Germany was not yet officially admitted-he was still being referred to as Signor Orlando Mazzota or His Excellency Mazzota-but he began to be known to more and more people in Berlin. Josef Goebbels wrote in his diary on 1 March:

> *We have succeeded in prevailing upon the Indian nationalist leader, Bose, to issue an imposing declaration of war against England. It will be published most prominently in the German press and commented upon. In that way we shall now begin our official fight on behalf of India, even though we don't as yet admit it openly.*

On 14 March, he remarked of Bose, "He is an excellent worker." The fall of Singapore was a signal for Netaji to broadcast his first official speech over the Free India Radio, repeating his vow to fight British imperialism until the end. This he followed with a declaration of war against England, although at that stage such a pronouncement could only be symbolic. Netaji had not yet obtained an Axis declaration in support of the freedom of India that he pressed for in the supplement of his first memorandum to the German government.

That government was of the opinion that the time was not ripe yet for such a declaration and unless a pronouncement of this nature could be supported by military action, it would not be of much value. Meanwhile, Japan proposed a tripartite declaration on India. Encouraged by this, Bose met Mussolini in Rome on 5 May, and persuaded him to obtain such a declaration in favour of Indian independence. Mussolini telegraphed the Germans, proposing proceeding at once with the declaration. To back his new proposal Mussolini told the Germans that he had urged Bose to set up a "counter-government" and to appear more conspicuously. The German reaction, which still remained guarded, is recorded by Dr. Goebbels in his diary on 11 May:

> *We don't like this idea very much, since we do not think the time has yet come for such a political manoeuvre. It does appear though that the Japanese are very eager for some such step. However, emigre governments must not live too long in a vacuum. Unless they have some actuality to support them, they only exist in the realm of theory.*

Netaji apparently was of the opinion that a tripartite declaration on Indian independence, followed up by a government-in-exile, would give some credibility to his declaration of war on England, push over the brink the imminent revolution in India, and legitimize the Indian legion. However, Hitler held a different view. During an interview at the Führer's field headquarters on 29 May, he told Netaii that a well-equipped army of a few thousand could control millions of unarmed revolutionaries, and there could be no political change in India until an external power knocked at her door. Germany could not yet do this.

To convince Netaji, he took him to a wall map, pointed to the German positions in Russia and to India. The immense distances were yet to be bridged before such a declaration could be made. The world would consider it premature, even coming from him, at this stage. Hitler was perhaps being realistic, but nevertheless it must have come as some sort of disappointment for Netaji. In July 1942, the Germans suggested that a contingent of the Irregular Company be sent for front-line propaganda against Indian troops at El Alamein; but Rommel, who did not like battlefields turned into proving grounds for

Foreign Office ideas, opposed the move. However, at the Lehrregiment manoeuvers in September, and on field exercises in October, the Indian performance won high praise.

By January 1943, it was realized that maintenance of the irregulars as a separate entity was not of much practical use, and the ninety Indian men, (excepting four under N.G. Swamy who were being trained for work within Indiaj were absorbed into the Legion. Since the supply of recruits from the Annaburg camp was fast being depleted, it was decided to hasten the shipment of prisoners of war from Italy.

According to an agreement between Italy and Germany, all Indian POWs were to be sent directly to Germany without being held in Italian camps. But, in the meanwhile, an unforseen impediment stood in the way. A long-time Indian resident in Rome, Iqbal Shedai, formed an Indian unit under the Italians, and began broadcasting from Rome with the aid of a few Indian prisoners. It is understood that he had conferred with Netaji a few times, but obviously had no intention of co-operating with him. From radio broadcasting, he advanced into forming an Indian military unit, although it was in clear violation of the Italo-German agreement. The unit was named the Centro Militare India, but existed only from April to November 1942.

During its brief period of existence, however, Shedai succeeded in diverting several hundred volunteers to Italian camps, who would normally have gone to Germany. In November the unit was three hundred and fifty strong, having been trained by Italian officers. On 9 November, after the Allied landing in North Africa, it was learnt that the men were being sent to fight in Libya, contrary to Shedai's promises. When they refused to go and mutinied, Shedai refused to intervene. Consequently, the Centro Militare India was disbanded.

It was never revived, and thus a barrier that stood in Netaji's way toward recruitment was removed. In August 1942, the Legion was moved to Koenigsbrueck, a large military training center in Saxony. This had been a regular training ground for the German infantry and motorized units for decades. Here the first contingents paraded before Netaji's eyes in October, and the growth was rapid. However, the rapid expansion of the Legion also posed the problem of finances. Hitherto, payment to soldiers was being made from the monthly grants to the Free India Center and its office. As the number of Legionaries grew, that source became insufficient. For this problem there could be but one solution: direct payment to the Legion by the Germans. This would mean hereafter that the Legionaries would receive promotions and precedence as soldiers of national socialist Germany, and would become, in fact, a regiment of the German army, while retaining its separate name and distinction. This was agreed upon between Netaji and the German government, necessitating the taking of a formal oath of loyalty to Adolph Hitler on the part of the Legionaries. Describing the ceremony, Hugh Toye writes:

> *Five hundred Legionaries were assembled. Their German commander, Lieutenant-Colonel Krappe, addressed them, and the oath was administered by German officers to six men at a time. All was done with solemnity, the soldiers touching their officer's sword as they spoke the German words: 'I swear by God this holy oath, that I will obey the leader of the German State and people, Adolph Hitler, as commander of the German Armed Forces, in the fight for freedom of India, in which fight the leader is Subhash Chandra Bose, and that as a brave soldier, I am willing to lay down my life for this oath.' Bose presented to the Legion its standard, a tricolor in the green, white and saffron of the Indian National Congress, superimposed with the figure of a springing tiger in place of the Congress spinning wheel. "Our names," he said, "will be written in gold letters in the history of free India; every martyr in this holy war will have a monument there." It was a brave, colorful show, and for Bose, a moment of pride and emotion. "I shall lead the army," he said, "when we march to India together." The Legionaries looked well in their new uniforms, the silken banner gleaming in their midst; their drill did them credit.*

What was Netaji's plan for leading this army to India? When the Germans launched out beyond Stalingrad into Central

Asia, the Indian irregulars, trained at Messeritz, would accompany their Tajik and Uzbek counterparts along with the German Troops. After Uzbekistan and Afghanistan were reached the Indian Company would leap ahead of the German advance to disrupt the British-Indian defenses in northwestern India. Netaji spoke of dropping parachute brigades, calling on the Indian peasantry to assist them. Through radio he issued warnings to British Indian soldiers and police to the effect that unless they assisted the liberation forces they would one day have to answer to the free Indian government for their criminal support of the British.

The effect of the Indian army of liberation marching into India along with the German forces would be such that the entire British Indian Army morale would collapse, coinciding with a revolutionary uprising against the British. The Legion would then be the nucleus of an expanding army of free India.

Netaji's plan, largely dependent on German Military successes in the Soviet Union, undoubtedly had a setback when the Wehrmacht was halted at Stalingrad. After the German retreat from that city, the plan for marching into India from the West had to be abandoned. The tide of war was turning swiftly, calling for devising new strategies on the part of Netaji. While the German army's second thrust into Russia encountered an unexpected counter-offensive at Stalingrad and thus was forced to turn back, in another part of the world the forces of another Axis partner were forging ahead, nearer and nearer to India.

Japan was achieving spectacular successes in the Far East and was ready to welcome Netaji as the leader of millions of Indians who lived in the countries of East and Southeast Asia. To Netaji, the Japanese attitude was extremely encouraging. Tolo, the Prime Minister, had issued statements in the Diet about Indian freedom early in 1942, and by March there was a Japanese proposal for a tripartite declaration on India. A small band of Indian National Army legionaires had already been in existence in the Southeast under Japanese patronage, although a few of its leaders, including Mohan Singh, had fallen out with the Japanese. Netaji would have no difficulty in reorganizing and expanding this organization. He would get the active support of millions of overseas Indians, and the many thousands of British Indian prisoners-of-war would provide him a greater opportunity for recruitment, and for thus organizing a formidable army of liberation that could immediately be deployed in forward positions as the Imperial Japanese Army kept on advancing through the steaming jungles of the Malayan peninsula and Burma.

During his meeting with Hitler on 29 May, the Führer had also suggested that in view of the prevalent world situation, Netaji should shift the center of his activities from Germany to the Far East.

Netaji could look back at his two years work in Germany with a sense of pride and accomplishment. Broadcasting, publications and propaganda were all extended. Azad Hind Radio had extended programmes in several languages, and reports indicated that they were being listened to with interest in target areas; Azad Hind, a bilingual journal, was being published regularly.

There were other papers for the Legion besides; the Free India Center had attained an acknowledged status in Germany. It was treated as a foreign mission, entitling its members to a higher scale of rations, and exemption from some of the Aliens' regulations. Netaji himself was given a good villa, a car and special rations for entertainment purposes. His personal allowance amounted to about eight hundred pounds a month. The monthly grant for the Free India Center rose from 1,200 pounds in 1941 to 3,200 pounds in 1944. All these Netaji stipulated as a loan from the German government, to be returned after India gained independence with the Axis assistance. However, the turn of events now demanded his presence in a different theatre-of-war.

What would happen to the Legion in Netaji's absence? It was now 3,500 strong, well trained and equipped, ready for action. Netaii consulted with his aides in Berlin. A.C.N. Nambiar, an Indian journalist who had been in Europe for some eighteen years prior to Netaji's arrival in Germany, was his right-hand man. While preparing for his journey to the Asian theatre-of-war, Netaji passed on to Nambiar his policy and instructions. As Hugh Toye writes:

> *There were plans for new branches of the Free India Center, for broadcasting, for Indians to study German police methods, and for the training of Indian seamen and airmen. As for the legion, it must be used actively as soon as possible, the German officers and NCOs must be quickly replaced by Indians, there must be no communalism. Legionaries were to be trained on all the most modern German equipment, including heavy artillery and tanks; Bose would send further instructions as opportunity offered.*

A few words must be added regarding the Indo-German cooperation and comradeship during the critical days of World War II when the Legion was formed. None could describe it better than Adalbert Seifriz, who was a German Officer in the training camp of the Legionaries. He writes:

> *Agreeing to the proposal of Bose was a magnificient concession and consideration shown to the great personality of Bose by the German Government in those critical times when all German efforts were concentrated on the war ... The mutual understanding and respect between Indians and Germans and the increasing contact between them in the interest of the common task made it possible for the Indian Legion to sustain and keep up discipline right up to the German capitulation in 1945. During the period of training and even afterwards the comradeship between Indians and Germans could not be destroyed ... A meeting with Subhash Bose was a special event for the German training staff.-We spent many evenings with him, discussing the future of India. He lives in the minds of the training staff members as an idealistic and fighting personality, never sparing himself in the service of his people and his country ... The most rewarding fact was the real comradeship which grew between Indians and Germans, which proved true in dangerous hours, and exists still today in numerous cases. The Indian Legion*

was a precious instrument in strengthening and consolidating Indo-German friendship.

A report of Hitler's visit to the Indian Legion headquarters in Dresden was given by Shantaram Vishnu Samanta (one of the Legionaries) during a press interview in India, after his release from an internment camp. According to his statement, Hitler addressed the soldiers of the Legion after Netaji had left for East Asia. He spoke in German and his speech was translated into Hindustani by an interpreter.

He said:

You are fortunate having been born in a country of glorious cultural traditions and a colossal manpower. I am impressed by the burning passion with which you and your Netaji seek to liberate your country from foreign domination. Your Netaji's status is even greater than mine. While I am the leader of eighty million Germans, he is the leader of 400 million Indians. In all respects he is a greater leader and a greater general than myself. I salute him, and Germany salutes him. It is the duty of all Indians to accept him as their führer and obey him implicitly. I have no doubt that if you do this, his guidance will lead India very soon to freedom.

A statement by another soldier of the Indian Legion, who remains anonymous, has a somewhat different version. It stated that both Netaji and Hitler took a joint salute of the Indian Legion and a German infantry. In addition to comments cited earlier, Hitler was reported to have made these remarks as well:

German civilians, soldiers and free Indians! I take this opportunity to welcome your acting Führer, Herr Subhash Chandra Bose. He has come here to guide all those free Indians who love their country and are determined to free it from foreign yoke. It is too much for me to dare to give you any instructions or advice because you are sons of a free country, and you would naturally like to obey implicitly the accredited leader of your own land.

However, reports of Hitler's visit and address to the Indian Legionaries are not confirmed from any other source. Netaji would be leaving Germany on 8 February 1943. On 26 January, "Independence Day for India," there was a great party in Berlin where hundreds of guests drank his health. On 28 January, which was set aside for observance as the "Legion Day" in honour of the Indian Legion, he addressed the Legion for the last time. It is believed that his departure was kept secret from his army.

So, there were no visible emotions among the men; no gesture of a farewell. The impression Netaji was leaving at the Free India Center, was that he was going on a prolonged tour. So there were no signs of any anxiety. Except for a few top-ranking German officers and his closest aides, hardly anybody was aware that within a week-and-a-half he would be embarking on the most perilous journey ever undertaken by man; a submarine voyage through mine-infested waters to the other side of the world.

In his absence, Nambiar settled down in his job as his successor and soon gained respect of the Legionaries. Two months after Netaii's departure, as a result of discussion between the German Army Command and the Free India Center, it was decided to transfer the Legion from Koenigsbrueck to a coastal region in Holland, to involve it in a practical coastal defense training. It was also in accordance with Netaji's Wishes. He had often expressed a desire to give his troops, whenever possible, some training in coastal defense. After the first battalion was given a hearty send-off, an untoward incident happened within the legion; two companies of the second battalion refused to move. It was soon found out that there were three main reasons for staging this minor rebellion. Some Legionaries were unhappy that they were not promoted, but their names had to be put on the waiting list; some simply did not want to leave Koenigsbrueck; some were influenced by a rumor that Netaji had abandoned them and had gone off leaving them entirely in German hands, who were now going to use them in the Western Front, instead of sending them to the East to fight for India's liberation.

However, the rebellion was soon quelled after a team of NCOs visited the officials of the Free India Center in Berlin and obtained clarification regarding the rebel Legionaries' grievances. The team went back to the camp and assured the men that they were not being sent to fight a war but were there purely for practical training purposes according to Netaji's wishes; that the promotions were not being passed up, they would follow in due course; and that Netaji had not abandoned them, and they would be informed about his whereabouts and plans as soon as possible.

In pursuance of military discipline, the ringleaders of this act of insubordination were sent to prison camps for a specified period. The Legion was stationed in the coastal areas of Holland for five months. Afterwards, there was a decision to move it to the coastal area of Bordeaux in France from the mouth of the Girond, opposite the fortification of Foyan to the Bay of Arcachon.

The Legion was taking charge here. The stay in France was utilized to give the Legionaries a thorough training in the weaponry required for the defense of the Atlantic Wall. In the spring of 1944, the first batch of twelve Indians were promoted to officers. Field Marshal Rommel, who took charge of the Atlantic Wall, once visited the area where the Indian contingent was located. Ganpulay writes:

> *... after having seen the work carried out by the Indians,, he exclaimed: "I am pleasantly surprised to find that in spite of very little training in coastal defense, the work done here is fairly satisfactory." While departing, he said to the Indian soldiers: "I am glad to see you have done good work; I wish you and your leader all the good luck!"*

In the spring of 1944, one company of the Legion was sent to North Italy at the request of some officers who were seeking an opportunity to confront the British forces. After the Normandy invasion by the Allied forces in June 1944, the military situation in Europe began to deteriorate. It eventually became so critical that the German High Command decided to order the Indian Legion to return to Germany.

So after about ten months of stay in the coastal region of Lacanau in France, the Indian Legion started its road back. It is to be understood at this point that with the landing of the Allied troops in France and their gradual advance through the French countryside, the French Maquis (underground) guerrillas had become very active, and along with the German troops they made the Legionaries as well the target of their attacks. After travelling a certain distance, the first battalion of the Legion was temporarily located in the area of Mansle near Poitiers, while the second and the third battalion were stationed in Angouleme and Poitiers respectively. After a rest for ten days in this region, during which period they had to ward off sporadic attacks by the French underground, the Legionaries took to the road once again.

In this long march back to Germany, the Legion demonstrated exemplary courage and fortitude, and underwent rigours and hardships of battlefield with equanimity.

At this time, British propaganda was directed to these men which was full of empty promises; some material was dropped from the air, while agents infiltrated into the ranks to persuade the men to desert. The propaganda promised the would-be deserters reinstatement in the British Indian army with full retroactive pay and pension, but the British hypocrisy was once again manifest in the fact that a few of the soldiers who had fallen victim to this bait were shot later by the French publicly in a market place in Poitiers without any trial, along with some German prisoners-of-war. In following the saga of the Indian Army of Liberation in the West, one has to remember that its fate was indissolubly linked with that of the Axis powers in Europe, especially Germany. The overpowering of the new revolutionary regimes of Europe by forces representing an alliance of capitalism and Marxism was an international tragedy which engulfed the Indian Legion in Europe as well.

During its retreat into Germany, it encountered the enemy forces on several occasions and fought rearguard action with British and French forces, displaying exemplary bravery. The German military training had converted the regiment not only into a highly disciplined body, but a hard-core fighting unit as well. It is indeed a historical irony that this superb force could not be utilized for the purpose and way its creator and leader, Subhash Chandra Bose, had dreamt of. Nevertheless, the 950th Indian Regiment, as the Legion was officially designated, left its footprints in the battlefields of France and Germany, as their many other gallant comrades of the German Army.

In the fall of 1944 until Christmas, the Indian Legion spent its time in the quiet villages of southern Germany. Between Christmas and the New Year 1945, the unit was ordered to move into the military camp at the garrison town of Heuberg. In the spring of 1945 the Allied forces crossed the Rhine. The Russians entered the East German provinces murdering and plundering cities, townships and villages. Heavy bomber formations began destroying German cities. Transport systems became completely disorganized and paralyzed. The end was near, and there was no point in remaining in the barracks. The Legion, therefore, left its winter quarters at Heuberg in March 1945, and headed for the Alpine passes. By that time all communications with the Free India Center in Berlin had been cut off. The Legion commanders took decisions independently.

The Legion had already reached the Alpine regions east of Bodensee. However, with the surrender of the German forces on 7 May, all hopes also ended for the Free India Army. While attempting to cross over to Switzerland, the legionaries were overwhelmed by American and French units and were made prisoners. Those who fell into the hands of the French had to suffer very cruel treatment. Several were shot, while others died in prison camps in miserable conditions.

The rest were eventually handed over to the British. Although thus swept into the maelstrom of the Axis disintegration in Europe, Netaji's army of liberation in the west had carved for itself a niche in history; for, indeed, it was a nucleus which would eventually precipitate a much larger fighting force elsewhere. Inspired by its leader, that force would march into India to set in motion a process that would eventually deliver the country from an alien bondage. One, therefore, must not regard the saga of the Indian National Army in

Europe as an isolated event that ended tragically. While its dream of crossing the Caucasus along with its allies, the German Armed Forces, and entering India from the Northwest, did not materialize in reality, its extension and successor, India's army of liberation in the east, did enter the country from the opposite direction, thus fulfilling the cherished dream of Netaji and his soldiers. Not only that, as we shall see subsequently, but that army made the mightiest contribution toward finally ending an imperialist rule in India. During his interview with Netaji, Hitler had suggested to him that since it would take at least another one or two years before Germany could gain direct influence in India, and while Japan's influence, in view of its spectacular successes in Southeast Asia, could come in a few months, Bose should negotiate with the Japanese.

The Führer warned Bose against an air journey which could compel him to a forced landing in British territory. He thought Bose was too important a personality to let his life be endangered by such an experiment. Hitler suggested that he could place a German submarine at his disposal which would take him to Bangkok on a journey around the Cape of Good Hope.

However, despite Hitler's suggestions, it is believed that the German Foreign Office showed some reluctance in the matter of Netaji's leaving Germany and going to Japan. Col. Yamamoto Bin, Japanese military attache in Berlin (and a good personal friend of Netaji) along with the Japanese ambassador Lieutenant-General Oshima Hiroshi, had met Netaji as early as October 1941 when the latter expressed hopes for enlisting Japanese aid in his plan for wresting Indian independence. This was the beginning of a series of such meetings.

After the entry of Japan in World War II in December, Netaji was more eager to go as soon as possible to East Asia and fight beside Japan for India's liberation. He reportedly urged Oshima to use his good offices to secure his passage to Asia. It was about at this point that both Oshima and Yamamoto encountered a feeling of reluctance in the matter on the part of the German Foreign Office. They had the feeling that

Germany was not to willing to let Japan lead India to independence. Bose was already a useful ally as an Indian patriot, and his propaganda broadcasts were effective in both India and Britain. The Indian Legion was already having a psychological impact in India and worrying the Allies. For these reasons, "they were guarding Bose like a tiger cub."

In the meantime, Ambassador Oshima had also met with Hitler and explained Bose's plan to him. According to Japanese records. The Führer readily agreed with Oshima that it was better for Bose to shift his activities to Southeast Asia now that his country's (Japan's) armies had overrun the area. The second problem was whether Bose would get enough support in Tokyo for his activities. On this, Oshima had contacted Tokyo many times but had not received any firm answer. Finally, Tokyo replied to Oshima that in principle it had no objection to Bose's visit to Japan.

The third problem was to provide Bose with a safe means of transport to Japan. Communication between Germany and Japan was impossible during those days. Passage by boat was ruled out; and it was decided to use a plane belonging to the Lufthansa Company to airlift Bose from Germany to Japan via the Soviet Union. Tojo (Japanese Prime Minister) objected to this on the grounds that this would amount to a breach of trust with the Soviet Union. An attempt was made by both Yamamoto and Bose to get an Italian plane, but this also did not work. Finally the choice fell on a submarine. Germany agreed to carry Bose up to a certain unknown point in the east and asked that a Japanese submarine be pressed into service thence forward. After a series of exchanges with his government, Oshima finally obtained Tokyo's approval of the plan and communicated it to Bose. Alexander Werth writes:

> *An interesting anecdote related to this historic journey may perhaps be mentioned here. Shortly before Bose's departure the Japanese Naval Command raised objections because of an internal Japanese regulation not permitting civilians to travel on a warship in wartime. When Adam von Trott (of the German Foreign Office) received this message by cable from the German*

Ambassador in Tokyo, he sent the following reply: "Subhash Chandra Bose is by no means a private person, but Commander-in-Chief of the Indian Liberation Army." Thus the bureaucratic interference was overcome.

On 8 February 1943, accompanied by Keppler, Nambiar and Werth, Netaji arrived at the port of Kiel where a German submarine under the command of Werner Musenberg was waiting for him. His would-be sole companion on this perilous voyage, Abid Hasan had travelled separately to Kiel in a special compartment without knowing his destination. Only after commencement of the journey was he to be informed of the itinerary. Netaji was leaving behind his chosen 3,500 soldiers of the Indian Legion, the 950th regiment of the German Army, specially trained and equipped for the task of liberating an India held in bondage by the British. We have already followed the history and fate of the Legion. Now let us turn to the East.

3

SUBHASH CHANDRA BOSE AND INA

The Indian National Army (INA) or Azad Hind Fauj was an armed force formed by Indian nationalists in 1942 in South east Asia during World War II. The aim of the army was to overthrow the British Raj in colonial India, with Japanese assistance. Initially composed of Indian prisoners of war captured by Japan in her Malayan campaign and at Singapore, it later drew large numbers of volunteers from Indian expatriate population in Malaya and Burma. Initially formed in 1942 immediately after the fall of Singapore under Capt. Mohan Singh, the first INA collapsed in December that year before it was revived under the leadership of Subhash Chandra Bose in 1943 and proclaimed the army of Bose's *Arzi Hukumat-e-Azad Hind* (The Provisional Government of Free India). This second INA fought along with the Imperial Japanese Army against the British and commonwealth forces in the campaigns in Burma, Imphal and Kohima, and later, against the successful Burma Campaign of the allies. The end of the war saw a large number of the troops repatriated to India where some faced trial for treason and became a galvanising point of the Indian Independence movement. After Indian independence, the ex-INA members, with some exceptions, were refused service in the Indian Army. However, a number of notable members later became involved in public life in India and in South East Asia.

The legacy of the INA is controversial given its associations with Imperial Japan, the course of Japanese occupations in Burma, Indonesia and other parts of South east Asia, her alliance with Nazi Germany and Fascist Italy, as well as Japanese war crimes and alleged complicity of the troops of the INA in these. Also, its relative insignificance in military terms, its obvious propaganda value to the Japanese, as well as war time British Intelligence propaganda of cowardice and stories that associated INA soldiers in mistreatment of captured allied troops, to a large extent mires the history of the army. However, after the war, the trials of captured INA officers in India provoked massive public outcries in support of their efforts to fight the Raj, eventually triggering mutinies in the British Indian forces. These events in the twilight of the Raj are accepted to have played a crucial role in its hasty end.

BACKGROUND

Within the Indian independence movement, the origins of the concept of an armed force fighting its way into India to overthrow the Raj goes back to the First World War, when the Ghadar Party in February 1915 planned to initiate rebellion in the British Indian Army from the Punjab through Bengal to Hong Kong with German assistance. This plan failed after the information was leaked to British Intelligence, but only after the Singapore Garrison had rebelled. Further German assistance in the form of arms, ammunitions and trained cadres (both European and Indian) came too late to make a difference. During the Second World War, this plan found revival, with a number of different leaders, units and movements formed over the duration of the war. These included "liberation armies" formed in and with the help of Italy, Germany as well as in Southeast Asia. Local movements also formed within India which guerrilla tactics and significantly hindered the British war effort by sabotage, civil unrest and propaganda. The southeast Asian theatre saw the concept of the Indian National Army initiated by the Indian Independence League, which came to be acted out in two phases: the formation and subsequent disbandment of the Indian National Army under Capt. Mohan Singh Deb, and the formation of the Arzi Hukumat-e-Azad Hind under Subhash Chandra Bose and the reformation of the INA as its army. The concept of INA as the Azad Hind Fauj that lives in Indian Public Memory, and indeed as it is analysed by historians, as a fighting force is essentially the INA as the army of the Azad Hind Government under Netaji Subhash Bose. Both these phases saw extensive support from the Japanese Government, militarily as well as politically.

THE FIRST INA

Japan, as well as South East Asia was a major refuge for Indian nationalists living in exile before the start of World War II who formed strong proponents of militant nationalism and also influenced Japanese policy significantly. Although Japanese intentions and policies with regards to India were far from concrete at the start of the war, Japan had sent intelligence missions, notably under Major I Fujiwara, into South Asia even before the start of the World War II to garner support from the Malayan Sultans, overseas Chinese, the Burmese resistance and the Indian movement.

These missions were successful establishing contacts with Indian nationalists in exile in Thailand and Malaya, supporting the establishment and organisation of the Indian Independence League. At the outbreak of World War II in South East Asia, 70,000 Indian troops were stationed in Malaya. After the start of the war, Japan's spectacular Malayan Campaign had brought under her control considerable of Indian Prisoners of War, notably nearly 55,000 after the Fall of Singapore. The conditions of service within the British Indian Army as well as the conditions in Malaya had fed dissension among these troops. From these troops, the First Indian National Army was formed under Mohan Singh Deb and received considerable Japanese aid and support. It was formally proclaimed in September 1942 and declared the subordinate military wing of the Indian Independence League in June that year. The unit was dissolved in December 1942 and Mohan Singh was arrested and exiled to Pulau Ubin after apprehensions of Japanese motives with regards to the INA led to disagreements, distrust and subsequently open hostility between Mohan Singh and INA leadership on one hand, and the leagues leadership, most notable Rash Behari Bose and the Japanese military command on the other. A large number of the initial volunteers chose to revert to Prisoner of War Status and large number of these were subsequently sent to work in the Death Railway or in New Guinea. From the end of December 1942 to February Rash Behari Bose struggled to hold the INA together.

THE SECOND INA

In a series of meetings between the INA leaders and the Japanese in 1943, it was decided to cede the leadership of the IIL and the INA to Subhash Chandra Bose, since a number of the officers and troops who had returned to PoW camps, or had not volunteered in the first place, made it known that they would be willing to join the INA only on the condition that it was led by Bose. Bose had, at the start of the war in Europe, escaped from house arrest to make his way to Germany, reaching Berlin on 2 April 1941. In Germany he convinced Hitler, in a series of conferences, to support the cause of Indian Independence, forming the Free India Legion and the Azad Hind Radio By early 1943, Bose had turned his attention to Southéast Asia.

With its large overseas Indian population, it was recognised that the region was fertile ground for establishing an anti-colonial force to fight the Raj. In January 1943, the Japanese invited Bose to lead the Indian nationalist movement in East Asia. He accepted and left Germany on 8 February. After a three-month journey by submarine, and a short stop in Singapore, he reached Tokyo on 11 May 1943, where he made a number of radio broadcasts to the Indian communities, exhorting them to join in the fight for India's Independence.

On 15 February 1943, the Army itself was put under the command of Lt. Col. M.Z. Kiani. The former ranks and badges were revived. A policy forming body was formed with the Director of the Military Bureau, Lt. Col Bhonsle, in charge and clearly placed under the authority of the IIL. Under Bhonsle served Lt. Col. Shah Nawaz Khan as Chief of General Staff, Major P.K. Sahgal as Military Secretary, Major Habib Ur Rahman as commandant of the Officers' Training School and Lt. Col. A.C. Chatterji (later Major A.D. Jahangir) as head of enlightenment and culture.

On 4 July 1943, two days after reaching Singapore, Subhash Chandra Bose assumed the leadership of the IIL and the INA in a ceremony at Cathay Building. Bose's influence was notable. His appeal not only re-invigorated the fledgling INA, which previously consisted mainly of POWs, his appeals also touched a chord with the Indian expatriates in South Asia as local civilians-ranging from barristers to plantation workers – had no military experience joined the INA, doubled its troop strength. An Officers' Training School for INA officers, led by Habib Ur Rahman, and the Azad School for the civilian volunteers were set up to provide training to the recruits. A youth wing of the INA, composed of 45 Young Indians personally chosen by Bose and affectionately known as the Tokyo Boys, were also sent to Japan's Imperial Military Academy to train as fighter pilots. Also, possibly the first time in Asia, and even the only time outside the USSR, a women's regiment, the Rani of Jhansi regiment was raised as a combat force.

TROOP STRENGTH

Although there are slight variations in estimates, the INA is considered to have comprised about 40,000 troops when it was disbanded. The following is an estimate attributed to Lt. Colonel G.D. Anderson of British intelligence:

> *There were 45,000 Indian troops from Malaya captured and assembled in Singapore when the Japanese captured it. Of these, about 5,000 refused to join the First INA. The INA at this time had 40,000 recruits. The Japanese were prepared to arm 16,000. When the "first INA" collapsed, about 4,000 withdrew. The Second INA, commanded by Subhash Chandra Bose, started with 12,000 troops. Further recruitment of ex-Indian army personnel added about 8,000-10,000. About 18,000 Indian civilians enlisted during this time. In 1945, at the end of the INA, it consisted of about 40,000 soldiers.*

ORDER OF BATTLE

The exact organisation of the INA and its troop strength is not known, as Fay notes, since its records were destroyed by the withdrawing Azad Hind Government before Rangoon fell. .Fay's account of the INA gives the following account.

- The 1st Division was under Mohammed Zaman Kiyani. It drew a large number of ex-Indian army PoWs who had joined Mohan Singh's first INA. In addition, it also drew PoWs who had not joined in 1942. The 1st division consisted of:
  - — The 2nd Guerrilla regiment, or the Gandhi Brigade under Col. Inayat Kiani, consisting of two infantry battalions.
  - — The 3rd Guerrilla regiment, or the Azad Brigade under Col. Gulzara Singh, consisting of three battalions.
  - — The 4th Guerrilla regiment, or the Nehru Brigade. This unit was later under the command of Lt. Col G S Dhillon.
  - — The 1st Guerrilla regiment, or the Subhash Brigade under Col. Shah Nawaz Khan, consisting of three infantry battalions. This unit was the first and the major commitment of the INA to the U Go Offensive.

The 1st Division was lightly armed. Each battalion was composed of five Companies of infantry. The individual companies were armed with six antitank rifles, six Bren guns and six Vickers machine guns. Some NCOs carried hand grenades, while men going forward on duty were issued British stocks of hand grenades by senior officer of the Bahadur groups attached to each unit. Mortars were available, but Fay points out these were not available at battalion level.

- The 2nd Division under Aziz Ahmed. The 2nd division was formed to a large extent after the Imphal offensive had started, and drew a large remnant of the Hindustan Field Force of the First INA. The 2nd Division consisted of.
  - — The 1st Infantry Regiment, later to be merged with the 5th Guerrilla regiment to form the 2nd Infantry Regiment. The 1st Infantry drew a large number of civilian volunteers from Burma and Malaya, and

came to ve equipped with the lions share of the heavy armament that the INA possessed.

— The 5th Guerilla regiment, later to be renamed the 2nd Infantry Regiment under Col Prem Sahgal. This unit drew a large number of the remnants of the Hindustan Field Force.

- An additional 3rd Division of the INA was composed chiefly of local volunteers in Malaya and Singapore. This unit disbanded before Japan Surrendered. There was also a motor transport division, but this known to not have had a significant capability or resources.
- The Rani of Jhansi Regiment, under Lakshmi Sahgal, composed of female volunteers from Malaya and Burma.

COMMAND STRUCTURE

The INA in Operation

As the Japanese offensive opened, the INA sent its first forces into battle. The INA's own strategy was to avoid set-piece battles for which it lacked arms, armament as well as manpower. Initially, it sought to obtain arms as well as increase its ranks from British Indian soldiers expected to defect to patriotic cause.

Once the Japanese forces were able to break the British defences at Imphal, the INA would cross the hills of North-East India into the Gangetic plain, where it was to work as a guerrilla army and expected to live off the land, garner support, supplies, and ranks from amongst the local populace to ultimately touch off a revolution.

Prem Kumar Sahgal, an officer of the INA once Military secretary to Subhash Bose and later tried in the first Red Fort trials, explained that although the war itself hung in balance and nobody was sure if the Japanese would win, initiating a popular revolution with grass-root support within India would ensure that even if Japan lost the war ultimately, Britain would not be in a position to re-assert its colonial authority, which was ultimately the aim of the INA and Azad Hind.

1944

The plans decided between Bose and Kawabe envisaged the INA was to be assigned an independent sector of its own in the U Go offensive and no INA unit was to operate less than a battalion strength. For operational purposes, the Subhash Brigade was assigned under the command of the Japanese general Head Quarters in Burma.

Advance parties of the Bahadur Group also went forward with the advanced Japanese units early during the offensive. As Japan opened its offensive towards India, the INA's first division, consisting of four Guerrilla regiments, was divided between the diversionary Ha Go offensive in Arakan 1944, with one battalion reaching as far as Mowdok in Chittagong.

A Bahadur group unit, led by Shaukat Malik, took the border enclave of Moirang in early April. The main body of the first division was however committed to the U Go Offensive directed towards Manipur, initially successfully protecting the Japanese flanks against Chin and Kashin guerrilas as the Mutaguchi's three divisions crossed the Chindwin river and the Naga Hills, and later directed towards the main offensive through Tamu in the direction of Imphal and Kohima.

However, by the time Khan's forces left Tamu, the offensive had been held, and the troops were redirected to Kohima. By the time Khan's forces reached Ukhrul in the vicinity of Kohima, Japanese forces had began their slow withdrawal Kohima.

The first division suffered the same fate as did Mutaguchi's Army when the siege of Imphal was broken. With little or no supplies and supply lines deluged by the Monsoon, harassed by Allied air-dominance and local Burmese irregulars, the INA began withdrawing when the 15th Army and Burma Area Army began withdrawing, and suffer the same terrible fate as wounded, starved and diseased men succumbed during the hasty withdrawal into Burma.

The INA lost a substantial amount of men and materiel in the retreat, and a number of units were disbanded or used to feed the newly formed units of the second division.

1945

As the allied Burma campaign began the following year, however, the INA remained committed to the defence of Burma, and was a part of the Japanese defensive deployments. The second division, tasked with the defence of Irrawaddy and the adjoining areas around Nangyu, was instrumental in opposing Messervy's 7th Indian Division when it attempted to cross the river at Pagan and Nyangyu during Irrwaddy operations. Later, during the Battles of Meiktila and Mandalay, the 2nd division was instrumental in denying the British 17th Division the area around Mount Popa that would have exposed the Flank of Kimura's forces attempting to retake Meiktila and Nyangyu.

Ultimately however, the division was obliterated. As the Japanese situation became precarious, Azad Hind withdrew from Rangoon with Ba Maw's government and the Japanese forces for Singapore along with the remnants of the first division and the Rani of Jhansi Regiment. Nearly 6000 troops amongst the surviving units of the Army remained in Rangoon under A.D Loganathan surrendered as Rangoon fell, and helped keep order till the allied forces entered the city.

The only Indian territory that the Azad Hind govt controlled were the Indian territories that fell during the Imphal offensive, and the islands of Andaman and Nicobar. However, the latter two were bases for the Japanese Navy, and the navy never really fully relinquished control. Enraged with the lack of administrative control, the Azad Hind Governor, Lt. Col Loganathan later relinquished his authority to return to the Government's head quarters in Rangoon. The Japanese forces is said to have carried out torture on thousands of local inhabitants during the occupation, and some historians inexplicably apportion the blame to Subhash Bose's provisional government.

End of the INA

As the Japanese withdrawal from Burma progressed, the other remnants began a long march over land and on foot towards Singapore, along with Subhash Chandra Bose. The withdrawing forces suffered casualties regularly in clashes with

Aung San's Burmese resistance, as well as Chinese guerrillas who harassed the Japanese troops. At the time of Japan's surrender in September 1945, Bose left for Manchuria to attempt to contact the advancing Soviet troops, and was reported to have died in an air crash near Taiwan.

REPATRIATION TO INDIA

Even before the end of the war in South Asia, the INA prisoners who were falling into allied hands were being evaluated by forward intelligence units for potential trials. The number of prisoners necessitated this selective policy which envisaged trials of those with the strongest commitment to Bose' ideologies, while those with less strong views and other extenuating circumstance may be dealt with more leniently, with the punishment proportional to their commitment or war crimes. For this purpose, the field intelligence units designated the captured troops as *Blacks* with strongest commitment to Azad Hind, *Greys* with varying commitment but also with enticing circumstances that led them to join the INA, and *Whites*, i.e., those who pressured into joining the INA under the circumstances but with no commitment to Azad Hind, INA, or Bose. The prisoners were transferred through transit camps in Bengal to Delhi and Punjab. The *whites* were released slowly over a period of time after the end of the war. From amongst the rest, the selection for those to face trial started.

THE RED FORT TRIAL

At the conclusion of the war, the government of British India brought some of the captured INA soldiers to trial on treason charges. The prisoners would potentially face the death penalty, life imprisonment or a fine as punishment if found guilty. It was initially believed by Auckinleck that no less than twenty death penalties were likely to be confirmed. Between November 1945 and May 1946, approximately ten courts-martial were held. The first of these, and the most celebrated one, was the joint court-martial of Colonel Prem Sahgal, Colonel Gurubaksh Singh Dhillon and Major General Shah Nawaz Khan held in a public trial at Red Fort. The then Advocate

General of India, Sir Naushirwan P Engineer was appointed the counsel for Prosecution nearly.

The defendants in the first trial were charged with *Waging against the King-Emperor* (the charge of treason did not exist in the Indian Army Act, 1911) as well as torture, murder and abetment to murder. The three defendants were defended by the INA Defence Committee formed by the Congress and include legal luminaries of India of the time including Jawaharlal Nehru, Bhulabhai Desai, Kailashnath Katju and others. The trials covered arguments based on Military Law, Constitutional Law, International Law, and Politics and much of the initial defence was based on the argument that they should be treated as prisoners of war as they were not paid mercenaries but *bona fide* soldiers of a legal government, the Provisional Government of Free India, or the Arzi Hukumate Azad Hind, "however misinformed or otherwise they had been in their notion of patriotic duty towards their country" and as such they recognized the free Indian state as their sovereign and not the British sovereign. Those charged later only faced trial for torture and murder or abetment of murder.

These trials attracted much publicity, and public sympathy for the defendants who were perceived as patriots in India. The Indian National Congress and the Muslim League both made the release of the three defendants an important political issue during the agitation for independence of 1945-6. Beyond the concurrent campaigns of noncooperation and nonviolent protest, this spread to include mutinies and wavering support within the British Indian Army. This movement marked the last major campaign in which the forces of the Congress and the Muslim League aligned together; the Congress tricolor and the green flag of the League were flown together at protests. In spite of this aggressive and widespread opposition, the court martial was carried out, and all three defendants were sentenced to deportation for life. This sentence, however, was never carried out, as the immense public pressure of the demonstrations and riots forced Claude Auchinleck, Commander-in-Chief of the Indian Army, to release all three defendants. Within three months, 11000 soldiers of the INA were released after cashiering and forfeiture of pay and allowance. On the recommendation of Lord Mountbatten, and agreed by Nehru, as a precondition for Independence the INA soldiers were not reinducted into the Indian Army.

Post 1947

Within India, the INA continued to posses a strong hold over the public psyche and the sentiments of the armed forces till as late as 1947. Some have said that Shah Nawaz Khan was instrumental in organising INA troops to train Congress volunteers on Nehru's request in late 1946 and early 1947. After 1947, some accounts suggest that the INA-veterans were involved in training civilian resistance forces against the Nizam's Razakars prior to the execution of Operation Polo and annexation of Hyderabad. There are also mentions of some INA veterans leading Pakistani irregulars during the First Kashmir war.

INA-veterans were not allowed to join the Indian Army after India's independence in August 1947. However, a few ex-INA members, notably the most prominent members or those closely associated with Subhash Bose or with the INA trials later have seen prominent public life or held important positions in independent India.

Shah Nawaz Khan served as a Minister of State for Rail in the First Indian cabinet. Lakshmi Sahgal, Minister for Women's affairs in the Azad Hind govt, is a well known and widely respected public figure in India. In 1971, she joined the CPIM and was later elected the leader of the All India Democratic Women's Association. In 2002, she was also nominated by the Communist bloc's for the post of President of India, when she lost to the candidature of Abdul Kalam. Abid Hasan, Subhash Bose's sole Indian companion in the U-Boat from Germany to Southeast Asia, joined the Indian Foreign Service in 1948 and served as the Indian Ambassador to a number of countries including Egypt and Denmark. Mohan Singh served for two terms in the Rajya Sabha of the Indian Parliament as a member of the Indian National Congress. Ram Singh Thakur, composer of a number of songs including the

INAs regimental march Kadam Kadam Badaye Ja, later composed the tune for the Indian National Anthem.

Amongst the very few ex-INA members who joined the Indian Armed Forces after 1947 was R S Benegal, a member of the Tokyo Boys who was allowed to join the Indian Air Force in 1952 and later rose to be an Air Commodore. Benegal saw action in both the 1965 and 1971 Indo-Pak war, earning a Maha Vir Chakra, India's second highest award for valour. A few members, including Gurubaksh Singh Dhillon and Lakshmi Sahgal were later awarded civilian honours of Padma Vibhushan by the Indian Government in the 1990s. Subhash Bose himself was posthumously awarded Bharat Ratna in 1992 but this was later withdrawn over the controversy over the circumstances of his death. Outside India, the Malaysian Indian Congress was founded in 1946 by, amongst others, notable members of the INA and of which John Thivy was the founding president. Janaky Athi Nahappan, Second in Command of the Rani of Jhansi Regiment was also a founding member of the MIC, and later was to become a noted welfare activist and a distinguished senator in the Dewan Negara of the Malaysian Parliament. Rasammah Bhupalan, also of the Rani of Jhansi Regiment, later became a noted welfare-activist and a widely respected champion for Women's Rights in Malayasia.

Impact

The INA's impact on the war and on British India after the war has been analysed in detail. The INA's role in military terms is considered to be relatively insignificant, given its small numerical strength, lack of heavy weapons (it utilised captured British and Dutch arms initially), relative dependence on Japanese logistics and planning as well as its lack of independent planning. Shah Nawaz claims in his personal memoirs that the INA was a very potent and motivated force. Fay however, reinforces the argument that the INA was relatively less significant in military terms. Its special services group played a significant part in halting the First Arakan Offensive while still under Mohan Singh's command. The propaganda threat of the INA, coupled with the lack of concrete intelligence on the unit early after the fall of Singapore made it a potent threat to Allied war plans in South East Asia. It threatened to destroy the Sepoy's loyalty in the British Indian Army and in fact was significant and successful enough during the First Arakan Offensive for the British intelligence to begin the Jiffs campaign as well as engage in campaign to improve morale and preserve the loyalty of the sepoy to consolidate and prepare for defense of Manipur. These measures included imposing newsban on Bose and the INA that was not lifted till four days after the all of Rangoon two years later.

Later, during the Japanese U-GO offensive towards Manipur in 1944, it played a crucial and successful role in the diversionary attacks in Arakan as well as in the Manipur Basin itself where it fought with Mutaguchi's 15th Army. It qualified itself well in the Battles in Arakan, Manipur, Imphal, and later during the withdrawal through Manipur and Burma. The commanders like L.S. Mishra, Raturi, Mansukhlal, M.Z. Kiyani, and others attracted the attention of the Japanese as well as the British forces. Later, during the Burma Campaign, it did play a notable role in the Battles of Irrawaddy and Meiktilla especially in the latter, supporting the Japanese offensive and tying down British troops. Fay also notes the published accounts of several veterans, including that of William Slim that portrays INA-troops as incapable fighters and untrustworthy, and points out the inconsistencies and conflicts between the different accounts to conclude that intelligence propaganda as well as institutional bias may have played a significant part in the portrayed opinions.

It is however noted that the INA did indeed suffer a number of notable incidences of desertion. Fay notes the significant ones amongst these were not during the offensives into Manipur and the subsequent retreat through Burma, when incidences of desertion did occur but at a far smaller numbers than the fourteenth army told its troops. The significant desertions, Fay notes, occurred around the Battles at Irrawaddy and later around Popa. During the fall of Rangoon, 6000 INA troops manned the city to maintain order before allied troops entered the city. Nevertheless, Fay argues, the INA was not significant enough to militarily beat the British Indian Army, and was moreover aware of this and formulated its own strategy of avoiding set-piece battles, garnering local and popular support within India and instigating revolt within the British Indian army to overthrow the Raj. Moreover, the Forward Bloc underground within India had been crushed well before the offensives opened in the Burma-Manipur theatre, depriving the army of any organised internal support.

It was, however, the INA trials that attracted more attention in India than the war time activities of the unit, and coupled to the decisions to hold the first trial in public, these became a rallying point for the independence movement from Autumn 1945, so much so that the release of INA prisoners and suspension of the trials came to be the dominant political campaign in precedence over the campaign for Freedom. Newspaper reports around November 1945 reported executions of INA troops, which deteriorated already volatile situations. Opposition to the trial of the officers for treason became a major public and political campaign, and the very opening of the first trial saw violence and series of riots in a scale later described as sensational. It also saw a campaign that defied communal barriers. Increasingly violent confrontations broke out between the police and the mass rallies being held all over India, culminating in public riotings in support of the INA men. The Raj also observed with increasing disquiet and unease the spread of pro-INA sympathies within the troops of the British Indian forces. In February 1946, while the trials were still going on, a general strike ratings of the Royal Indian Navy rapidly deteriorated into a mutiny, incorporating ships and shore establishments of the RIN throughout India, from Karachi to Bombay and from Vizag to Calcutta. Amongst the rallying cries of the ratings the central one was the INA trials and slogans invoking Subhash Bose. Significantly, the mutiny received massive militant public support. At some places, NCOs in the British Indian Army started ignoring orders from British superiors.

In Madras and Pune, the British garrisons had to face revolts within the ranks of the British Indian Army. Another

Army mutiny took place at Jabalpur during the last week of February 1946, soon after the Navy mutiny at Bombay. This was suppressed by force, including the use of the bayonet by British troops. It lasted about two weeks. After the mutiny, about 45 persons were tried by court martial. 41 were sentenced to varying terms of imprisonment or dismissal. In addition, a large number were discharged on administrative grounds. Fay records Auckinleck as having sent a "Personal and Secret" letter to all senior British officers as having explained the remissions of the sentences in the First trial as:

> *"...practically all are sure that any attempt to enforce the sentence would have led to chaos in the country at large, and probably to mutiny and dissension in the Army, culminating in its dissolution"*

Later historians have pointed out that the INA trials and its after effects brought the decisive shift in British policy. The viceroy's journal describes the autumn and Winter 1945-45 as "The Edge of a Volcano". Intelligence reports at the time noted widespread public interest and sympathy that turned into what has been described as "Patriotic Fury" that was beyond the communal barriers in India at the time. Particularly disturbing was overt and public support for the INA by the soldiers of the Indian army. In addition, the use of Indian troops for the restoration of Dutch and French rule in Vietnam and Indonesia also fed growing resentment within the forces. The Raj had every reason to fear a revival of the Quit Indian movement, especially given the Congress rhetoric preceding the elections and rapidly realised that the Indian army, unlike in 1942, could not be used to suppress such a movement owing largely to nationalistic and political consciousness in the forces which was ascribed to the INA.

The political effects of the INA trials was enormous and were felt around India as late as 1948, much to the chagrin of the then Indian government. Clement Atlee, the then British Prime Minister, reflecting on the factors that guided the British decision to relinquish the Raj in India, is said to have cited the effects of the INA and Bose's activities on the British Indian Army and the Bombay Mutiny as the most important. After the war ended, the story of the INA and the Free India Legion was seen as so inflammatory that, fearing mass revolts and uprisings—not just in India, but across its empire—the British Government forbad the BBC from broadcasting their story.

Relations

The army's relationship to the Japanese was an uncomfortable one. Bose wished to establish his political independence from the regime that sponsored him (he had, in fact, led protests against the Japanese expansion into Manchuria, and supported Chiang Kai-shek during the 1930s), but his complete dependence on them for arms and resources made this difficult. On the Japanese side, members of the high command had been personally impressed by Bose, and were thus willing to grant him some latitude; more importantly, the Japanese were interested in maintaining the support of a man who had been able to mobilize large numbers of Indian expatriates—including, most importantly, 40,000 of the 45,000 Indians captured by the Japanese at Singapore.

The INA's interactions with the British Indian Army occurred over two distinct phases. The first of these was December 1942-March 1943, during the First Arakan offensive at a time that the morale of the sepoy was low and the knowledge about the INA was minimal. The INAs Special services agents led a successful operation during this time in encouraging the Indian troops to defect to the INA, while those who returned to India beaten in the field took back horrific if unbelievable stories of Japanese troops using their parachutes not only to drop from the skies, but to go back up again.

The threat of the INA at this time was significant and successful enough for the British intelligence to begin the Jiffs campaign as well as engage in campaign to improve morale and preserve the loyalty of the sepoy. General newsban on reporting the INA allowed the British Indian Army to consolidate and prepare for defense of Manipur, which it successfully did. By the end of March 1945, the sepoy of the British Indian Army was reinvigorated and perceived the men of the INA little more than savage turncoats and cowards. Bayly and Harper mentions that a number of times, the sepoys in the field units shot captured or wounded INA men, relieving their British officers of the complex task of formulating a formal plan for captured men. After Singapore was retaken, Mountbatten ordered the INA's war memorial to its fallen soldiers to be blown up.

However, the INA's most significant interaction with the British Indian Army occurred not in the battle field, but after the end of the war. The lifting of the newsban after the fall of Rangoon led to the INA story breaking in India which, within a matter of months if not weeks, had captured the public imagination within India. This nationalistic euphoria swept through the armed forces as well, generally destabilising the Sepoys loyalty to both the Raj and his regiments. Fay notes that even before Japan surrendered preparations were underway for the trial of selected among the INA men. The predominant feeling in the Indian officer corps at this time was a resentment was that so *few* were being tried. This changed dramatically over the following months as the further information on the INA began emerging in the Press and its true extent, as well as the stories of its campaigns came to be known. The general feeling within the British Indian army at this time is described by some is that of guilt for having fought for the British and against the INA. The revolts and mutinies within the armed forces in early 1946, during the trial and in a situation of volatile nationalist public mood, are held to be a significant factor in precipitating the end of the Raj.

Although the British Indian Army remained the largest volunteer force during the World War II and saw action from the theatres of North-Africa to Europe and New Guinea to Maniour, in India today, the stories of the INA form a much more prominent aspect of both appreciation as well as analysis of her role in World War II.

Controversies

The integral associations of the INA's history with that of the war in South East Asia especially the Japanese occupation of South East Asian countries, the renunciations of the oath to the King, as well as wartime propaganda and later allegations of torture by INA soldiers have inspired a number of controversies. Principal among these is the Intelligence propaganda during the war implied alleged torture at a massive scale of Indian and Allied Prisoners of War by the INA troops in collaboration with the Japanese.

A very opposing view that has emerged after the war, especially within India, are also based on the motivations of the troops who formed the INA, where a predominant view was held, and still holds, the INA as patriots and revolutionaries. Outside India it is not widely known and the accounts and views on the INA, especially among the allied servicemen who served in Burma, are diametrically opposite. However, almost no account of the Indian independence movement ignore the INA. Other controversies have risen on the contributions of the INA to India's independence, the treatment of INA troops in Independent India, as well as the conditions of expatriate Indians who joined the INA.

Motivations

Different historians have cited other reasons for the INA's recruits volunteering to serve with the Japanese enemy. These included both the high ideal of patriotism, the inevitable desire not to be interned in the POW Camp, as well as ambition. Some cite the destruction and devaluation of the Raj's prestige and authority in the Malayan debacle and the humiliating surrender at Singapore that first shook the Sepoy's loyalty to the Raj and more importantly to the notion of supremacy of the Sahib.

In addition, a number of authors have cited the disparity in the service conditions (including scopes of progression in the army) and treatment of White and Indian troops within the army as another reason for ill-feelings within the Indian troops. Further reason cited by Both Fay and Lebra and other authors indicate monetary and situational scopes, as well as the resentment at the abandonment of the Indian troops at Singapore by their White comrades and the officers. Controversy exists as to what was actually said by Hunt in the first of the three speeches at Farrer Park. Fay writes in 1993 that a number of the troops gathered at the park remembers Hunt as having told the troops that they now belonged to the Japanese army and should obey their orders while Hunt only remembers having said that they were all Prisoners of War of the Japanese Nevertheless, Fay also points out that the fact that they were all POWs was already self-evident, and the fact that they were addressed separately implies some significance. A number of INA veterans present have said that this also fed a feeling of devaluation (handed over like cattle, as Shah Nawaz Khan later put it), abandonment and of dishonour on part of the British high command that they perceived to have served loyalty. In the days and years to come, a number of INA men cited this act of abandonment a major reason to join the first INA. Others, especially ICOs and VCOs have said that they initially joined the first INA to prevent any possible ill-treatment of their subordinate Indian soldiers. However, all authors agree that Subhash Chandra Bose's charismatic leadership and persona was probably also amongst the most significant factors that drew the recruits of the second INA and was key in transforming it into a cohesive fighting force.

Axis Collaboration

During the war, the associations of the INA with the Japanese, and circulating stories of it being a small force of turn coats, of participations in outrages by Japanese forces and other stories meant that a number of Congress Leaders viewed what it knew about the INA as a traitor army. In addition, a number of Congress Leaders, including Gandhi, announced the Japanese as unwelcome. Other political forces, including the communist party and its members viewed the INA as fascist-collaborators, and was instrumental in helping the security forces track down INA agents landed by submarine or Parachute.

The army intelligence, when it became aware of the establishment and existence of the INA, was also faced with the possibilities of the sepoys of the Eastern Army (as the 14th army was called then) deserting. It was also during this time that the intelligence started coming in possession of accounts of torture and ill-treatment meted out to Allied troops and PoWs by the Japanese forces in Burma. During the war, the existence of the INA was alluded to by the commanders to frontline Indian troops. These also included references that the army was an auxiliary force to the Japanese forces, as well as that they were collaborators and traitors. After the war, Allied PoWs, as well as Indian PoWs who did not join the INA describe bitter memories of labour camps and ill-treatment in the hands of Japanese forces. In addition, the war time intelligence work and propaganda had described the INA, incorrectly, as a small force of deserters from among a large majority of Indian PoWs who remained loyal to the Raj and refused to join. In addition, the propaganda work also associated the INA with Japanese atrocities on allied PoWs and local populace.

Allegations of Torture

The INA is not widely known or described outside India, beyond those who fought in Southeast Asia. The predominant opinion within this group, especially in the accounts of the war in the popular accounts of British and Australian servicemen of the war in Burma, is of a contemptuous auxiliary force that was a totally ineffective fighting force and composed of cowards and brutes who sought opportunities to desert Allegations of torture by the INA had been made. Fay, however, notes that these allegations were not borne out by the number of men charged with torture at the Red Fort trials, nor by the charges against them.

In the first INA trials, Fay notes the three men were charged with Murder and abetment to murder of troops of the INA itself who had attempted to desert, and argues that this had been in an open process based on the INA's own laws, drawn from the Indian Army Act,1911, noting the court found the three men not guilty. However, Fay also describes the some of later ones of the ten or so trials, including those of Burhan-ud-Din and others, where the allegations by Fay's account are justified. Nevertheless, Fay argues that these made up a few instances and by no means match up to the large scale torture alleged and concludes these to be wartime intelligence manouevres. Some have also made allegations of complicity in the Selarang Barracks Incident at Singapore in 1942, where

INA guards are alleged to have shot four Australian PoWs who had attempted to escape from Changi Prison.

INDIAN INDEPENDENCE

It has been argued by a number of Historians, contemporary and modern, that the preparations for withdrawal from India had begun already, and the INA or the movements arising out of it achieved nothing. Others have however argued that although the will to relinquish the Raj may have existed already, but the events of the Red Fort trials, the Bombay mutiny and destabilisation within the armed forces were a principal reason for the hasty end to the Raj even in the face of dismal political scene. Within India, the story of the Army was seen at the time, and still seen, both as fascinating story as well as a turning-point in the movement for Independence.

After the ban on the INA was lifted on the 10th of May, it was seen as the first "national" force not decreed by caste and religion. As Sumit Sarkar puts it, its biggest impact was on the patriotic imagination of an army fighting for the country's liberation, led by a Bengalee-the least "Martial" of India's "races" in traditional British stereotype. When the accounts of the Red Fort trials and of the tales of the INA started being reported, both in the national press as well as the vernacular press, much public agitations and support emerged for the troops and quickly became a major driving force in the closing days of the Independence Movement. The INA's war cries of "*Chalo Delhi*" (on to Delhi) and most of all "*Jai Hind*" became the cries of the Freedom movement, and of protesters demanding their release. Jai Hind has since been adopted as India's National slogan, an official salutation in the Indian Armed Forces, as well as the closing salutation of the Prime Minister's Independence day address at Red Fort. It is also an extremely popular patriotic greeting.

INA AND INDEPENDENT INDIA

A further controversy exists, especially within India, with regards to the attitude and treatment towards the INA by the Post 1947 Governments of India as well as the omission of the events of September 1945-46 from the historical records of the Freedom movement. Nehru, in 1948, refused to readmit the men of the INA to the Indian Army after independence. He cited the break in the service of the ex-INA men, as well as the effects on the Indian Army of taking ex-INA troops into their ranks. However, it has been noted that as late as 1948, considerable pro-INA sentiments existed in the army as well as public psyche, attracting strong dissatisfactions from members of Nehru's cabinet, Defence Minister Sardar Baldev Singh is on record as having commented on the need to strengthen the morale of the Indian army "which in recent months has been somewhat tried for internal discipline and perverse lauding of the "Indian National Army" and its role in the war against the Allies in Asia."

Also, although Nehru promised pensions, the men of the INA were however not eligible for the Freedom Fighters Pension till 1972. A number of people, notably ex-members of the INA and sympathetic groups have accused the Nehru, Mountbatten, and subsequently successive Congress governments, of largely ignoring and not-recognising the role of the INA, as well as the events surrounding it between 1945-46, in the History of the Independence movement. These have been compounded by a number of conspiracy-theories and news reports in the past on agreements between the Indian political leadership to hand over its leader Subhash Chandra Bose as a War Criminal if he was found to be alive. Other historians have suggested a systemic bias of the. Later historians have, however, argued that given the political aim and nature of the entire Azad Hind movement especially the Indian National Army, Nehru's decisions may have been to prevent politicisation of the army and assert civilian authority over the military.

Further criticisms have been made in recent years for the general hardships and apathy surrounding the conditions of ex-INA troops including, for example, the circumstances surrounding the death and funeral of Ram Singh Thakur, the composer of India's National Anthem. Also, criticisms have been made for not recognising as freedom-fighters for India the expatriate Indians, notably Burmese Indians, who joined the

INA and were not repatriated to India at the end of the war. Most are not recognised as Indian citizens, and not recognised as citizens in their adopted countries, effectively being stateless people.

COMMEMORATIONS

Memorials

Subhash Chandra Bose laying foundation stone of INA War Memorial, Singapore, 8 July 1945.

- The INA War Memorial at Singapore to commemorate the "*Unknown Warrior*" of the INA. Started on 8 July 1945 the memorial was situated at the Esplanade Park. It was destroyed on Mountbatten's orders when allied troops reoccupied the city. The words inscribed upon the War Memorial were the motto of the INA: *Ittefaq* (Unity), *Etmad* (Faith) and *Kurbani* (Sacrifice).
- The Former Indian National Army Monument, was established in 1995 by the National Heritage Board of Singapore at the site where the old memorial stood with financial donations from the Indian community in Singapore. The site is now officially one of the Historical sites in Singapore.
- The Indian National Army Memorial at Moirang, Manipur commemorates the place where the flag of Azad Hind was raised by Col. Shaukat Hayat Malik. Moirang was the first Indian Territory captured by the INA. The memorial suffered damage in an insurgent attack in 2004 when the Statue of the Springing Tiger on the entrance was blown up.
- *Swatantrata Sainani Smarak* (Memorial to the soldiers of the Independence Army) is an Indian National Army (INA) memorial at the Salimgarh Fort, at Delhi, adjacent to the Red Fort, on the banks of the Yamuna. The site has been neglected for a number of years now and fallen into disrepair. Its exhibits include the Indian National Army uniform worn by Colonel Prem Sahgal, riding boots and coat buttons of Colonel Gurbaksh Singh

Dhillon, photographs of Subhash Chandra Bose. In addition, a separate gallery also holds material and photographs from excavations carried out by the Archaeological Survey of India inside the fort in 1995.

Postage and Philately

- Jai Hind, the INA's battle cry, became Independent India's first commemorative post mark on 15 August 1947.
- The first postage stamp issued by Independent India shows the Indian Flag with the letters Jai Hind in the top right hand corner.

These were a pat of the *Jai Hind* series of stamps issued on 15 August 1947.

- Commemorative postage stamps were issued by the Indian government in 1968 and 1993 respectively to commemorate the 25th and the 50th anniversaries of the establishment of Azad Hind at Singapore.

The Indian Postal Department also includes the six unused Azad Hind Stamps in its commemorative book *India's Freedom Struggle through India Postage Stamps.*

Works on the INA

The Indian National Army, from the time it came into public perception in India around the time of the Red Fort Trials, and from the time it found its way into the works of Military Historians around the world, has been the subject of a number of projects, both of academic, historical and of popular nature. Some of these are critical of the army, some-especially of the ex-INA men are biographical or auto-biographical, while still others are works of History and politics that tell the story of the INA. A large number of these give a large analysis of Subhash Chandra Bose and his work with the INA.

Literary Works

The first literary works on the INA were published as early as 1946. Some were works of fiction with the INA as the central theme and subject, others the records of the INA that the authors were able to obtain from the ex-servicemen, or from what information was available from the trials and from what the British Intelligence possessed and that the authors had access to. Some of the literature focused on the first INA trial itself.

The notable work on INA include:

- *Two Historic Trials at Red Fort* by Moti Ram. (New Delhi: Roxy Printing Press, 1946). This was one of the first published account of any sort of the INA and describes the Trial of Major General Shah Nawaz Khan, Col Prem Sahgal, and Col G.S Dhillon that took place between November and December, 1946. Moti Ram was the staff correspondent of the Hindustan Times at the first Red Fort Trial and wrote his book on what information was available at the trial, and from interviews with the defendants, Sahgal, Khan and Dhillon. The book also provides an account of the 1858 trial of Bahadur Shah Zafar.
- *Jai Hind, the Diary of a Rebel Daughter of India. Bombay, 1945* (fiction) by Amritlal Seth. The book is a work of fiction narrating the story of a recruit of the Rani of Jhansi Regiment. It is believed to be loosely based on the story of Lakshmi Sahgal.
- *The Day of the Scorpion* and *The Towers of Silence*, second and third respectively of Paul Scott's *Raj Quartet* that mentions *Jiffs* in the political and social context in which the term found use in the Eastern Army during the war.
- *The Glass Palace* by Amitav Ghosh chronicles the fictional life of a Rangoon Teak trader and describes the occupation of Rangoon and the Indian perspectives and efforts In the book, Uma Dey is a widow and Indian Independence League activist. Her appearance in the later half of the book is used as a device to characterize the post-colonial divisions for the remainder of the novel. The novel describes the Burma front in some detail, examining the motivations of those Indian officers who joined the INA and those who did not)

Historical literary works on the INA includes:

- *My memories of I.N.A. & its Netaji'* by Shah Nawaz Khan.
- *The Indian National Army-Second Front of the Indian Independence Movement* by Kalyan Ghosh.
- *Jungle Alliance: Japan and the Indian National Army.* by Joyce C Lebra.
- *The Forgotten Army: India's Armed Struggle for Independence, 1942-1945.* by Peter Fay.

Visual Media

Notable works on the INA in the visual and electronic media include:

- *The War of The Springing Tiger* (1984)-made by Granada Television for Channel 4. It examines the role of the Indian National Army during the Second World War. The documentary focuses on a number of aspects, including why the PoWs chose to join the INA, its role in the Burma and Imphal Campaign, as well as exploring its role in the independence movement. The documentary took contributions from Lakhsmi and Prem Sahgal.
- *The Forgotten Army*-(1999)-Film India. This was a documentary directed by Kabir Khan and produced by Akhil Bakshi following their famous *Azad Hind Expedition* in 1994-95. The expedition retraced the route taken by the troops of the INA from Singapore to Imphal and ends at Red Fort, where the famous trial of the officers were held. The expedition team had among its members Col G.S Dhillon who himself was one of the famous accused in the first trial, Captain Lakshmi Sahgal, who commanded the Rani of Jhansi Regiment and was also the minister in Charge of Women's affairs in the Azad Hind Govt and Captain S.S. Yadava, an INA veteran and once the general secretary of All India INA Committee, as well as prominent members of the Indian Parliament. The expedition met, and honoured, a number of INA veterans residing in South East Asia.

The then Indian Prime Minister PV Narasimha Rao sent through the expedition team goodwill messages to the heads of state of the countries it went through. The documentary went on to win the Grand Jury Prize at the Film South Asia festival in 1999.

- *Hitler's secret Indian army* (2004)-BBC-By Mike Thomson. This traces briefly the story of Bose's Azad Hind Legion in Europe, but does not attempt to distinguish or explain the differences between the Legion and the INA.
- *Historical Journey of the Indian National Army*-From the National Archives of Singapore.
- *Indian National Army in East Asia*-Hindustan Times.

Cinema

INA has also been the source of or a significant context of a number of movies in a number of Indian languages. Notable amongst these include

- *Pahla Admi*, a 1950 film by Bimal Roy and INA veteran Nazir Ahmed.
- *Samadhi*, a 1950 Hindi film by Ramesh Saigal. The movie was a fictional drama set in Singapore around the time the second INA was rising. The lead character of Shekhar, played by Ashok Kumar, is a young recruit to the INA.
- *Indian*, a 1996 Tamil film directed by S. Shankar. The plot describes one of the main character, Senapathy, as an ex-soldier in the INA.
- *Netaji: The Forgotten Hero*, a 2004 movie by Shyam Benegal, traces the last five years of Subhash Chandra Bose, who was the Supreme Commander of the second INA and was instrumental in reorganising it. The film describes the story of the INA but focuses on its leader. The film was also widely noted for A R Rahman's music.

In music, *Kadam Kadam Badaye Ja...*, the INA's marching song, has since become a famous patriotic song in India. Today, it is in use as the Regimental quickmarch of the Indian Army as well as its Para Regiments. The music was composed by Ram Singh Thakur, from whose composition was later derived the tune for India's national anthem Jana Gana Mana. Other mentions of the INA in popular culture abound through India, including:

- The Azad Hind Fauj Marg, in New Delhi, is named after the INA, and houses the Netaji Subhash Institute of Technology named after Netaji Subhash Chandra Bose.

INDISCHE LEGION

The Legion Freies Indien, or the Indische Legion, variously known as the Tiger Legion, the Free India Legion (in English), the Azad Hind Legion, and the Indische Freiwilligen-Legion Regiment 950 or the I.R 950 (*Indisches Infanterie Regiment 950*) was an Indian armed unit raised in 1941 attached to the Wehrmacht, ostensibly according to the concept of an Indian Liberation force during World War II by Subhash Chandra Bose in Nazi Germany. The initial recruits were Indian student volunteers resident in Germany at the time, and a handful from the Indian PoWs captured by Rommel during his North Africa Campaign. It would later draw a larger number of Indian PoWs as volunteers.

Raised initially as an assault group that would form a pathfinder to a German/Indian invasion of the western frontiers of British India, only a small contingent was ever put to its original intended purpose when a hundred of the Legionnaires were parachuted into eastern Iran to infiltrate into India through Baluchistan and commence sabotage operations against the British in preparation for the anticipated national revolt. A majority of the troops of the Free India Legion were only ever stationed in Europe-mostly in non-combat duties-from Netherlands, to Atlantic Wall duties in France till the Allied invasion of France. A small contingent, including the leadership and the officer corps, was also transferred to Azad Hind after its formation and saw action in the INA's Burma Campaign. Although it has been alleged to have been a collaborationist Heer Unit, the unit was not deployed as a part of the German

War effort or defences in Europe but did see actions against British and Polish troops and also undertook anti-partisan operations in Italy in 1944. At the time of the surrender of the Third Reich in 1945, remaining troops of the Free India Legion made efforts to march to Neutral Switzerland over the Alps, but these efforts proved futile as they were captured by American and French troops and eventually shipped back to India to face charges of treason.

BACKGROUND

The origins of the idea of raising an armed force that would fight its way into India to bring down the Raj goes back to the First World War, when the Ghadar Party and the nascent embryo of the Indian Independence League formulated plans to initiate rebellion in the British Indian Army from Punjab to Hong Kong with German Support. This plan failed after the information was leaked to British Intelligence, but only after the Hong Kong Garrison had rebelled.

However, during World War II, all the three major Axis Powers, at some stage of their campaign against Britain, sought to support/exploit the armed revolutionary activities within India and aided the recruitment of a military force from disaffected Indian prisoners-of war captured while serving with the British Commonwealth forces and Indian expatriates, of which the most famous, and successful, was probably the Indian National Army that came into being with Japanese Support in the Far East. Italy had in 1942 created the Battaglione Azad Hindoustan, with ex-Indian Army personnel and Italians previously resident in India and Persia, that ultimately served under Ragruppamento Centri Militari. However, these efforts proved unsuccessful, given the overtly propagandist nature of their efforts that ultimately found little acceptance among the constituent soldiers, and the lack of a leadership that would deemed legitimate by the troops. By November 1942, following the defeats in El Alamein, the Italian efforts had failed.

However at this time in India, although the Congress Party had passed resolutions conditionally supporting the fight against fascism, Indian public opinion was more hostile at

Britain's unilateral decision to declare India a belligerent on the side of the Allies. Among the more rebellious amongst Indian political leaders of the time was Subhash Chandra Bose, who was viewed as a potent threat enough that when the war started, the Raj put him under arrest, and later, house arrest. Bose escaped from under British surveillance at his house in Calcutta on January 19, 1941, with the help of family members, members of his party-the Forward Bloc-and later the Abwehr, he made his way through Afghanistan to the Soviet Union. Once in Russia the NKVD transported Bose to Moscow where he hoped that Russia's traditional enmity to British rule in India would result in support for his plans for a popular rising in India. However, Bose found the Soviets' response disappointing and was rapidly passed over to the German Ambassador in Moscow, Count von der Schulenberg, who arranged for Bose to be sent to Berlin at the beginning of April where he met Rippentrop and later, Hitler. In Berlin, Bose set up the Azad Hind Radio and the Free India Centre which commenced broadcasting to Indians in short wave frequencies. The Azad Hind Radio broadcasts were estimated to have regularly been received by 30,000 Indians who possessed the requisite receiver. However, soon, Bose's aim became to raise an army that he imagined would march to India's NWFP with German forces through the Caucasus and trigger the downfall of the Raj.

ORIGIN

The first troops of the Free India Legion were derived from Rommel's Indian PoWs captured at El Mekili, Libya during the Battles for Tobruk. Initially a core group of 27 officers were selected in May 1941 and flown to Berlin. A larger PoW camp of about 10,000 was also set up in Annaburg where Subhash Bose met Indian PoWs.

From these, a group of approximately 6,000 men were transferred to the Frankenburg Camp, from which a further core of 300 soldiers were sent to Königsbrück for training and induction. It was at Königsbrück that uniforms were issued, in German feldgrau with the badge of the Leaping Tiger of

Azad Hind. The formation of the Indian National Army was announced by the German Propaganda Ministry in January 1942. It did not, however, take oath until 26 August 1942, as the Legion Freies Indien of the German Army. By May of 1943, the numbers had been swelled, aided by the enlistment as volunteers of Indian expatriates in Germany.

ORGANIZATION

The British Indian Army, possibly as an extension of the divide and rule policy, organized regiments and units on the basis of religion and regional identity. Bose, from very early on, sought to eradicate this practice to build on an unified Indian identity. Consequently, the Free India Legion was organized as mixed units so that Moslems, Hindus, Sikhs, Jats, Rajputs, Marathas and Garhwalis all served side-by-side.

Approximately two-thirds of the Legion's members were Muslim and one-third Hindu and other religions, including a large number of Sikhs.. That Bose's idea of developing a unified nationalist identity was successful is evident from the fact that when Himmler proposed in late 1943-after Bose's Departure to the Far East-that the Muslim soldiers of the I.R. 950 be recruited into the 13th Waffen Mountain Division of the SS Handschar (1st Croatian) that was formed at the time, the head of the SS Head office Gottlob Berger was obliged to point out that while the Bosnians perceived themselves as people of an European identity, the Muslims perceived themselves as Indians.

UNIFORM AND STANDARD

The uniform issued to the Free India Legion were the standard German Army uniform of feldgrau in winter and Khaki in Summer. Additionally, the troops wore on their right upper arm a specially designed arm badge in the shape of the shield with three horizontal stripes of the saffron, white and green-the colours of the flag of Azad Hind-and featuring a leaping tiger on the white middle band. The legend Freies Indien inscribed in black featured on a white background above the tricolor. A saffron, white and green transfer was also worn on the left side of their helmets. Sikhs in the Legion were permitted to wear a turban, of a colour appropriate to their uniform as dictated by their religion instead of the usual peaked field cap. The standard of the Free India Legion-presented as regimental colours in 1942-featured the same design as the arm badge of the IR 950 consisting of saffron, white and green horizontal bands in the stated order from top to bottom. The white middle band was approximately three times the width of the two colored bands.

The words "AZAD" and "HIND" in white were inscribed over the saffron and green bands respectively. Also over the white middle band featured a leaping tiger. This is essentially the same design that the Azad Hind Government later adopted as their flag, although photographic evidence shows that the later Indian National Army, at least during the Burma Campaign, may not have carried it as their Battle Standard, opting for the Flag of the Congress instead

STRUCTURE AND UNITS

Free India Legion was organized as a standard German army infantry regiment of three battalions of four companies each, with, at least initially all the commissioned officers German. It has been later referred to as Panzergrenadier Regiment 950 (indische), indicating the unit was partially motorized. It was equipped with 81 motor vehicles and 700 horses. In this structure, the legion came to consist of

- I. Bataillon | Infanterie Kompanien 1 to 4
- II. Bataillon | Infanterie Kompanien 5 to 8
- III. Bataillon | Infanterie Kompanien 9 to 12
- 13th Infanteriegeschütz Kompanie (Infantry-Gun Company | consisting of six 7.5cm leichtes Infanteriegeschütz 18)
- 14th Panzerjäger Kompanie (Anti-tank Company | consisting of six Panzerabwehrkanone)
- 15th Pionier Kompanie (Engineer Company)
- Ehrenwachkompanie (Honour Guard Company)

It also consisted of Hospital staff and Training & Maintenance Staff (Ausbildungs und Betreutungsstab)

FREIES INDIEN IN OPERATION

It is doubtful that Subhash Chandra Bose envisaged the Free India Legion (or Azad Hind Legion as it came to be more popularly known by the time he left Germany for the far east) as an army sufficient or strong enough to conduct a campaign across Persia into India on its own. Instead, most historians accept that the IR 950 was to become the path finder would precede a much larger Indo-German force in a caucasian campaign into the western frontiers of British India that would encourage public resentment of the Raj and incite the British Indian army into revolt. To this end, Operation Bajadere was launched in January 1942 when a detachment of the Freies Indien, numbering about one hundred and having trained with the German Special Forces, were paradropped into Eastern Persia tasked to infiltrate into India through Baluchistan. They were also tasked to commence sabotage operations in preparation for the anticipated national revolt. Information passed on to Abwehr headquarters in Berlin from their office in Kabul indicate that they were successful.

Following German defeat in Europe at Stalingrad and in North Africa at El Alamein it became clear that an Axis assault through Iran or even USSR was unlikely. Bose had in the mean time travelled to the Far East where the Japanese troops were threatening India. Bose's army in the South Asia, the Indian National Army successfully engaged the allies along with the Japanese 15th Army in Burma and ultimately entered India through Moirang to lay siege on Imphal. The German Naval High Command at this time made the decision to transfer the leadership and a segment of the Freies Indien to the Azad Hind Government in South Asia and on 21 January, it was formally made a part of the Indian National Army.

Holland and France

A majority of the troops of the Indian Legion, however, were to remain in Europe through the war and was never utilized in their original perceived role over Persia and Central Asia. The Legion was transferred to Zeeland in the Netherlands in April 1943 as part of the Atlantic Wall duties and later to

France in September 1943, attached to 344 Infanterie-Division, and later the 159 Infanterie-Division of the Wehrmacht. From Beverloo in Belgium, I Battalion was reassigned to Zandvoort in May 1943 were they stayed till relieved by Georgian troops in August. In September 1943, the battalion was deployed on the Atlantic coast of Bordeaux on the Bay of Biscay. The II Battalion moved from Beverloo to the island of Texel in May 1943 and stayed there till relived in September of that year. From here, it was deployed to Les Sables d'Olonne in France.. The III Battalion remained at Oldebroek as Corps Reserve till the end of September 1943. Where they gained a "wild and loathsome" reputation amongst the natives.

Indische Freiwilligen Legion der Waffen SS

The Legion was stationed in the Lacanau region of Bordeaux at the time of the Normandy landings and remained there for up to two months after D-Day. On the 8th of August its control was transferred to the Waffen SS (as was that of every other volunteer unit of the Wehrmacht). Command of the legion was very shortly transferred from Kurt Krapp to Heinz Bertling. The Indian personnel noticed a change of command was at hand and started to complain. Noting he wasn't "wanted" Bertling kindly refused the assignment and headed back to Berlin. On 15 August, 1944, the unit pulled out of Lacanau to make its way back to Germany. It was in the second leg of this journey, from Poitier to Chatrou that it suffered its first combat casualty (Lt. Ali Khan) while engaging French Regular forces in the town of Dun. The unit also engaged with allied armour at Nuis St. Georges while retreating across the Loire to Dijon. It was regularly harassed by the French Resistance, suffering two more casualties (Lt. Kalu Ram and Capt. Mela Ram). The unit moved from Remisemont, through Alsace, to Oberhofen near the town of Heuberg in Germany in the winter of 1944, where it stayed till March 1945.

Italy

II Battalion, 9th Company, of the Legion also saw action in Italy. Having been deployed in the spring of 1944, it faced the British 5th Corps and the Polish 2nd Corps before it was withdrawn from the front to be used in antipartisan operations. It surrendered to the Allied forces April 1945, still in Italy.

END OF THE LEGION FREIES INDIEN

With the defeat of the Third Reich imminent in May 1945, the Indian Legion sought sanctuary in neutral Switzerland. The remainder of the unit undertook a desperate march along the shores of Lake Constance, attempting to enter Switzerland via the alpine passes. This was, however, unsuccessful and the Legion was captured by US and French forces and delivered to British and Indian forces in Europe. There is some evidence that some of these Indian troops were shot by French Moroccan troops in the town of Immenstadt after their capture. The captured troops would later be shipped back to India where a number of the troops would stand trial for treason. It is alleged that a number of the Indian soldiers were shot by French troops before their delivery to British Forces.

LEGACY OF THE FREE INDIA LEGION

The integral associations of the Free India Legion with Nazi Germany and (later) Japan means its legacy is judged from two distinct view points-one of a collaborationist army of the Third Reich, and the other as the realization of a liberation army against the British Raj in India. The Free India Legion was conceived with the same doctrine as the Indian National Army and the entire Azad Hind movement, it has found little exposure since the end of the war even in Independent India, possibly due to a perception that their fight was far removed from the Battlefields of Burma, a land much closer to India where the troops of the INA fought and died and caught the public imagination. To consider the legacy of Free India Legion, however, one has to consider both the Azad Hind Movement (of which the Legion was possibly a birth mother, and certainly an integral plan of Bose's initial plans) and the events that happened at the time, both in and away from the public eye. Abandoned by its proclaimed leader, the politician Subhash Chandra Bose, and disillusioned by his naive assessment of the political situation the legion surrendered to the British and the Americans soon after.

PERCEPTIONS AS COLLABORATORS

In considering the history of the Free India Legion and the ramifications of its creation, the most controversial aspect comes to be its integral link to the Nazi Germany, with a prevailing perception among some historians that they were mere mercenaries and collaborators of the Third Reich by the virtue of their uniform, oath and field of operation. To properly assess this, one has to first assess what actions it is that may be termed collaborationist. Throughout Europe, during and after the war, collaboration came to be defined broadly as; being party to the Nazi philosophy of Aryan-and even more so, German-supremacy as a race; actively supporting and participating in the Nazi atrocities against *inferior* races and occupied people in support of furthering the Nazi ideology, and; actively supporting the Nazi war effort.

As a prologue to the main debate on these issues, it is necessary to consider the views of the founder and leader of the Free India Legion, Subhash Chandra Bose (for Bose was the life blood of the entire Free India Movement in Germany, and later in South Asia). Bose, in 1931, had organized and led protest marches against the Japanese invasion of Manchuria and of China itself in 1938 when he was Congress president. In 1937 he published an article attacking Japanese Imperialism in the Far East, although he betrayed some admiration for other aspects of the Japanese regime. Bose's earlier correspondence (prior to 1939) also reflects his deep disapproval of the racist practices of, and annulment of democratic institutions in Nazi Germany. He also, however, expressed admiration for the authoritarian methods (though not the racial ideologies) which he saw in Italy and Germany during the 1930s, and thought they could be used in building an independent India .

However, this does not address whether the men of the Freies Indien were party to or in collaboration with the Nazi machinery. In these contexts, it is doubtful that the Indian PoWs were party to or held any loyalty to the Nazi ideology of racial supremacy. Although, the Nazis regarded Indians as members of the Aryan race, the small number of Indians and their particular usefulness in Germany's situation resulted in Indians not receiving the best treatment. It is also fallacious to say that the soldiers of the Free India Legion were mere mercenaries who fought with the Reich, for money or power.

Indeed, when the first PoWs were brought to Annaburg camp and met by Subhash Chandra Bose, there was marked open hostility towards him as a Nazi propaganda puppet. Subsequent to this, at a time when Bose's efforts and views had gained more sympathy, a persistent query among the (then) PoWs had been "How would the Legionary stand in relation to the German soldier?". Neither were they prepared to fight Germany's war for Germany's people for Germany's interests. Italy had in 1942 created the Battaglione Azad Hindoustan, with Indian PoWs captured by Italy, and Italians previously resident in India and Persia and led by an Indian resident in Rome for a long-time, Iqbal Shedai, whose rallying cry was to raise an Indian Unit to fight for India. In November 1942 the unit was three hundred and fifty strong, having been trained by Italian officers. Much has been said of the "dubious loyalty" of this unit. On 9 November, after the Allied landing in North Africa, the Italian high command made the decision to send the men to Libya to fight the allies instead of to India to fight for India's freedom, contrary to Shedai's promises. The men refused to go and mutinied, insisting that they were only willing to fight for the Indian cause Shedai refused to intervene. Consequently, the Centro Militare India was disbanded. The men of the Battaglione Azad Hindoustan are later said to have been either integrated into the Free India Legion or sent back to PoW camps. In another instance, immediately prior to the first deployment of the Free India Legion in Holland in April 1943, after departure of I Battalion from Koenigsbrueck, two Companies within the II Battalion refused to move.

The Free India Centre-in charge of the Legion after the departure of Bose in January 1943 for South Asia-came to face a number of grievances, prime of which stood out two in particular; some were influenced by a rumour that Netaji had abandoned them and had gone off leaving them entirely in German hands; a second grievance was a perception that the

Wehrmacht was now going to use them in the Western Front, instead of sending them to the East to fight for India's liberation. Even in the east, where the Indian National Army took its colossal shape, the first efforts under Capt. Mohan Singh came to nought essentially because Rash Behari Bose, who led the Indian Independence League (of which the first INA in the east was integrally linked) lost credence among the troops, appearing as a Japanese pawn. These goes to show that the men never possessed loyalty either to the Fascist or the Nazi cause or ideology and that their motivation was to fight for India' liberation, their loyalty lay to India. They were unwilling to fight for an alien nation and for a cause that was distant to the sacrosanct one for which they had abandoned their oath to the King Emperor. These, at the least, indicate that the Free India Legion was not a lovechild of desire to serve the Reich or its philosophy, wed to an opportunity to do so. If anything, Bose sought from early on to ensure that the troops were seen and treated as equal to their German counterparts

As for having participated in the Nazi war effort, in Europe the unit's deployments in Holland and France appear to be solely for training purposes, according to Bose's plans for the unit to be trained in some aspects of coastal defence. Bose had also had the German High Command committed to not deploying the unit for purposes of German military interests and strategy.. Indeed after the invasion of France by the Allies, the unit was ordered back to Germany. It has been suggested that the unit participated in atrocities, especially in the French town of Ruffec. This may require more authentication. The allegations that the Free India Legion was nothing more than a collaborationist Heer unit is therefore a very simplistic view of a formation of men who possibly imagined themselves as patriots and pioneers and not as Nazis or collaborators. However, the effects of the limited actions the unit undertook in anti-partisan role in Italy also ought to be considered while making a definitive conclusion.

A LIBERATION ARMY

The Free India Legion did not engage in its original conceived role in the western front of British India, so it is not possible to hold any arguments as to whether they did-or could have-fulfilled the destiny that the men of the Legion had dreamt of. Moreover, the Legion was, and still remains, far removed from public perception in India because it did not engage its enemy, the British Raj as did the Indian National Army in Burma, which was much closer to the home of the common Indian. Even the 9th Company's engagements in Italy with British forces are hardly known outside those circles with an interest in World War II history. Was, then, Bose's plans for Azad Hind Legion too grandiose for its own capability? In terms of military capability, that answer is a definitive yes, for the fate of Free India Legion was tied like a corpse to that of the Axis.

But in political terms, to consider the Azad Hind Legion a paper tiger can be debated, for it ignores a number of events that occurred within India and more specifically the British Indian Armed Forces in the postwar demobilisation scenario. To consider the effects that the legion had, it is necessary however, to consider the effects that the *entire* Azad Hind movement (for they were a part of the same strategy and movement) had on the culmination of British Raj in India.

After the war ended, the stories of the INA and the Free India Legion were seen as so inflammatory that, fearing mass revolts and uprisings—not just in India, but across its empire—the British Government forbid the BBC from broadcasting their story.. The Raj also brought to trial soldiers and officers of the INA (as well as the Free India Legion, of which not much is known). However, the stories of the trials at the Red Fort filtered through. The Raj observed with alarm the turnaround in the perception of Azad Hind and its army as traitors and collaborators to the greatest among the patriots.

During the trial, inspired to a large extent by the stories of the INA soldiers that were going around the country at the time mutiny broke out in the Royal Indian Navy(the mutiny had other underlying social and political causes as well; see article), incorporating ships and shore establishments of the RIN throughout India, from Karachi to Bombay and from Vizag to Calcutta. The most significant, if disconcerting factor for the

Raj, was the significant militant public support that it received.. A wave of nationalist sentiments swept through the Indian troops who had fought with the allies and were in the process of being de-mobilized. The navy mutiny was followed up by another among the ground crew in the Royal Indian Air Force. Another Army mutiny took place at Jabalpur during the last week of February 1946, soon after the Navy mutiny at Bombay. This was suppressed by force, including the use of the bayonet by British troops. It lasted about two weeks. After the mutiny, about 45 persons were tried by court martial. 41 were sentenced to varying terms of imprisonment or dismissal. In addition, a large number were discharged on administrative grounds.

In the after-effect of the mutiny, Weekly intelligence summary issued on the 25th of March, 1946 admitted that the Indian army, navy and air force units were no longer trust worthy, and, for the army, "only day to day estimates of steadiness could be made".. It was decided that; if wide-scale public unrest took shape, the armed forces (including the airforce-for Quit India had shown how it could turn violent) could not be relied upon to support counter-insurgency operations as they had been during the Quit India movement of 1942, and drawing from experiences of the Tiger Legion and the INA, their actions could not be predicted from their oath to the King emperor .

Reflecting on the factors that guided the British decision to relinquish the Raj in India, Clement Attlee, the then British prime minister, cited several reasons, the most important of which were: which were the INA activities of Netaji Subhash Chandra Bose, which weakened the Indian Army-the foundation of the British Empire in India-and the RIN Mutiny that made the British realize that the Indian armed forces could no longer be trusted to prop up the *Raj*. .

Although Britain had made, at the time of the Cripps' mission in 1942, a commitment to grant dominion status to India after the war; these events and views held in 1946 by the administrations of the Raj would suggest to the reader that, contrary to the usual narrative of India's independence struggle, (which generally focuses on Congress and Mahatma Gandhi), the INA and the revolts, mutinies, and public resentment it germinated were an important factor in the complete withdrawal of the Raj from India. In the same breath, whether awarded any credit for India's independence or not, the events at the time show that the strategy of Azad Hind (derived from the embryo of the Free India Legion) of achieving independence from Britain by fermenting revolts and public unrests-although a militarily a failure-remains, politically a significant and historic success.

AZAD HIND RADIO

Azad Hind Radio was a radio service that was started in leadership of Netaji Subhash Chandra Bose in Germany in 1942 to unite Indians to fight for freedom. Though initially based in Germany, its headquarters were shifted to Singapore and later Rangoon following the course of the war in South East Asia. Following Netaji's departure to South East Asia, the German operations were continued by A.C.N. Nambiar, the head of the Indian Legion (in Germany) and later Ambassador of the Arzi Hukumate Azad Hind in Germany.

The radio broadcast weekly news bulletins in English, Hindi, Tamil, Bengali, Marathi, Punjabi, Pashtu, and Urdu only as these were the languages of the people volunteering and serving the Indian Legion in Germany and the Indian National Army in Southeast Asia. The majority of the volunteers spoke these Indian languages only. Azad Hind Radio served to counter the misinformation and blackout of politically sensitive information as done by the BBC. As a retort and response to the periodic misinformation on the conditions prevalent in British India, as broadcast by the BBC, Netaji had on the Azad Hind Radio referred the British Broadcasting Corporation as the "Bluff and Bluster Corporation."

ARZI HUKUMAT-E-AZAD HIND

Arzi Hukumat-e-Azad Hind the Provisional Government of Free India), or simply Azad Hind, was an Indian Government-in-Exile established in Singapore in 1943. It was a part of a political movement originating in the 1940s outside of India with a purpose of freeing India from British Rule. Established by Indian nationalists-in-exile during the latter part of the second world war in Singapore with monetary, military and political assistance from Imperial Japan, ostensibly to posit and portray legitimacy for the campaign of the Indian National Army as a liberation force against British Rule in India. Founded on October 21, 1943,the government was inspired along the concepts of Netaji Subhash Chandra Bose who was also the leader of the government and the Head of State of this Provisional Indian Government in Exile. The government proclaimed authority over Indian civilian and military personnel in Southeast Asian British colonial territory and prospective authority over Indian territory to fall to the Japanese forces and the Indian National Army during the offensive to India during the Second World War. The government of Azad Hind had its own currency, court and civil code, and in the eyes of many Indians its existence gave a greater legitimacy to the independence struggle against the British.

However, while it possessed all the nominal requisites of a legitimate government, it lacked large and definite areas of sovereign territory until the government assumed control of the Andaman and Nicobar Islands from Japan in 1943 and the occupation of parts of Manipur and Nagaland. Throughout its existence, it remained heavily dependent on Japanese support.

Immediately after the formation of the government-in-exile, Azad Hind declared war against the Anglo-American allied forces on the Indo-Burma Front. Its army, the "Azad Hind Fauj", (Indian National Army or the *INA*) went into action against the British Indian Army and the allied forces alongside the Imperial Japanese Army in the Imphal-Kohima sector. The INA was to make its mark in the battle of Imphal where along with the Japanese 15th Army it breached the British defences in Kohima, reaching the salient of Moirang before Allied air dominance and compromised supply lines forced both the Japanese and the INA to lift the siege.

The existence of Azad Hind was essentially coterminous with the existence of the Indian National Army. While the government itself continued until the civil administration of the Andaman Islands was returned to the jurisdiction of the British towards the end of the war, the limited power of Azad Hind was effectively ended with the surrender of the last major contingent of INA troops in Rangoon. The supposed death of Bose is seen as culmination of the entire Azad Hind Movement. The allies at the time, as also some postwar historians claim the Government as a puppet state on the grounds of the lack of universal political recognition (the government was not recognised by allied governments and Vichy France), almost ineffective control of the Andaman and Nicobar Islands, as well as the continued dependency on Japan for support and survival.

The legacy of Azad Hind is, however, open to judgment. After the war, the Raj observed with alarm the turnaround in the perception of Azad Hind and its army as traitors and collaborators to "the greatest among the patriots". Given the tide of militant nationalism that swept through India and the resentment and revolts it inspired, it is arguable that its overarching aim-to germinate public resentment and revolts within the Indian forces of the British Indian Army to overthrow the Raj was ultimately, if belatedly for Azad Hind, successful.

ESTABLISHMENT

The direct origins of Azad Hind can be linked to two conferences of Indian expatriates from across Southeast Asia, the first of which was held in Tokyo in March of 1942. At this conference, convened by Rash Behari Bose, an Indian expatriate living in Japan, the Indian Independence League was established as the first move towards an independent Indian state politically aligned with the Empire of Japan. Rash also moved to create a sort of liberation army that would assist in driving the British from India-this force would later become the Indian National Army. The second conference, held later that year in Bangkok, invited Subhash Chandra Bose to participate in the leadership of the League. Bose was living in Germany at the time and made the trip to Japan via submarine. Rash Behari Bose, who was already ageing by the time the League was founded, struggled to keep the League organized and failed to secure resources for the establishment of the Indian National

Army. He was replaced as president of the Indian Independence League by Subhash Chandra Bose; there is some controversy as to whether he stepped down of his own volition or by pressure from the Japanese who needed a more energetic and focused presence leading the Indian nationalists.

Bose arrived in Tokyo on June 13, 1943, and declared his intent to make an assault against the eastern provinces of India in an attempt to oust the British from control of the subcontinent. Bose arrived in Singapore on July 2nd, and in October of 1943 formally announced the establishment of the Provisional Government of Free India.

In defining the tasks of this new political establishment, Subhash declared: "It will be the task of the Provisional Government to launch and conduct the struggle that will bring about the expulsion of the British and their allies from the soil of India." Bose, taking formal command of the demoralized and undermanned Indian National Army from Rash Bose, turned it into a professional army with the help of the Japanese. He recruited Indian civilians living in Japanese-occupied territories of Southeast Asia, and incorporated vast numbers of Indian POWs from British forces in Singapore, Malaya and Hong Kong to man the brigades of the INA.

MINISTERS

The Provisional Government of Free India consisted of a Cabinet headed by Netaji Subhash Chandra Bose as the *Head of the State, The Prime Minister and the Minister for War and Foreign Affairs*.

Captain Doctor Lakshmi Swaminathan (later married as Lakshmi Sehgal) was the *Minister in Charge of Women's Organization*. She held this position over and above her command of the *Rani Jhansi Regiment*, a brigade of women soldiers fighting for the Indian National Army. For a regular Asian army, this women's regiment was quite visionary; it was the first of its kind established on the continent. Dr. Lakshmi was one of the most popular and prosperous gynaecologists in Singapore before she gave up her fabulous practice to lead the troops of the Rani of Jhansi Regiment. Other public administration ministers of the Provisional Government of Free India included:

- Mr. S. A. Ayer-the Minister of Broadcasting and Publicity
- Lt. Col. A. C. Chatterji-the Minister of Finance

The Indian National Army was represented by Armed Forces ministers, including:

- Lt. Col. Aziz Ahmed
- Lt. Col. N. S. Bhagat
- Lt. Col. J. K. Bhonsle
- Lt. Colonel Guizara Singh
- Lt. Col. M.Z. Kiani
- Lt. Col. A. D. Loganathan
- Lt. Col. Ehsan Qadir
- Lt. Col. Shahnawaz Khan

The Provisional Government was also constituted and administered by a number of Secretaries and Advisors to Subhash Chandra Bose, including:

- A.N. Sahay-Secretary
- Karim Ghani
- Debnath Das
- D.M. Khan
- A. Yellapa
- J. Thivy
- Sirdar Isher Singh
- A. N. Sarkar-the government's official Legal Advisor

All of these Secretaries and Advisory officials held Ministerial rank in the Provisional Government. The extent of the Provisional Government's day-to-day management of affairs for Azad Hind is not entirely well-documented, so their specific functions as government officials for the state outside of their positions as support ministers for Subhash Chandra Bose is not entirely certain.

RECOGNITION

Azad Hind had diplomatic relations with nine countries: Nazi Germany, the Empire of Japan, Fascist Italy, the Independent State of Croatia, Wang Jingwei's Government in Nanjing, Thailand, Burma, Manchukuo and the Philippines. On the declaration of its formation in Singapore, President Eamon de Valera of the Irish Free State sent a note of congratulations to Bose. Vichy France, however, although being an Axis collaborator, never gave formal political recognition to Azad Hind. Recent researches have shown that the USSR too had recognised the Provisional Government of Free India. This government participated as a delegate or observer in the Greater East Asia Co-Prosperity Sphere.

GOVERNMENT ADMINISTRATION AND THE WAR

The same night that Bose declared the existence of Azad Hind, the government took action to declare war against the United States and Britain. The government consisted of a Cabinet ministry acting as an advisory board to Subhash Bose, who was given the title "Netaji" (translating roughly to "leader") and was no doubt the dominant figure in the Provisional Government. He exercised virtual authoritarian control over the government and the army. With regards to the government's first issuances of war declarations, the "Cabinet had not been unanimous about the inclusion of the U.S.A. Bose had shown impatience and displeasure-there was never any question then or later of his absolute authority: the Cabinet had no responsibility and could only tender advice..."

At the end of October of 1943, Bose flew to Tokyo to participate in the Greater East Asia Conference as an observer to Japan's Greater East Asia Co-Prosperity Sphere; it could not function as a delegate because India had technically fallen outside the jurisdiction of Japan's definition of "Greater East Asia", but Bose gave speeches in opposition to Western colonialism and imperialism at the conference. By the end of the conference, Azad Hind had been given a limited form of governmental jurisdiction over the Andaman and Nicobar Islands, which had been captured by the Imperial Japanese

Navy early on in the war. Once under the jurisdiction of Azad Hind, the islands formed the government's first claims to territory. The islands themselves were renamed "Shaheed" and "Swaraj", meaning "martyr" and "self-rule" respectively. Bose placed the islands under the governorship of Lt. Col A. D Loganathan, and had limited involvement with the official governorship of the territory, instead involving himself in plans to expand the Indian National Army, ensure adequate men and materiel, and formulate its course of actions and the administrations and relations of the Indian population in south east Asia and determining Japanese designs in India and his provisional government.

In theory the government itself had the power to levy taxes on the local populace, and to make and enforce laws: in practice they were enforced by the police force under Japanese control. Indians were willing to pay these taxes at first, but became less inclined to do so towards the end of the war when the Provisional Government enacted legislation for higher wartime taxes to fund the INA.

During his interrogation after the war Loganathan admitted that he had only had full control over the islands' vestigial education department, as the Japanese had retained full control over the police force, and in protest he had refused to accept responsibility for any other areas of Government. He was powerless to prevent the Homfreyganj massacre of the 30th January 1944, where forty-four Indian civilians were shot by the Japanese on suspicion of spying. Many of them were members of the Indian Independence League, whose leader in Port Blair, Dr. Diwan Singh, had already been tortured to death in the Cellular Jail after doing his best to protect the islanders from Japanese atrocities during the first two years of the occupation. Azad Hind's military forces in the form of the INA saw some successes against the British, and moved with the Japanese army to lay siege to the town of Imphal in eastern India. Plans to march towards Delhi, gaining support and fresh recruits along the way, stalled both with the onset of monsoon season and the failure to capture Imphal. British bombing seriously reduced morale, and the Japanese along with the INA forces began their withdrawal from India. In addition to these setbacks, the INA was faced with a formidable challenge when the troops were left to defend Rangoon without the assistance of the Japanese in the winter of 1944-1945. Loganathan was relocated from the Andaman Islands to act as field commander. With the INA garrison about 6,000 strong, he manned the Burmese capital in the absence of any other police force or troops during the period between the departure of the Japanese and the arrival of the British. He was successful in maintaining law and order to the extent that there was not a single case of dacoity or of loot during the period from April 24th to May 4th, 1945.

INDIAN AREAS UNDER THE ADMINISTRATION OF THE PROVISIONAL GOVERNMENT

Almost all of the territory of the Provisional Government lay in the Andaman Islands, although the Provisional Government was allowed some authority over Indian enclaves in Japanese-occupied territories. Provisional Government civil authority was never enacted in areas occupied by the INA; instead, Japanese military authority prevailed and responsibility for administration of occupied areas of India was shared between the Japanese and the Indian forces.

THE DEFEAT OF THE INA AND THE COLLAPSE OF THE PROVISIONAL GOVERNMENT

Left to defend Rangoon from the British advance without support from the Japanese, the INA was soundly defeated. Bose had fled Burma and returned to Singapore before the fall of Rangoon; the government Azad Hind had established on the Andaman and Nicobar Islands collapsed when the island garrisons of Japanese and Indian troops were defeated by British troops and the islands themselves retaken. Bose himself was killed in a plane crash departing from Taiwan attempting to escape to Russia. The Provisional Government of Free India ceased to exist with the deaths of the Axis, the INA, and Netaji Bose in 1945. The troops who manned the brigades of the Indian National Army were taken as prisoners of war by the

British. A number of these prisoners were brought to India and tried by British courts for treason, including a number of high ranking officers such as Colonel Gurbaksh Singh Dhillon. The defense of these individuals from prosecution by the British became a central point of contention between the British Raj and the Indian Independence Movement in the postwar years.

RELATIONS WITH JAPAN AND VIEW OF AZAD HIND AS AXIS COLLABORATOR

Netaji Subhash Chandra Bose, while an ally of Japan throughout the war, has become a controversial figure for his stances against racism and imperialism which would run in opposition against what was generally recognized as Japanese imperialism in Asia during World War II. Bose himself opposed all manner of such colonial practices, but saw Britain as hypocritical in "fighting a war for democracy" but refusing to extend the same respect for democracy and equal rights to their colonial subjects in India. As such, he is sometimes cited by revisionist Japanese historians as proof of the legitimacy of Japanese assertions that their brand of imperialism was in the best interests of Asian nations oppressed by Western colonialists. Criticism of Bose remains, with some accusing him of fascism, citing his strict control over the Provisional Government as evidence of this; some accused him of wanting to establish a totalitarian state in India with the blessings of the Axis powers. It is inaccurate to term Bose solely as a fascist, but it is true that Bose openly admired fascism in the Axis countries and used it as a way to organize the Provisional Government; he believed that parliamentary democracy was unsuitable for India, and that a centrally organized, self-sufficient, semi-socialist India under the firm control of a single party was the best course for Indian government. Some of his ideas would help shape Indian governmental policy in the aftermath of the country's independence from Britain.

The fact that Azad Hind was aligned politically with Japan may have little to do with explicit agreement and support for Japanese policy in Asia, and more with what Bose saw as a pragmatic approach to Indian independence. Disillusioned with

Gandhi's philosophies of nonviolence, Bose was clearly of the camp that supported exploiting British weakness to gain Indian independence.

Throughout the existence of Azad Hind, Bose sought to distance himself from Japanese collaboration and become more self-sufficient, but found this difficult since the existence of Azad Hind as a governmental entity had only come about with the support of the Japanese, and on whom the government and army of Azad Hind were entirely dependent. Bose, however, remains a hero in present-day India and is remembered as a man who fought fiercely for Indian independence.

Although Japanese troops saw much of the combat in India against the British, the INA was certainly by itself an effective combat force, having faced British and allied troops and making their mark in the Battle of Imphal. On 18 April 1944 the suicide squads led by Col. Shaukat Malik broke through the British defence and captured Moirang in Manipur. The Azad Hind administration took control of the this independent Indian territory.

Following Moirang, the advancing INA breached the Kohima road, posing a threat to the British positions in both Silchar and Kohima. Col. Gulzara Singh's column had penetrated 250 miles into India. The Azad Brigade advanced, by outflanking the Anglo-American positions. However, INA's most serious, and ultimately fatal, limitations were the reliance on Japanese logistics and supplies and the total air-dominance of the allies,-which, along with a supply line deluged by torrential rain, frustrated the INA'S and the Japanese bid to take Imphal.

With the siege of Imphal failing, the Japanese began to shift priority for resource allocation from South Asia to the Pacific, where they were fighting United States troops advancing from island to island against Japanese holdings there. When it had become clear that Bose's plans to advance to Delhi from the borders of Burma would never materialize due to the defeat of the INA at Imphal and the halt of Japanese armies by British aerial and later naval superiority in the region, Japanese support for Azad Hind declined.

CONTRIBUTIONS TO THE INDIAN INDEPENDENCE

The true judgement of success or failure of the movement remains open to historians. However, the true extent to which the INA's activities influenced the decision to leave India is mirrored by the views of Clement Atlee, the British Prime Minister at the time of India's Independence. Attlee cites several reasons, the most important of which were the INA activities of Netaji Subhash Chandra Bose, which weakened the very foundation of the British Empire in India, and the RIN Mutiny which made the British realise that the support of the Indian armed forces could no longer be relied upon

WHAT INDIANS FEEL ABOUT AZAD HIND, THE AZAD HIND FAUJ AND ITS LEGACY

During the war, Indians had only intermittent information (through radio broadcasts) about the activities of Subhash Chandra Bose and the Indian National Army. The Azad Hind Radio broadcasts were estimated to have regularly been received by 30,000 Indians who possessed the requisite receiver. However, it was during the trials of the INA's officers in 1945-6 that they really burst upon the public consciousness, and Congress and the Muslim League allied for the last time to secure their release. Independent India's attitude to the soldiers remain however, mired in controversy within its own population. The ex-soldiers of the INA were not allowed to enlist in the Indian Army of independent India, ostensibly at Nehru's decision on the advice of Mountbatten A pension was awarded to the ex-soldiers of INA only in 1972. Bose himself remains a cult figure in India, widely seen as a man whose leadership of the INA was a crucial factor in shaking the foundations of the British Empire in India. Had India been under Bose's leadership during and after Independence in 1947 the history of modern India and its society would have been very different

Those who experienced the rule of the Provisional Government of Free India, namely the population of the Andaman and Nicobar Islands, had largely bitter memories of the Japanese occupation, during which 2,000 people, or 10% of the population of the Andamans, died, about half of whom were tortured and killed by the Japanese. The *Arzi Hukumat-e Azad Hind* was powerless to prevent this.. Many historians have, however, argued that it was the INA and the mutinies it inspired among the British Indian Armed forces that was the true driving force for India's independence. The stories of the Azad Hind movement and its army, that came into public limelight during the trials of soldiers of the INA in 1945 were seen as so inflammatory that, fearing mass revolts and uprisings-not just in India, but across its empire, the British Government forbade the BBC from broadcasting their story. Newspapers reported at the time of summary execution of INA soldiers held at Red Fort During and after the trial, mutinies broke out in the British Indian Army, most notably in the Royal Indian Navy which found public support throughout India, from Karachi to Bombay and from Vizag to Calcutta.

A wave of nationalist sentiments swept through the Indian troops who had fought with the allies and were in the process of being de-mobilised. The navy mutiny was followed up by another among the ground crew in the Royal Indian Air Force. Another Army mutiny took place at Jabalpur during the last week of February 1946, soon after the Navy mutiny at Bombay. This was suppressed by force, including the use of the bayonet by British troops.

It lasted about two weeks. After the mutiny, about 45 persons were tried by court martial. 41 were sentenced to varying terms of imprisonment or dismissal. In addition, a large number were discharged on administrative grounds. In the after-effect of the mutiny, Weekly intelligence summary issued on the 25th of March, 1946 admitted that the Indian army, navy and air force units were no longer trust worthy, and, for the army, "only day to day estimates of steadiness could be made". It was decided that; if wide-scale public unrest took shape, the armed forces (including the air force) for Quit India had shown how it could turn violent) could not be relied upon to support counter-insurgency operations as they had been during the Quit India movement of 1942, and drawing from experiences of the Tiger Legion and the INA, their actions could not be predicted from their oath to the King emperor.

These suggest that the ultimate goal of the Azad Hind Movement, to germinate public resentment and revolts within the Indian forces of the British Indian Army to ultimately overthrow the Raj was, if belatedly for Azad Hind, successful.

MOHAN SINGH DEB

General Mohan Singh Deb (1909-1989) was an Indian Millitary officer and member of the Indian Independence Movement most famous for his role in organising and leading the First Indian National Army in South East Asia during World War II. Following Indian independence, Mohan Singh later served in Public life as a Member of Parliament in the *Rajya Sabha* (Upper House) of the Indian Parliament.

Early Life

He was born the only son of Tara Singh and Hukam Kaur, a peasant couple of Ugoke village, near Sialkot (now in Pakistan). His father died two months before his birth and his mother shifted to her parents home in Badiana in the same district, where Mohan Singh was born and brought up.

Military Career

As he passed high school, he joined the 14th Punjab Regiment of the Indian Army in 1927. After the completion of his recruit training at Hrozpur, Mohan Singh was posted to the 2nd Battalion of the Regiment, then serving in the North-West Frontier Province. He was selected as a potential officer in 1931, and after six months' training in Kitchener College, Nowgong (Madhya Pradesh), and another two and a half years in the Indian Military Academy, Dehra Dun, he received his commission in 1934 and was posted for a year to a British unit, the 2nd Border Regiment, and then to 1st Battalion of his former 14th Punjab Regiment, which at that time happened to be at Jhelum. World War II broke out in 1939. Mohan Singh had been promoted to Captain when his battalion was earmarked for operational service in the Far East. The battalion was still carrying out intensive training at Secunderabad when he married, in December 1940, Jasvant Kaur, sister of a brother officer. He left for Malaya with his unit on 4 March 1941.

Second World War

Japan entered the War with her surprise attack on the American air base at Pearl Harbour, Hawaii, on 7 December 1941 and overran the entire South East Asia within a few weeks. The Japanese IGHQ in October set up the Fujiwara Kikan, or the F-kikan, in Bangkok, Headed by the Major Fujiwara Iwaichi, chief of intelligence of the 15th army. Tasked with intelligence gathering and contacting the Indian independence movement, the overseas Chinese and the Malayan Sultan with the aim of encouraging friendship and cooperation with Japan, Fujiwara's staff included five commissioned officers and two Hindi-speaking interpreters. His initial contact was with Giani Pritam Singh.

Action in Malaya

The British force in the northern part of the Malaya Peninsula including Captain Mohan Singh's battalion, 1/14 Punjab Regiment, was fleeing towards the south. Mohan Singh's own forces had been outgunned and destroyed by superior Japanese forces at Jitra. Captured by Japanese troops after several days in the Jungle, Singh was taken to Alor Star to Fujiwara and Pritam Singh at a joint office of the F-Kikan and the IIL. Fujiwara, later self-described as "Lawrence of the Indian National Army" (after Lawrence of Arabia) is said to have been a man committed to the values which his office was supposed to convey to the expatriate nationalist leaders, and found acceptance among them.

Although Pritam Singh was involved to a large extent, it was Fujiwara who, with his sincerity of purpose and belief, convinced Mohan Singh to betray his oath to the Crown by uniting with the Japanese mission for the greater motive of Indian freedom. This included the promise that he would be treated as an ally and a friend, and not a PoW. Initially helping Fujiwara to take control of the situation of looting and arson that had developed in Alor Star, Singh was in December 1941, after meeting with the Japanese commanding general, convinced of the feasibility of raising an armed Indian unit. Between himself, Pritam Singh and Fujiwara, Mohan Singh set about contacting Indians in the British Indian Army in Southeast Asia, and also began recruiting from amongst those captured by the Japanese in Malaya. All Indian prisoners of war and stragglers were placed under his charge and he was asked to restore order in the town of Alor Star. Thus the nucleus what came to be the Indian National Army was born. Kuala Lumpur fell on 11 January 1942 with 3,500 Indian prisoners of war, and Singapore on 15 February with 85,000 British troops, of whom 45,000 were Indians. Mohan Singh asked for volunteers who would form the *Azad Hind Fauj* (Free India Army) to fight for liberating India from the British rule.

A large number of men, mostly Sikhs, came forward to join what came to be termed as the *Azad Hind Fauj* (National Army of independent India). The new set-up came into being on 1 September 1942 by which time the strength of volunteers had reached 40,000. Mohan Singh, now designated a general, was to command it. Already in a conference held at Bangkok during 15-23 June 1942, the Indian Independence League under the leadership of Rash Behari Bose, an Indian revolutionary who had escaped to Japan in June 1915 and who had been living there ever since, had been inaugurated. Through one of the 35 resolutions passed by the conference, Mohan Singh was appointed commander-in-chief of the "Army of Liberation for India," *i.e.* the Indian National Army.

Disagreements with Japan

General Mohan Singh was soon disenchanted regarding the intentions of the Japanese who, it appeared, wanted to use Indian National Army only as a pawn and who were deliberately withholding recognition and public proclamation about its entity as an independent liberation army. On 29 December 1942, General Mohan Singh was removed from his command and taken into custody by the Japanese military police. It was only after the arrival of another Indian leader of great political standing, Subhash Chandra Bose, from Germany to the Far-Eastern front in June 1943 that the Indian National Army was revived and Mohan Singh reinstated to his former command with Subhash as the supreme commander in his capacity as president of the Provisional Government of Azad Hind.

The Indian National Army participated in the Japanese offensive on the Indo-Burma front in 1944 and gave a good account of itself. But the British forces withstood the offensive and in fact launched a counter-attack during the winter of 1944-45. The Japanese as well as the Indian National Army, retreated fast, and the war ended with Japan's surrender on 14 August 1945. Even before that during May-June 1945, most officers and men of the *Azad Hind Fauj* (I.N.A.), numbering about 20,000, including General Mohan Singh, had been made prisoners by the British and brought back to India. They were all set free during 1945. General Mohan Singh and his comrades of the Indian National Army were acclaimed by Indians for their patriotism.

Post 1947

Mohan Singh's dream of liberation was realized with India's Independence on 15 August 1947, but this was accompanied by the partition of the country into India and Pakistan. Mohan Singh had to leave his hearth and home in what then became Pakistan and came to India a homeless refugee. He was allotted some land in the village of Jugiana, near Ludhiana, where he settled permanently. He entered politics and joined the Indian National Congress. After a stint as a legislator in the Punjab, he was elected to *Rajya Sabha*, the upper house of Indian Parliament, for two terms. In and out of Parliament he strove for the recognition of the members of his *Azad Hind Fauj* as "freedom fighters" in the cause of the nation's liberation . General Mohan Singh died at Jugiana on 26 December 1989.

RASH BEHARI BOSE

Rashbehari Bose May 25, 1886–January 21, 1945 was a revolutionary leader against the British Raj in India and was one of the key organisers of the Ghadar conspiracy and later, the Indian National Army.

Early Life

Bose was born in the Subaldaha village of Burdwan, in the province of Bengal. He had his education in Chandannagar, where his father, Vinodebehari Bose, was stationed.

Revolutionary Activities

Though interested in revolutionary activities early in his life, he left Bengal to shun the Alipore bomb case (1908). At Dehradun he worked as a head clerk at the Forest Research Institute. There, through Amarendra Chatterjee of the Jugantar led by Jatin Mukherjee, he secretly got involved with the revolutionaries of Bengal and, thanks to Jatindra Nath Banerjee alias Niralamba Swami-the earliest political disciple of Sri Aurobindo-he came across eminent revolutionary members of the Arya Samaj in the United Provinces(currently U.P.) and the Punjab. Following the attempt to assassinate Lord Hardinge, Rash Behari was forced to go into hiding.

He was hunted by the colonial police due to his active participation in the failed bomb throwing attempt directed at the Governor General and Viceroy Lord Charles Hardinge in Delhi (the bomb was actually thrown by Basanta Kumar Biswas, a disciple of Amarendra Chatterjee). He returned to Dehra Dun by the night train and joined the office the next day as though nothing had happened. Further, he organised a meeting of loyal citizens of Dehradun to condemn the dastardly attack on the Viceroy. Who on earth could imagine that he was the same person who had masterminded and executed the most outstanding revolutionary action.

Lord Hardinge in his *My Indian Years* has described the whole incident in an interesting way. During the flood relief work in Bengal, in 1913, he came in contact with Jatin Mukherjee in whom he "discovered a real leader of men," who "added a new impulse" to Rash Behari's failing zeal. Thus,during WW I he became extensively involved as one of the leading figures of the Ghadar Conspiracy that attempted to trigger a mutiny in Inda in February 1915. Trusted and tried Ghadrites were sent to several cantonments to infiltrate into the army. The idea of the Jugantar leaders was that with the war raging in Europe most of the soldiers had gone out of India and the rest could be easily won over. The revolution failed and most of the revolutionaries were arrested. But Rash Behari managed to escape British intelligence and reached Japan in 1915.

Bose was instrumental in persuading the Japanese authorities to stand by the Indian nationalists and ultimately to support actively the Indian freedom struggle abroad. Bose convened a conference in Tokyo on March 28-30, 1942, which decided to establish the *Indian Independence League*. At the conference he moved a motion to raise an army for Indian liberation. He convened the second conference of the League at Bangkok on June 22, 1942. It was at this conference that a resolution was adopted to invite Subhash Chandra Bose to join the League and take its command as its president.

The Indian prisoners of war captured by the Japanese in the Malaya and Burma fronts were encouraged to join the Indian Independence League and become the soldiers of the Indian National Army (INA), the military wing of Bose's Indian National League. But his rise to actual power and glory was unfortunately terminated by an action of the Japanese military command, which expelled him and his general Mohan Singh from the INA leadership. But though he fell from grace, his organisational structure remained, and it was on the organisational spadework of Rashbehari Bose that Subhash Chandra Bose later built the Indian National Army (also called 'Azad Hind Fauj'). Before his death, the Japanese Government honoured him with the 'Second Order of the Merit of the Rising Sun'.

BATTAGLIONE AZAD HINDUSTAN

The Battaglione Azad Hindustan was a unit of Indian troops formed in Fascist Italy under the Raggruppamento Centri Militari in July 1942. The unit, raised initially as the Centro I, was headed by Iqbal Shedai-a long term Indian resident of Rome-and was formed of Indian ex-prisoners-of-war and Italians from India. Raised along with units dedicated to Tunisia (Centro T), the Arabs (Centro A), it was tasked to intelligence gathering and sabotage operations behind enemy lines. By the time of its disbandment in November 1942, the Battaglione Azad Hindustan came to be between three hundred and fifty to four hundred strong. A part of the Centro I was renamed Battaglione Azad Hindustan in August 1942 when the Raggruppamento

Centri Militari itself was redesignated as Ragruppamento Frecce Rosse (Red Arrows Group) The modus operandi of infiltration of the units of the Ragruppamento Frecce Rosse were intended to be means of infiltration on the ground, via submarine and by parachute. Accordingly, a further unit was raised within the Battaglione Azad Hindustan to form the Platone Paracadutisti or the Parachute Platoon. The chosen troops were sent for Paratroop combat training to the Parachute School at Tarquinia.

Uniform

The soldiers of the Battaglione Azad Hindustan were attired in standard Italian military uniform. However, unlike the troops of the Legion Freies Indien who wore peaked field caps, all the troops of the Battaglione Azad Hindustan wore a turban of the colour of the Italian Sahariana Tunic. Additionally, the troops wore on their tunics collar patches with three vertical stripes in the saffron, white and green (reflecting the colours of the Indian National Congress that was at the time focus of the nationalist movement). Italians serving in the Battaglione Azad Hindustan were distinguished by stars on the collar patches that was not worn by the Indian troops. The Tarquinia detachment sent for parachute training wore their own collar patches above paratroop pattern patches, as well as the paratroop badge depicting an open yellow parachute embroidered in rayon thread on the left upper arm.

Structure

The order of battle of the Battaglione Azad Hindustan in August 1942 was

- Compagnie Fucilieri, a motorized rifle company.
- Compagnie Mitraglieri, a motorized machinegun company.
- Platone Paracadutisti, Parachute Platoon
- Overseas Italian Platoon

INDIAN NATIONAL ARMY OF LIBERATION IN THE EAST

On 15 February 1942, Singapore fell to the Japanese army advancing southward from the Malayan peninsula. Two days later, in an impressive ceremony held at Farrar Park in the heart of the town, Indian troops were handed over to the Japanese as prisoners-of-war by their commanding officer, Colonel Hunt.

Major Fujiwara took them over on behalf of the victorious Japanese, and then announced that he was handing them over to Captain Mohan Singh of the Indian contingents, who should be obeyed by them as their Supreme Commander. Mohan Singh then spoke to the Indian POWs, expressing his intention of raising an Indian national army out of them to fight for India's freedom.

He held a preliminary discussion with some prominent Indians in Malay and Burma in a meeting in Singapore on 9 and 10 March, which was attended by Rashbehari Bose, a veteran Indian revolutionary exile living in Japan for the last quarter of a century. Bose then called a conference in Tokyo, which was held 28-30 March.

The delegates representing several East and Southeast Asian countries present at the conference, decided to form the Indian Independence League to organize an Indian independence movement in East Asia. Bose was recognized as head of the organization.

The conference further resolved that "militay action against the British in India will be taken only by the INA and under Indian command, together with such military, naval and air cooperation and assistance as may be requested from the Japanese by the Council of Action" and further, "after the liberation of India, the framing of the future constitution of India will be left entirely to the representatives of the people of India."

On 15 June 1942, a conference opened in Bangkok with over a hundred delegates of the IIL attending from all over Asia. By the close of the nine-day conference a resolution was unanimously adopted setting forth the policies of the independence movement in East Asia. The III, was proclaimed the organization to work for India's freedom; the Indian National Army was declared the military arm of the movement with

Mohan Singh as the Commander-in-chief and Rashbehari Bose was elected president of the Council of Action.

It was further decided that Singapore would be the headquarters of the IIL. Netaji had stated in a message to the conference that his personal experience had convinced him that Japan, Italy and Germany were sworn enemies of British imperialism; yet, independence could come only through the efforts of Indians themselves. India's freedom would mean the rout of British imperialism. The Indian National Army was officially inaugurated in September 1942.

Unfortunately, at this point a distrust began to grow within the Indian group against Rashbehari Bose's leadership. Some thought that having been long associated with Japan, he gave precedence to the Japanese interests over Indian interests. According to Japanese records:

> *Some even thought that he was just the protege of the Japanese, and that the latter was exploiting Indians for their own ends. Such resentment finally resulted in a revolt of a group of leaders headed by Captain Mohan Singh within the INA in November 1942. As a consequence, Mohan Singh and his associate, Colonel Gill were both arrested by the Japanese and the Indian Army was disbanded. However, in 1943 a new Indian Army was organized, put under the command of Lt. Col. Bhonsle, who held this post until the final dissolution of the army.*

Describing the revived INA. Joyce Lebra writes:

> *On 15 February 1943, the INA was reorganized and former ranks and badges revived. The Director of the Military Bureau, Lieutenant-Colonel Bhonsle, was clearly placed under the authority of the III. to avoid any repetition of IIIANA rivalry. Under Bhonsle was Lt. Col. Shah Nawaz Khan as Chief of General Staff-, Major P.K. Sahgal as Military Secretary; Major Habibur Rahman as commandant of the Officers' Training School; and Lt. Col. A.C. Chatterji, and later Major A.D. Jahangir, as head of enlightenment and culture.*

Apart from this policy-forming body was the Army itself, under the command of Lt. Col. M.Z. Kiani. This was the organization which held the INA together until the arrival of Subhash Chandra Bose from Berlin, six months later.

In February, the Japanese military officer Iwakuro had called a meeting of about three hundred officers of the INA at Bidadri camp in Singapore and spoke to them about the advisability of joining the army, but with no effect. According to Ghosh, "Later on, in a 'Heart to heart talk' with some officers, it emerged that a large number of officers and men would be willing to continue in the INA on the express condition that Netaji would be coming to Singapore." The story of Netaji's exploits in Germany and the history of the Indian Legion was known to Indian revolutionaries of the IIL in East Asia for some time now, and they awaited his arrival eagerly. As the first INA wavered, faltered and was finally disbanded, and as its successor merely continued to exist, the need for Netaji's leadership began to be felt more keenly. Mohan Singh had mentioned his name to General Fujiwara as early as 1941. In all conferences the need of his guidance had been emphasized by the delegates.

While Netaji and Abid Hasan continued to push toward the East making a wide sweep out into the Atlantic, by pre-arrangement, a Japanese submarine left Penang Island on 20 April for the tip of Africa, under strict orders not to attack or risk detection. The two submarines had a rendevous four hundred miles south-southwest of Madagascar on 26 April.

After sighting each other and confirming their identity, the submarines waited for a day for the sea to become calm. Then on 28 April, in what was known to be the only known submarine-to-submarine transfer of passengers (in the annals of World War II) in an area dominated by the enemy's air and naval strength, Netaji and Abid Hasan were transhipped into the Japanese submarine via a rubber raft. Travelling across the ocean, the Japanese 1-29 reached Sabang on 6 May, 1943. It was an isolated offshore islet north of Sumatra.

There, Netaji was welcomed by Colonel Yamamoto, who was the head of the Hikari Kikan, the Japanese-Indian liaison group. From Sabang, Netaji and Yamamoto left for Tokyo by plane, stopping en route at Penang, Manila, Saigon and Taiwan.

The plane landed in Tokyo on 16 May. All throughout his submarine voyage from Germany and for about a month after his arrival in Tokyo, Netaji's identity and presence was kept a secret. He was supposed to be a Japanese VIP named Matsuda.

Although he remained incognito during the first few weeks in Japan, Netaji did not waste any time by just waiting. From 17 May onwards, he met Japanese Army and Navy Chiefs-of-Staff, Navy Minister and Foreign Minister in rapid succession. However, he had to wait for nearly three weeks before Japanese Prime Minister Tojo granted him an interview.

But Tojo was so impressed with Netaji's personality that he offered to meet him again after four days. Two days later, on 16 June, Netaji was invited to visit the Diet (the Japanese Parliament) where Tojo surprised him with his historic declaration on India:

> *We are indignant about the fact that India is still under the ruthless suppression of Britain and are in full sympathy with her desperate struggle for independence. We are determined to extend every possible assistance to the cause of India's independence. It is our belief that the day is not far off when India will enjoy freedom and prosperity after winning independence.*

It was not until 18 June that Tokyo Radio announced Netaji's arrival. The news was reported in the Tokyo press the following day. At this announcement, the atmosphere was electrified overnight. The Axis press and radio stressed the significance of the event.

The INA and the Indian independence movement suddenly assumed far greater importance in the eyes of all. On 19 June, Netaji held a press conference. This was followed by two broadcasts to publicize further his presence in East Asia, and during the course of these he unfolded his plan of action. As Ghosh describes, Bose's plan stood for the coordination of the nationalist forces within India and abroad to make it a gigantic movement powerful enough to overthrow the British rulers of India. The assumption on which Bose seemed to have based his grand scheme was that the internal conditions in India were ripe for a revolt. The no-cooperation movement must turn into an active revolt.

And to quote Netaji's own words during the press conference: "Civil disobedience must develop into armed struggle. And only when the Indian people have received the baptism of fire on a large scale would they be qualified to achieve freedom." Netaji then embarked upon a series of meetings, press conferences radio broadcasts and lectures in order to explain his immediate task to the people concerned, and the world.

Accompanied by Rashbehari Bose, Netaji arrived at Singapore from Tokyo on 27 June. He was given a tumultuous welcome by the resident Indians and was profusely 'garlanded' wherever he went.

His speeches kept the listeners spellbound. By now, a legend had grown around him, and its magic infected his audiences. Addressing representatives of the Indian communities in East Asia on 4 July he said:

> *Not content with a civil disobedience campaign, Indian people are now morally prepared to employ other means for achieving their liberation. The time has therefore come to pass on to the next stage of our campaign. All organizations whether inside India or outside, must now transform themselves into a disciplined fighting organization under one leadership. The aim and purpose of this organization should be to take up arms against British imperialism when the time is ripe and signal is given.*

At a public meeting where Netaji spoke these words, Rashbehari Bose formally handed over to Subhash Chandra Bose the leadership of the III, and command of the INA. The hall was packed to capacity. In his last speech as leader of the movement Rashbehari Bose said:

Friends! This is one of the happiest moments in my life. I have brought you one of the most outstanding personalities of our great Motherland to participate in our campaign. In your presence today, I resign my office as president of the Indian Independence League in East Asia. From now on, Subhash Chandra Bose is your president, your leader in the fight for India's independence, and I am confident that under his leadership, you will march on to battle and to victory.

In that meeting Netaji announced his plan to organize a Provisional Government of Free India. It will be the task of this provisional government to lead the Indian Revolution to its successful conclusion ... The Provisional Government will have to prepare the Indian people, inside and outside India, for an armed struggle which will be the culmination of all our national efforts since 1883. We have a grim fight ahead of us. In this final march to freedom, you will have to face danger, thirst, privation, forced marches-and death. Only when you pass this test will freedom be yours. The next day, on 5 July, Netaji took over the command of the Indian National Army, now christened Azad Hind Fauj (Free India Army). Tojo arrived from Manila in time to review the parade of troops standing alongside with Bose. Addressing the soldiers, Netaji said:

Throughout my pubic career, I have always felt that, though India is otherwise ripe for independence in every way, she has lacked one thing, namely, an army of liberation. George Washington of America could fight and win freedom, because he had his army. Garibaldi could liberate Italy because he had his armed volunteers behind him. It is your privilege and honour to be the first to come forward and organize India's national army.

By doing so you have removed the last obstacle in our path to freedom... When France declared war on Germany in 1939 and the campaign began, there was but one cry which rose from the lips of German soldiers-"To Paris! To Paris!" When the brave soldiers of Nippon set out on their march in December 1941, there was but one cry which rose from their lips-"To

Singapore! To Singapore!" Comrades! My soldiers! Let your battle-cry be-"To Delhi! To Delhil"

How many of us will individually survive this war of freedom, I do not know. But I do know this, that we shall ultimately win and our task will not end until our surviving heroes hold the victory parade on another graveyard of the British Empire-Lal Kila or the Red Fortress of ancient Delhi.

On 27 July, Netaji left Singapore for a 17-day, tour of the East Asian and Southeast Asian countries. The prime objective of this tour was to enlist moral and monetary support for his movement from other countries, as well as the resident Indian communities. He was given a rousing reception in Rangoon, where he attended the Burmese independence on 1 August; from Rangoon Netaji went to Bangkok and met Thai Prime Minister Pilbulsongram.

He won the moral support of Thailand and tumultuous ovation from the Indian community. He then flew to Saigon and addressed Indians there. Returning to Singapore for a brief rest, he flew to Penang to address a rally of 15,000 Indians. Everywhere, he held his audience spellbound for hours with his superb oratory, and at the conclusion of his speech the people raced to reach the platform and pile up all they had before him-a total of two million dollars.

This scene was repeated over and over in towns and cities all over Southeast Asia, when Netaji stood before thousands of people like a prophet, addressing them for the cause of India's freedom. Merchants, traders, businessmen and women came forward everywhere and donated their wealth and ornaments in abundance, to enable their leader to fulfil his mission. In his plan for total mobilization, Netaji had outlined a grandiose scheme for an army of three million men. However, the immediate target was set at 50,000. The Major part of this number would be from the Indian POWs and the rest from civilian volunteers.

According to Bose's plan there would be three divisions from thirty thousand regulars and another unit of twenty thousand mainly from civilian volunteers. The Japanese authorities informea Netaji at that time that it could provide arms for thirty thousand men only. However, by 1945, it was authoritatively known that the actual strength of the INA rose to not less than 45,000 men. After completing the task of reorganizing the Indian Independence League and launching preparations for revolutionizing the army, and after conducting a successful campaign to mobilize the support of the Indian communities throughout Southeast Asia-a phase which lasted from July to October Netaji turned toward formation of the Provisional Government of Azad Hind (Free India).

This had to be done before the army could be sent for action in the battlefield. This government was officially proclaimed in Singapore at a mass rally on 21 October 1943 where Netaji was unanimously elected as the Head of the State and The Supreme Commander of the Indian National Army. While taking the oath he said:

> *In the name of God, I take this sacred oath that to liberate India and the three hundred eighty million of my countrymen, L Subhash Chandra Bose, will continue the sacred war of freedom till the last breath of my life. I shall remain always a servant of India, and to look after the welfare of three hundred eighty million of Indian brothers and sisters shall be for me my highest duty. Even after winning freedom, I will always be prepared to shed even the last drop of my blood for the preservation of India's freedom.*

The Provisional Government of Free India had five Ministers with Netaji as the Head of the State, Prime Minister and Minister for War and advisers representing the Indian communities in East Asia.

The first momentous decision which the new government took was its declaration of war on Britain and the United States, which was decided on the night of 22-23 October. Toye writes: "The Cabinet had not been unanimous about the inclusion of the U.S.A. Bose had shown impatience and displeasure-there was never any question then or later of his absolute authority: the Cabinet had no responsibility and could only tender advice.

Recognition of the Provisional Government came quickly from nine countries-the Axis powers and their allies. They were: Japan, Burma, Croatia, Germany, the Philippines, Nanking China, Manchuto, Italy and Siam (Thailand), but for some unknown reasons, Vichy France withheld its recognition. The Japanese Army promised all-out support for the provisional government.

Toward the end of October, Netaji flew to Tokyo again to meet Tojo and to attend the greater East Asia Conference. Since India technically did not fall within this sphere, he attended as an observer. He made an impressive speech at the conference, stressing the creation of a new Asia where all vestiges of colonialism and imperialism would be eliminated.

The Japanese navy had captured the Andaman and Nicober islands in the Bay of Bengal during the early months of war. As a result of Netaji's requests, Prime Minister Tojo announced at the conference that Japan had decided to place the two islands under the jurisdiction of the Provisional Government of Free India, thereby giving it its first sovereignty over a territory.

The ceremonial transfer took place in December, and Netaji named Lieutenant-Colonel Loganathan, an officer in the Medical Services, as the chief commissioner in charge of the civil administration of the islands. Soon thereafter, preparations began for sending the army to the front and moving the provisional government headquarters to Rangoon, in Burma. In the meantime, Netaji announced the formation of a women's brigade within the INA, and named it "Rani of Jhansi Regiment," after the celebrated queen of Jhansi, Laxmibai, who had led her soldiers against the British in an uprising during the First War of Independence in 1857.

Coincidentially, another Laxmi, Lieutenant-Col. Laxmi, was placed in charge of this regiment by Netaji. In November it was agreed between Netaji and the Japanese militay headquarters, that the INA first division and the civil and military headquarters would move to Burma in January 1944.

THE IMPHAL CAMPAIGN

The Imphal Campaign, including the battle of Kohima—the first major town to be captured by the INA inside India—will perhaps go down as one of the most daring and disastrous campaigns in the annals of world military history. General Mutaguchi, commander of the Japanese forces in North Burma since 1943, had been convinced that Imphal should be attacked.

The objects of such an offensive were to forestall any invasion of Burma in 1944 and to establish the Japanese defenses on the frontier mountains. The idea would be first to overwhelm the British in Arakan, involving all their reserves in battle for Chittagong and the gateway to eastern Bengal.

Then, by April, Kohima and Imphal could be conquered at leisure, without danger of their being reinforced. The monsoon, beginning in May, would postpone operations, and after the rains were over, in the absence of a new British defense posture east of the river Brahmaputra, the entire Assam and East Bengal would lie open to the Indian National Army and the Japanese.

Imphal, the capital of the state of Manipur, lay on a flat, nearly treeless plateau just inside the Indian border. Its elevation was about 3,000 feet, surrounded on all sides by impassable mountains. The mountain range in the east with 2,000-4,000 foot peaks above the plateau stretches some five hundred miles. To the West and South are the Chin hills of the Arakan range, a formidable stretch of inhospitable terrain.

The jungle surrounding this basin is hostile to human habitation. The northern access to the plain from India and Assam lay through Dimapur and the steep Kohima Road. From Dimapur, a single track railway swept through Assam and Bengal and was an important military objective to both armies.

For the INA the importance of the Imphal campaign was that it was the only major battle in which it would participate with the object of achieving freedom for India. As Salto and Hayashida writes:

> *The Imphal Operation was the final offensive of the East Asia War, mounted by three Burma-based Japanese*

divisions, and one INA division. The campaign lasted from 15 March to 9 July 1944. The operation has often been compared to the operation Wacht am Rhein or the Battle of the Bulge, which was the final all-out drive launched by Germany towards Ardennes on the Western Front, from December 1944 to January 1945. Both operations al most succeeded and both are termed "gambles" by historians today. If the German push towards Ardennes was Wacht am Rhein, the Japanese-Indian thrust against Imphal might be called "Wacht am Chindwin" although the official Japanese code-name for the action was most prosaic: Operation "U".

River Chindwin lay across the Indo-Burmese border, and its crossing from the east by an army would signal an invasion of India.

Execution orders for Operation U became operative on 7 January 1944, coinciding with completion of the shifting of the Provisional Government headquarters in Rangoon. In the evening of the same day, Lt. General Masakazy Kawabe, commanding the overall Burma headquarters, held a welcome party in honour of Netaji and his staff officers.

Netaji spoke, and concluded his speech with these words. "My only prayer to the Almighty at this moment is that we may be given the earliest opportunity to pay for our freedom with our own blood.', One INA Division, named after Netaji as Subhash Regiment, was readied for action at the front with the Japanese. Toye writes.

... He spent the whole days... with the Subhash Regiment, reviewing, watching it at exercises and on parade, talking to its officers, exerting his magic on it in a way that he had not attempted before. These were his comrades, the men by whose means he would uphold the rights and honour of India. Everything depended on their achievement in battle; they must absorb all his feelings of confidence, feel the whole of his personal force. On 3 February he bade them farewell: "Blood is calling for blood. Arise! We have no time to lose. Take up your arms. There in front of you is the road. our pioneers have built. We shall march along that road. We shall carve our way through enemy's ranks, or, if God wills, we shall die a martyr's death. And in our last sleep we shall kiss the road which will bring our Army to Delhi. The road to Delhi is the road to Freedom. On to Delhi!"

Mutaguchi set 15 March as the D-day for the beginning of the Imphal campaign. The deployment of well over 120,000 troops along the Chindwin river, a front of some 200 kilometres, went on smoothly and undetected by British spies planted in the area. In the meantime, Netaji received some good news. The Arakan offensive, launched on 4 February, had cut off the 7th Indian Division of the British Army in Mayu valley. Contributing to this success was the reconnaissance and subversion of an Indian outpost position by Major Misra, the INA Commander in Arakan. At the same time, he received messages from the underground network working inside India under his direction, whose selected trained spies had been sent by submarine.

On D-day, Mutaguchi assembled the war correspondents at his headquarters in central Burma and declared: "I am firmly convinced that my three divisions will reduce Imphal in one month. In order that they can march fast, they carry the lightest possible equipment and food enough for three weeks. Ali, they will get everything from the British supplies and dumps. Boys! See you again in Imphal at the celebration of the Emperor's birthday on 29 April."

The Japanese-Indian offensive took the British by complete surprise. The Japanese and INA troops literally galloped through mountains and jungles routing the enemy on the way. Prior to the Imphal offensive, an INA detachment under Colonel Saligal had created a breach through the British lines in the Arakan sector. Now the INA's deployment was extended to the Imphal sector.

As the INA under Netaji's command set foot on the Indian soil, the main Japanese force also defeated the obstinate resistance of the enemy on 22 March, broke through the India-Burma border, and advanced from the north and west to encircle Imphal. The initial success of the INA at the Arakan front generated much enthusiasm. In a Special Order of the Day, Netaji referred to the "Glorious and brilliant actions of the brave forces of the Azad Hind Fauj."

On 8 April, Japanese Imperial Headquarters issued a communique which said: "Japanese troops, fighting side by side with the Indian National Army, captured Kohima early on 6 April. A jubilant Netaji at this time started talking with the Japanese about the administration of the liberated and soon-to-be-liberated territories in India.

In response to a call by Netaji, Prime Minister Tojo made an announcement clarifying that all areas of India occupied as a result of Japanese advance would be placed under the jurisdiction of the Provisional Government. This was followed by Netaji's announcement that he was appointing the Finance Minister of his cabinet, Major-General A.C. Chatterjee, as the governor of the newly liberated areas. Netaji described the march of the INA into India as the event of the century.

He had also just declared the Legion in Europe to be part of the INA and had appointed Nambiar to be a Minister in the Provisional Government; his Chief Commissioner had been installed in the Andamans, his first heroes from the Arakan front had been decorated, and the, INA troops had raised the national standard of free India in Kohima; and now, the fall of Imphal seemed very near. Did the Imphal Campaign come almost two years too late? What would have happened if Netaji had arrived in East Asia a year earlier? by the end of 1942, the Axis had scored successes everywhere.

Rommel was in Egypt, the German invasion of Russia had gone smoothly, Nationalist China was on her knees, and India and Australia were expecting a Japanese invasion. Prospects for the Allies were dark in the Pacific and the Rising Sun was at its zenith from Japan to the Bay of Bengal ... Britain was unable to dispute with the Japanese Navy, and there were not enough British and Indian troops in India to assure its defense. Even air protection was inadequte ... Japanese forces had not pursued retreating British troops beyond the Chindwin river in Burma in May 1942, allegedly because "an invasion was likely to arouse ill-feelings amongst the Indian masses." ... So the Japanese remained east of the Chindwin river, leaving British Indian forces to build up their strength in the Imphal plain.

But above all, in that moment of a golden opportunity, the towering leadership of Netaji, a provisional government, and an Indian national army worthy of its name—all these were non-existent in East Asia. Japan by itself simply lacked the motivation for extending war into India, let alone think of its independence. The fact remains, however, that the Imphal campaign was indeed first conceived in 1942, right after the conquest of Burma. According to the official history of the British Armed Forces in the Second World War, Soon after the completion of the Japanese conquest of Burma in June 1942, a certain Lt. Col. Hayashi had advocated an attack on Imphal. He considered that the Japanese should strike against India without giving time to the defenders to recuperate from their disastrous retreat, and Imphal's capture would rob them of the best base for launching a counter-offensive against Burma ... 18th division argued that the jungles of Burma were impassable for large bodies of operational troops and that any attack on Indian territory would provoke anti-Japanese feelings in India. About December 1942, therefore, the plan was abandoned.

Lieutenant-General Kuroda Shigetoku, Southern Army Chief of Staff, stated later that if the operation had been carried out in 1942 when first conceived, rather than in 1944, it would have succeeded. According to Lebra, "General Tojo stated in the spring of 1945 that he regretted Japan had missed the opportunity in 1942."

As the INA and the Japanese forces continued to lay siege on Imphal, the Allied air superiority gained strength and the enemy was preparing for counterattack. Shah Nawaz, commanding two battalions of the Subhash Regiment in the Chin Hills, told of the hardships his men were suffering as a result of disease and of supply and transport difficulties. However, owing to communication problems, the news of difficulties his men were undergoing at the front did not reach Netaji in detail.

While there was a stalemate in the front and the offensive came to a halt, there were meetings and jubilations at Rangoon where Netaji collected money and donations in other forms for the conduct of his campaign. He offered to send additional INA regiments to the Front and more troops were despatched. For about a month Operation U went according to plan. Enemy forces were successfully encircled in the Imphal area.

Suddenly, in the middle of April, the military balance began to shift against Japan and the INA. Wingate's airborne unit had already been attacking from air over Burma supply routes. British forces were being supplied by airlift into the besieged Imphal, and reinforcements began to flow in. British forces were being sent to Kohima to the north by both rail and air. Japan had no matching air power to strike back at enemy air operations. By the end of April the battle strength of Japanese and INA divisions was decreased forty percent. Time for success by surprise attack had already passed and gradually the offensive turned into a defensive battle. The monsoon that followed, brought the ultimate disaster.

As roads became impassable, all supply routes were cut off. Muddy streams flooded roads and valleys, and rivers swelled to sweep away tanks and ammunition. In the wake of the monsoon, disease became rampant. Cholera, malaria, dysentery, beriberi and jungle sores began to take their toll. The INA and the Japanese started living on rations consisting of rice mixed with jungle grass. The 33rd Division had fought desperately for forty days without being able to penetrate the British lines at Imphal. And now that vast amounts of military supplies were reaching the beleaguered garrison at Imphal, there was virtually no hope for a renewed offensive. On 8 July, on the recommendation of top-ranking Generals including Kawabe and Mutaguchi, Prime Minister Tajo issued the order to halt the operation.

The story of retreat from Imphal is one of the greatest tragedies of World War II. It is a story of misery, hunger and death. Japanese and INA troops, bottled up in the Kawab valley between the Chin Hills in the west and the Chindwin river in the west, began their long trek back through jungles and mountains, headed by division commanders and guards in jeeps and horses.

Officers, supply, communication and medical units followed. Behind them marched thousands of stragglers: rain-soaked, emaciated with fever and malnutrition. Soon, corpses began accumulating along the trek, and they had to be left unburied. Of the 220,000 Japanese troops who began the Imphal Campaign, only 130,000 survived, and of these only 70,000 remained at the front to retreat. INA casualties were over fifty percent. It was a disaster equal in magnitude to Dunkirk and Stalingrad. Lebra writes:

> *When Bose heard the order to retreat he was stunned. He drew himself up and said to Kawabe in ringing tones: "Though the Japanese Army has given up the operation, we will continue it. We will not repent even if the advance of our revolutionary army to attain independence of our homeland is completely defeated. Increase in casualties, cessation of supplies, and famine are not reasons enough to stop marching.*

Even if the whole army becomes only spirit we will not stop advancing toward our homeland. This is the spirit of our revolutionary army." In an article in Azad Hind on 6 November 1944, after the retreat from Imphal, Bose was reported to have "reiterated his firm conviction that final victory in this war would belong to Japan and Germany ... that a new phase of war was approaching in which the initiative would again lie in the hands of the Japanese.-"

Each Japanese commander gave his own analysis of the causes of the failure of Operation U, like the problem of the chain of command, lack of air power, on dispersal rather than concentration of forces. However, Netaji thought it was timing, with respect to the monsoon. He felt that the only chance to take Imphal was before the rains came, and most strategists agreed on this point. From the historic perspective, however, Fujiwara perhaps was the most correct. According to him, the Imphal disaster could have been avoided had the operation been undertaken a year earlier, at a time when the British power in the region was weak.

The delay in launching the Imphal offensive was no doubt due to Netaji's late arrival from Europe to East Asia. The Imphal campaign should have been undertaken at a time when the Axis victories had reached their zenith and the Allied forces were on retreat everywhere. During the last three months of 1944, Japanese forces had withdrawn to the banks of the Irrawaddy in Burma, where they intended to make a stand. Netaji enthusiastically offered the reorganized INA First Division, when the Japanese 15th division was ordered to oppose the British. Subsquently, the 2nd Division was also readied for action. In February 1945, the INA held some positions in the region of Mandalay in Burma, giving battle to the advancing enemy.

This was the second campaign of Netaji's army, and it held out tenaciously at Nyaungu for some time. However, allied troops later crossed the Irrawaddy at several points and the Japanese and INA units were surrounded. There were some desertions. Despite unique examples of heroism and Netaji's presence in the battlefields, risking his own life in the face of enemy attacks, the second campaign of the INA (which was purely a defensive one) finally had to give way to the gradual reconquest of Burma by the British.

The end of this campaign was followed by a chain of events that included the final Japanese defeat, an alleged plane crash in Formosa in which Netaji reportedly perished, the surrender of the INA to the allied forces and the trial of their leaders at the Red Fort in Delhi, staged by the British. However, all these fateful events, occurring during the final phase of World War II and its aftermath, should be considered parts of an altogether different episode relating to Subhash Chandra Bose and the Indian National Army.

In the present episode we have examined the historical tasks fulfilled by Netaji and his army in Europe and Asia during World War II, and their significance. In recognition of Netaji's historically significant role as a war leader, Guy Wint pays him a rare tribute with these words: "He played ... an extraordinarily decisive part. By accident, and by seizing an exceptional opportunity, he was able to cut a figure which made him outstanding among the comparatively small number of men who influenced the course of the war by their individual qualities." The Myth of "Freedom through Nonviolence under Gandhi's Leadership" Modern historians in India are taking a second look at the way the country's freedom was achieved, and in that process are demolishing a number of theories, assumptions and myths preached by the "court historians."

However, in order to grasp the magnitude of the issue, with its many ramifications, it is essential to understand first the concept of freedom as envisaged by Netaji—the ideal which motivated him to wrest it from the hands of the British by the force of arms.

In his entire political career, Subhash Chandra Bose was guided by two cardinal principles in his quest for his country's emancipation: that there could be no compromise with alien colonialists on the issue, and that on no account would the country be partitioned. The Indian geographical unity was to be maintained at all costs. As we have already seen, the unfortunate turn of events during World War II prevented Netaji's dream of his victorious march to Delhi at the head of his Indian National Army from becoming a reality.

In his and his army's absence in a postwar India, politicians under the leadership of Gandhi and Nehru did exactly what Netaji never wanted: they negotiated and compromised with the British on the issue of freedom, and in their haste to get into power, agreed to a formula of partitioning India presented to them by the British. The transfer of power was followed by two more developments that were alien to Netaji's philosophy and his blueprint for a free India: introduction of a parliamentary democratic system by Nehru and his decision to keep India in the British Commonwealth of Nations. It was a truncated freedom, achieved over the bloodbath of millions who had perished in fratricidal religious rioting during the process of partition, as the erstwhile India emerged on the world map as the two nations of India and Pakistan.

Even so, the fragmented freedom that fell as India's share after the British had skilfully played their age-old game of divide and rule came not as a result of Gandhi's civil disobedience and nonviolent movement as the court historians would have us believe; nor was it due to persistent negotiations by Nehru and other Indian National Congress leaders on the conference table, which the British found so easy to keep stalling.

The British finally quit when they began to feel the foundations of loyalty being shaken among the British Indian soldiers-the mainstay of the colonial power-as a result of the INA exploits that became known to the world after the cessation of hostilities in East Asia.

Ramesh Chandra Majumdar, the eminent Indian historian who passed away recently, and who by virtue of his challenges to several historical myths can rightly be called the Dean of new historians in India, observed in his book *Three Phases of India's Struggle for Freedom*:

> *There is, however, no basis for the claim that the Civil Disobedience Movement directly led to independence. The campaigns of Gandhi ... came to an ignoble end about fourteen years before India achieved independence ... During the First World War the Indian revolutionaries sought to take advantage of German help in the shape of war materials to free the country by armed revolt. But the attempt did not succeed. During the Second World War Subhash Bose followed the same method and created the INA. In spite of brilliant planning and initial success, the violent campaigns of Subhash Bose failed ... The Battles for India's freedom were also being fought against Britain, though indirectly, by Hitler in Europe and Japan in Asia. None of these scored direct success, but few would deny that it was the cumulative effect of all the three that brought freedom to India. In particular, the revelations made by the INA trial, and the reaction it produced in India, made it quite plain to the British, already exhausted by the war, that they could no longer depend upon the loyalty of the seapoys for maintaining their authority in India. This had probably the greatest influence upon their final decision to quit India.*

Despite Japan's defeat and the consequent withering away of the Indian National Army on the India-Burma front, both Subhash Chandra Bose and his INA became household names throughout the country as the returning soldiers were sought to be prosecuted by the British. By then, the Congress leadership under Gandhi and Nehru had pre-empted itself, and the year 1945 seemed relatively calm and uneventful.

However, Netaji and his legend worked up a movement all over the country which even a Gandhi could never produce. Echoing this mass upsurge Michael Edwardes wrote in his *Last Years of British India*:

> *The Government of India had hoped, by prosecuting members of the INA, to reinforce the morale of the Indian army. It succeeded only in creating unease, in making the soldiers feel slightly ashamed that they themselves had supported the British. If Bose and his men had been on the right side-and all India now confirmed that they were-then Indians in the Indian army must have been on the wrong side. It slowly dawned upon the Government of India that the backbone of the British rule, the Indian army, might now no longer be trustworthy. The ghost of Subhash Bose, like Hamlet's father, walked the battlements of the Red Fort (where the INA soldiers were being tried), and his suddenly amplified figure overawed the conference that was to lead to independence.*

Apart from revisionist historians, it was none other than Lord Clement Atlee himself, the British Prime Minster responsible for conceding independence to India, who gave a shattering blow to the myth sought to be perpetuated by court historians, that Gandhi and his movement had led the country to freedom.

Chief justice P.B. Chakrabarty of Calcutta High Court, who had also served as the acting Governor of West Bengal in India, disclosed the following in a letter addressed to the publisher of Dr. R.C. Majumdar's book *A History of Bengal*. The Chief Justice wrote:

You have fulfilled a noble task by persuading Dr. Majumdar to write this history of Bengal and publishing it ... In the preface of the book Dr. Majumdar has written that he could not accept the thesis that Indian independence was brought about solely, or predominantly by the nonviolent civil disobedience movement of Gandhi. When I was the acting Governor, Lord Atlee, who had given us independence by withdrawing the British rule from India, spent two days in the Governor's palace at Calcutta during his tour of India. At that time I had a prolonged discussion with him regarding the real factors that had led the British to quit India. My direct question to him was that since Gandhi's "Quit India" movement had tapered off quite some time ago and in 1947 no such new compelling situation had arisen that would necessitate a hasty British departure, why did they have to leave? In his reply Atlee cited several reasons, the principal among them being the erosion of loyalty to the British Crown among the Indian army and navy personnel as a result of the military activities of Netaji. Toward the end of our discussion I asked Atlee what was the extent of Gandhi's influence upon the British decision to quit India. Hearing this question, Atlee's lips became twisted in a sarcastic smile as he slowly chewed out the word, "m-i-n-i-m-a-l!"

When the new version of the history of the Twentieth Century India, and especially the episode of the country's unique struggle for independence comes to be written, it will no doubt single out but one person who made the most significant and outstanding contribution among all his compatriots toward the emancipation of his motherland from the shackles of an alien bondage. During World War II this man strode across two continents like a colossus, and the footsteps of his army of liberation reverberated through the forests and plains of Europe and the jungles and mountains of Asia. His armed assaults shook the very foundations of the British Empire. His name was Subhash Chandra Bose.

On the Transfer of Power from Britain to India-from 'The Freedom Struggle and the Dravidian Movement' by P.Ramamurti, Orient Longman, 1987

"We have seen that no nonviolent struggle conducted by Mahatma Gandhi in the course of the freedom struggle had achieved its objective. In 1921, the non-cooperation movement was withdrawn before it was started. In 1930 the Civil Disobedience Movement was withdrawn without achieving its limited objective. In 1932, the Civil Disobedience Movement was suspended at Gandhiji's instance and was never revived. In 1941 individual satyagraha for the right of freedom of speech ended in six months without achieving its aim. The 1942 countrywide struggle for freedom was never started by Gandhiji. How is it then that the British Government transferred power to the Congress and Muslim League leaders in 1947?

For an answer to this question, one must look into the countrywide upsurge in which military personnel also participated en masse, as anticipated by the communists at the end of the war.

First, there was the trial of the Indian National Army. Consequent to the surrender of Japan, the Government arrested the sepoys of the Indian National Army and started a trial on charges of attempting to overthrow the Government established by Law in the Red Fort at New Delhi.

The Communist Party of India gave a call for countrywide hartals and strikes. The call was responded to in cities, towns and in big villages. In Calcutta the hartals and strikes lasted a week and the people took to the streets demanding the unconditional release of the I.N.A. prisoners. The Government was forced to release them unconditionally.

When Pandit Jawaharlal Nehru set foot in Jammu and Kashmir, he was arrested by the Princely Raj. Immediately the Communist Party called for countrywide protest demonstrations. The Kashmir Government was forced to release him.

Next came the strikes of police personnel in many provinces, supported by the Communist Party. This was followed by strikes in military cantonments all over the country. The Indian soldiers and air force personnel left the barracks, and held massive rallies in nearby towns shouting slogans like 'Down with British Government" 'Down with Imperialism' and 'Inquilab Zindabad'.

From Kashmir to Travancore, the people of the princely states were fighting to end princely rule. The crowning event of these struggles was the strike by the navymen of the naval ship 'Talwar' stationed near Bombay on 19th February 1946. The British Union Jack was removed and in its place the Congress-League and Communist Party's flags fluttered proudly.

The naval ship 'Hindustan' was ordered to proceed to Bombay to quell the revolt. On reaching Bombay, the navymen of 'Hindustan' refused to fire on their brothers. Then Admiral Godfrey through a radio broadcast ordered the navymen of 'Talwar' and 'Hindustan' to surrender within 24 hours, failing which, he said, 'The entire might of the British Royal Navy would be used to crush the revolt; it does not matter if the entire Indian navy is destroyed in the proces.'

Sardar Patel, on behalf of the Congress, supported Admiral Godfrey and said, 'Discipline in the Navy is of utmost importance and the men should obey the orders of the officers without questioning.' The fighting navymen had formed a struggle committee which appealed to the Congress, Muslim League and the Communist Party to lend their support. The Communist Party appealed to the people all over the country to demonstrate in support of the struggle; demonstrations and strikes took place all over the country. In Karachi, Cochin, Madras, Calcutta and Chittagong, there was complete strike in all naval establishments.

Sardar Patel, on behalf of the Congress, issued an order to the working class of Bombay not to respond to the call of the Communist Party. The people ignored Sardar Patel's call, struck work, observed hartal, demonstrated with the tri-colour flags of the Congress, the green flag of the Muslim League and the red flag of the Communist Party shouting slogans like 'Hindus and Muslims Unite; down, down the British Government', 'Down with imperialism', 'Inquilab Zindabad', etc.

Sardar Patel lamented in a statement that the Congress prestige was sinking. Troops manned by British soldiers were sent to Bombay to quell the demonstrators. They started shooting at unarmed demonstrators indiscriminately. Yet the demonstrations lasted for many days. The official statement of the Central Legislature was that 130 people were killed, which was a conservative estimate. No one knows how many died and how many were wounded since most of the people were not taken to hospitals.

Gandhiji, who was quiet during the struggle, later issued a statement:

> *'I can understand if there was unity from top to bottom in this struggle. Only the people at the lower levels were united. This will only lead the country into the hands of the rabble; I would prefer to die in the fire than to live for hundred and twenty five years.'*

Four days after the naval revolt started, on the night of the 23rd February 1946, the British Cabinet held an emergency meeting and decided to transfer political power to the Congress and League leaders. The British Prime Minister Attlee announced the decision the next day in the House of Commons. The former Prime Minister Churchill and his conservative colleagues bitterly opposed the decision. While replying to the debate, Prime Minister Attlee said:

> *"In the conditions prevailing in India today, old remedies are of no use. It is meaningless to talk about them now. The heat in **1946** is not the same as that of **1920** (non-cooperation movement), **1930** (first civil disobedience movement) or **1942** (when the Quit India resolution was passed). (Emphasis mine.)*

"Nothing intensifies the national feelings and aspirations of a colonial people like a great war. Those who have had anything to do with the two wars, know what effect the 1914-18 a world war had on the feelings and aspirations of the Indian people. National waves which rise slowly or are accelerated during wartime. and rise very high after the war. During the war, they are controlled to some extent; but after the war, they break all shackles and rise very high. Today, in India, no, in the whole Asian continent, they are dashing against the stones and, rocks, breaking them to pieces. I have no doubt about it. "India alone has to decide what its future will be and what its status will be in the world. I hope that India will decide to stay in the Commonwealth. Instead, if it decides to be an independent country, it is our duty to work for peaceful transfer of power in the interim period and make it easy. India has a right to he a sovereign independent country."

Sir Stafford Cripps, intervening in the debate made the position crystal clear. He said:

> *"...The Indian Army in India is not obeying the British officers. We have recruited our workers for the war; they have been demobilised after the war. They are required to repair the factories damaged by Hitler's bombers. Moreover, they want to join their kith and kin after five and a half years of separation. Their kith and kin also want to join them. In these conditions if we have to rule India for a long time, we have to keep a permanent British army for a long time in a vast country of four hundred millions. We have no such army...."*

The countrywide opposition to British rule in which the Indian personnel of the three armies participated, crowned by the naval mutiny, was the direct cause of the decision to transfer power. The Congress had nothing to do with the entire upsurge. These facts are obscured by Congressmen today. Subsequently, a cabinet mission arrived in India and held talks with both Congress and League leaders. It used the differences between the Congress and the Muslims; Lord Wavel was replaced as Viceroy by Lord Mountbatten, and an interim Government dominated by the Congress and the League was formed.

Riots were engineered between Hindus and Sikhs on the one hand, and Hindus and Muslims on the other. On August 15th, United India was divided into India and Pakistan, and power was tranferred to the Congress in India, and the League in Pakistan. India and Pakistan attained independence in the midst of the worst instance in history of mutual killing by two communities."

Death of Subhash Chandra Bose-An enduring political mystery-Anthony Paul, Straits Times, 1 June 2005

Three days after Japan's surrender ended World War II, a Japanese Mitsubishi Ki.21 medium bomber reportedly took off from Taihoku, a Taipei airfield. The most important of several VIPs on its passenger list was a man who was then one of India's most famous sons-Subhash Chandra Bose, or Netaji (or Revered Leader), of the anti-British Provisional Government of Free India.

To this day, Indians dispute passionately what happened next.

Most accept the official version of events: For reasons unknown, the plane burst into flames on take-off. Badly burnt, Netaji Bose died later that day-Aug 18, 1945.

What are said to be his remains-bone fragments, some teeth and parts of the skull and jaw-were taken to Tokyo and housed at the suburban Renkoji Temple. Singapore also venerates him indirectly: A modest monument to his greatest accomplishment-the Indian National Army (INA), mobilised in Singapore in the early 1940s for the purpose of driving the British from India-occupies an honoured place on the Esplanade.

But a small, persistent minority of Indians insists that the story of Netaji Bose's death was an elaborate subterfuge. They can point to some fresh support: Earlier this year, an official Indian inquiry, the third since 1956, turned up evidence in Taipei indicating that whatever happened to Netaji Bose, he did not die in a plane crash that day. According to Taipei's current mayor, there are no official records of any such crash. The conspiracy theorists have several alternative histories, all tortuous. One of the most quoted: Those death reports were a ruse by the leader, his aides and the Japanese to have him escape from victors' justice and flee unscathed to Manchuria. From there, say Netaji Bose's fans, he most probably made his way to the Soviet Union.

Dictator Joseph Stalin, whom he may have met in Moscow in 1941, probably kept him in safe custody, they say, for the day on which he could continue his lifelong struggle against the

British imperialists. Fear of the mischief the anti-British firebrand would cause if he managed to get back to India kept Britain from following up various intelligence leads to Netaji Bose's whereabouts, those sceptical about the official story claim. And Bose's political rivals-those devious accomplices of the British, Mahatma Gandhi and Prime Minister Jawaharlal Nehru-went along with the cover-up.

The Revered Leader is unlikely to be returning to Indian politics-if alive, he would now be 108. Nevertheless, books and newspaper articles, often passionately pro-Bose, continue to be written about India's most enduring political mystery. Author Anuj Dhar (*Back From The Dead: Inside The Subhash Bose Mystery*; Manas Publications, 2005) tells The Straits Times: 'People may or may not like Netaji, but they have a right to know what happened to him-how he died and where.'

Over the past few months, two developments have brought Netaji Bose back into the headlines.

First, there is a much-trumpeted three-hour-long movie with a US$5 million (S$8.3 million) budget. Bose: The Forgotten Hero took more than three years to shoot.

Second, the Indian government has extended for six more months the inquiry into the circumstances of Netaji Bose's death or disappearance. In Calcutta, on June 10, the Mukherjee Commission, named after its sole commissioner, retired Supreme Court Justice M. K. Mukherjee, will resume its inquiry, now six years long, into the affair. Subhash Bose was born in 1896, the son of a well-to-do Bengali lawyer. After securing a Cambridge University honours degree, he returned to India and involved himself in left-wing politics.

A powerful orator, he was elected Indian National Congress president in 1938, but was soon forced to resign after a dispute with Mohandas K. Gandhi. Bose advocated the militant overthrow of British rule; Gandhi and acolyte Nehru preferred nonviolent resistance.

Placed under house arrest by the British for his pro-Axis sympathies, he escaped in 1941 and, with clandestine German and Italian help, fled to Germany. From there on, as a biographer puts it, 'his life reads as though written for Hollywood'. He saw Britain's war with Germany as a chance to wrest India from British rule. Thus in Berlin, this Indian nationalist sought an alliance with Adolph Hitler.

Their one meeting cannot have been very comfortable. In Mein Kampf, the German's racist sermon to his Nazi Party, Hitler had declared: 'Indian agitators...will never achieve (freedom from Britain).'

This view, the Fuhrer had written, was 'quite aside from the fact that I, as a man of Germanic blood, would, in spite of everything, rather see India under English rule than under any other'.

A German information officer's account of the meeting says that Hitler refused attempts by Bose to discuss Mein Kampf's offensive passage. The Fuhrer is reported also to have told the Revered Leader that India 'would not be able to rule itself for another 150 years'.

Nevertheless, Bose received permission to establish a Free India Centre in Berlin and recruit, for an 'Indian Legion', Indians in British uniform whom the Germans had captured, mostly in North Africa.

But the Nazis' racism got in the way of Bose's grander plans-for an Axis-Indian army on the European and Middle Eastern fronts. So he turned to the Japanese.

With his fellow-Asians, then promoting the Greater East Asia Co-Prosperity Sphere, he was somewhat more successful.

In 1943, in an extraordinarily hazardous journey across three oceans, German and Japanese U-boats delivered him to Singapore. Over Japanese-controlled Radio Singapore, he broadcast a stirring appeal to India and the Indian diaspora: 'Give me blood and I will give you freedom!'

At the Capitol Theatre on Oct 21, 1943, he proclaimed the creation of a Japanese-sponsored 'provisional government of Free India' and organised the INA, a force ultimately comprising three divisions totalling about 30,000 troops. Both government and troops hailed him as 'Netaji', an honorific many Indians still use for him today. Singapore's National Archives' oral history files hold recordings of INA veterans who speak emotionally of those heady days. At the archives last week, I listened to Sikh intelligence officer Mohinder Singh recall with pride and affection his leader's oratory at Singapore's Padang as he addressed troops who would soon be in combat.

'He was a great man, very popular, a great orator,' the old soldier recalled. 'He had a remarkable memory. He would speak first in Hindustani. Then he would repeat the speech word for word in English...But he knew little about military matters.'

In November 1943, the Japanese and the INA captured the Andaman and Nicobar Islands. Suddenly, about two million (of about 400 million then) Indians were no longer under British rule. Netaji moved his headquarters to Yangon. Four months later, spurred by his war cry Chalo Delhi! (On to Delhi!) the INA crossed the Myanmar border and raised its flag on Indian soil.

But the moment did not last long. Unknown to the Japan-Free India alliance, the British had cracked Axis codes. When the INA infiltrated fifth columnists into India, the British picked them up. British forces also acquired air superiority.

Moreover, according to Mr Mohinder Singh, the British, playing for time, were soon joined by a South Asian ally for which the Japanese were unprepared. 'That was 'General Monsoon',' said Mr Singh. 'The Japanese were running out of supplies, and the rains turned their supply routes into mud.' Even before two atomic bombs in August 1945 ended the war, Japanese and Indian forces in Southeast Asia were effectively at a standstill. But the Japan-India axis put a brave face on events. In the war's last months, *a large cenotaph dedicated to an 'Unknown Warrior' of the INA was raised on the Esplanade.*(in Singapore)

Several months after the British returned to Singapore, their army dynamited the pillar. Erected on the site by Singapore's National Heritage Board in 1995, the new INA monument is thus, in the words of one tourist brochure, 'a monument to a monument'.

Mr Mohinder Singh told the National Archives that he believed the official story of his leader's death-that he perished in the plane crash. But the recording adds an intriguing detail in support of the notion that Bose might have been trying to reach out to the Russians.

The Soviet Union did not declare war on Japan until Aug 9, 1945. Before this had happened, Mr Singh told his interviewer, a 'Japanese admiral (in Singapore) suggested to Netaji that he might find the Soviet Union would help India'.

Of course, if Bose had been making his way to Manchuria and then Russia on Aug. 18, he could not have been unaware that Moscow now stood with the British-American allies against Japan. But that has not stopped rumours of the Indian being spotted in the Soviet Union over the past half-century.

According to India's Outlook magazine, scholars from Calcutta's Asiatic Society researching India-Soviet ties in Moscow came across recently declassified Soviet files 'that hinted at Bose having been in the USSR after 1945'.

One of the scholars, Dr. Purobi Roy, was quoted as saying Soviet military archives mentioned Stalin and foreign minister Vyacheslav Molotov discussing in 1946 whether Bose should stay in the Soviet Union or leave.

The quest for the truth continues. The Mukherjee Commission has now taken evidence from 127 witnesses and depositions.

The commission's priority will be visiting Russia. Author Dhar told The Straits Times: 'They already have evidence in the form of official papers, affidavits, depositions, etc., all hinting that an inquiry in Russia is most necessary.'

INA War Memorial at the Esplanade, Singapore

Historical Journey of Indian National Army

On 8 July 1945, Bose laid the foundation stone of the INA War Memorial at the Esplanade, Singapore to commemorate the "Unknown Warrior" of the INA. The words inscribed upon the War Memorial were the motto of the INA: Unity (Ittefaq),

Faith (Etmad) and Sacrifice (Kurbani). While paying homage to the martyrs of the INA, he said:

> *"The future generations of Indians who will be born, not as slaves but as free men, because of your colossal sacrifice, will bless your names and proudly proclaim to the world that you, their forbears, fought and suffered reverses in the battle of Manipur, Assam and Burma. But through temporary failure you paved the way to ultimate success and glory."*

When the British returned to Singapore in 1945, Lord Mountbatten, Head of Southeast Asia Command, ordered the INA Memorial to be destroyed.

In 1995, the site where the INA Memorial once stood was marked by the National Heritage Board of Singapore and new memorial was erected-a monument to a monument'.

The inscription in English reads:

"In the final months of the Japanese Occupation of Singapore a memorial dedicated to the "Unknown Warrior" of the Indian National Army (INA) was constructed at this site.

The local INA was formed in 1942 with Japanese support. It sought to liberate India from the British and consisted mainly of prisoners of war from the British Indian Army. Subhash Chandra Bose who led the INA from 1943 onwards laid a foundation stone at the monument in July 1945. The Urdu words inscribed on the monument read Unity (Ittefaq), Faith (Etmad) and Sacrifice (Kurbani) When the British returned to Singapore, they demolished the memorial barely two months after its installation."

Aurobindo, Chitranjan Das & Subhash Chandra Bose-Excerpt from *The Relevance Of Aurobindo: Early Political Life & Teachings* by Nadesan Satyendra:

> *".... Aurobindo also inspired the young lawyer, Chitranjan Das who had defended him in the Alipore trial. Chitranjan Das, later known as Deshabandu became a fearless fighter for India's freedom and served as President of the Indian National Congress in 1920.*

Another young Bengalee, Subhash Chandra Bose followed Aurobindo's footsteps by spurning the Indian Civil Service after having passed the examination in 1920 from Fitzwilliam Hall in Cambridge University. Subhash wrote to his brother Sarat on 22 September 1920, in words reminiscent of Aurobindo:

"You will readily understand my mental condition as I stand on the threshold of what the man-in-the-street would call a promising career. There is much to be said in favour of such service. It solves once for all what is the paramount problem for each of us-the problem of bread and butter... But for a man of my temperament who has been feeding on ideas which might be called eccentric-the line of least resistance is not the best line to follow... it is not possible to serve one's country in the best and fullest manner if one is chained to the (Indian) Civil Service. In short, national and spiritual aspirations are not compatible with obedience to Civil Service conditions."

Subhash Chandra Bose wrote again to his brother on 23 February 1921:

"The principle of serving an alien bureacracy is one to which I cannot reconcile myself. Besides the first step towards equiping oneself for public service is to sacrifice all worldly interests-to burn one's boats as it were-and devote oneself whole heartedly to the national cause... The illustrious example of Aurobindo Ghosh *looms large before my vision. I feel that I am ready to earlier.*

"I had the privilege to be in the same jail with him (Deshabandu Chitranjan Das) for eight months in 1921-22. For a couple of months we were in the Presidency Jail occupying two adjacent celss, and the remaining six months we were in one big hall... in the Alipore Central Jail... That Swaraj in India meant primarily the uplift of the masses... was a matter of conviction with the Deshabandu... Ofcourse, thirty years ago *Swami Vivekananda* spoke in that vein in his book entitled 'Bartaman Bharat', but that message of Swamiji was never echoed from our political platforms...

....another reason for the extraordinary influence which he (Deshabandu) wielded.... was (his) constant experience that through all his actions he had succeeded in establishing Vaishanavism which was very much part of his religious life. Thanks to a fine synthesis between his ideal and his practical life, his entire being was getting progressively saturated with this synthesis... As a result of inner purity, which follows the pursuit of action without caring for results, *man loses the awareness of the ego. And when the ego is transcended he becomes an instrument for the expression of the Divine Will.."* (Subhash Chandra Bose, letter dated 20 February 1926 to Hemendra Nath Dasgupta-The Essential Writings of Netaji Subhash Chandra Bose, Edited by Sisir K.Bose and Sugata Bose, Oxford University Press, 1997)

Sri Aurobindo, in a significant sense inspired both the spritual and militant aspects of India's struggle for freedom. He was a worthy son of a Bengal which had also given birth to *Ramakrishna Paramahamsa, Swami Vivekananda* and *Rabindranath Tagore*-and that is not to mention *Satyendranath Bose*."

Netaji Subhash Chandra Bose: While the Gandhi / Nehru faction of Congress has garnered much of the credit for India's freedom struggle, it is important to remember that India's freedom movement was in fact a movement of the masses and there were a number of great leaders with fierce patriotism and great visionary ideas who sacrificed their entire lives for the nation's cause. We continue our series on the freedom fighters, on the occasion of Netaji's 102nd birthday.

-Jyotsna Kamat

January 26, 1999

India's Republic Day

Known as *Netaji* (leader), Mr. Bose was a fierce and popular leader in the political scene in pre-independence India. He was the president of the Indian National Congress in 1937 and 1939, and founded a nationalist force called the Indian National

Army. He was acclaimed as a semigod, akin to the many mythological heroes like Rama or Krishna, and continues as a legend in Indian mind.

Subhash Chandra was born on January 23rd 1897 in Cuttack (in present day Orissa) as the ninth child among fourteen, of Janakinath Bose, an advocate, and Prabhavatidevi, a pious and God-fearing lady. A brilliant student, he topped the matriculation examination of Calcutta province and passed his B.A. in Philosophy from the Presidency College in Calcutta. He was strongly influenced by Swami Vivekananda's teachings and was known for his patriotic zeal as a student. His parents' wishes kept him away from the Indian freedom struggle and led him into studies for the Indian Civil Service in England. Although he finished those examinations also at the top of his class (4th), he could not complete his aprecentship and returned to India, being deeply disturbed by the Jallianwalla Bagh massacre. He came under the influence of Mahatma Gandhi and joined the Indian National Congress (a.k.a. Congress). Gandhiji directed him to work with Deshbandhu Chittaranjan Das, the Bengali leader whom Bose acknowledged as his political guru.

Bose was outspoken in his anti-British stance and was jailed 11 (eleven) times between 1920 and 1941 for periods varying between six months and three years. He was the leader of the youth wing of the Congress Party, in the forefront of the trade union movement in India and organized *Service League*, another wing of Congress. He was admired for his great skills in organization development.

THE INFLUENCE OF BOSE

Bose advocated complete freedom for India at the earliest, whereas the Congress Committee wanted it in phases, through a Dominion status. Other younger leaders including Jawaharlal Nehru supported Bose and finally at the historic Lahore Congress convention, the Congress had to adopt *Poorna Swaraj* (complete freedom) as its motto. Bhagat Singh's martyrdom and the inability of the Congress leaders to save his life infuriated Bose and he started a movement opposing the Gandhi-

Irvin Peace Pact. He was imprisoned and expelled from India. But defying the ban, he came back to India and was imprisoned again!

Clouds of World War II were gathering fast and Bose warned the Indian people and the British against dragging India into the war and the material losses she could incur. He was elected president of the Indian National Congress twice in 1937 and in 1939, the second time defeating Gandhiji's nominee. He brought a resolution to give the British six months to hand India over to the Indians, failing which there would be a revolt. There was much opposition to his rigid stand, and he resigned from the post of president and formed a progressive group known as the *Forward Block* (1939).

The second World War broke out in September of 1939, and just as predicted by Bose, India was declared as a warring state (on behalf of the British) by the Governor General, without consulting Indian leaders. The Congress party was in power in seven major states and all state governments resigned in protest.

Subhash Chandra Bose now started a mass movement against utilizing Indian resources and men for the great war. To him, it made no sense to further bleed poor Indians for the sake of colonial and imperial nations. There was a tremendous response to his call and the British promptly imprisoned him. He took to a hunger-strike, and after his health deteriorated on the 11th day of fasting, he was freed and was placed under house arrest. The British were afraid of violent reactions in India, should something happen to Bose in prison.

The Mystery Begins...

Bose suddenly disappeared in the beginning of 1941 and it was not until many days that authorities realized Bose was not inside the house they were guarding! He travelled by foot, car and train and resurfaced in Kabul (now in Afghanistan), only to disappear once again. In November 1941, his broadcast from German radio sent shock waves among the British and electrified the Indian masses who realized that their leader was working on a master plan to free their motherland. It also gave fresh confidence to the revolutionaries in India who were challenging the British in many ways. The Axis powers (mainly Germany) assured Bose military and other help to fight the British. Japan by this time had grown into another strong world power, occupying key colonies of Dutch, French, and British colonies in Asia.

Bose had struck alliance with Germany and Japan. He rightly felt that his presence in the East would help his countrymen in freedom struggle and second phase of his saga began. It is told that he was last seen on land near Keil canal in Germany, in the beginning of 1943. A most hazardous journey was undertaken by him under water, covering thousands of miles, crossing enemy territories. He was in the Atlantic, the Middle East, Madagascar and the Indian ocean. Battles were being fought over land, in the air and there were mines in the sea. At one stage he travelled 400 miles in a rubber dinghy to reach a Japanese submarine, which took him to Tokyo. He was warmly received in Japan and was declared the head of the Indian army, which consisted of about 40,000 soldiers from Singapore and other eastern regions. Bose called it the Indian National Army (INA) and a government by the name "*Azad Hind Government*" was declared on the 21st of October 1943. INA freed the Andaman and Nicobar islands from the British, and were renamed as *Swaraj* and *Shaheed* islands. The Government started functioning.

EARLY SUCCESS AND TRAGIC END

Bose wanted to free India from the Eastern front. He had taken care that Japanese interference was not present from any angle. Army leadership, administration and communications were managed only by Indians. Subhash Brigade, Azad Brigade and Gandhi Brigade were formed. INA marched through Burma and occupied Coxtown on the Indian Border. A touching scene ensued when the solders entered their 'free' motherland. Some lay down and kissed, some placed pieces of mother earth on their heads, others wept. They were now inside of India and were determined to drive out the British! *Delhi Chalo* (Let's march to Delhi) was the war cry.

The bombing of Hiroshima and Nagasaki changed the history of mankind. Japan had to surrender. Bose was in Singapore at that time and decided to go to Tokyo for his next course of action. Unfortunately, the plane he boarded crashed near Taipei and he died in the hospital of severe burns. He was just 48. The Indian people were so much enamored of Bose's oratory and leadership qualities, fealressness and mysterious adventures, that he had become a legend. They refused to believe that he died in the plane crash. The famous Red Fort trial wherein Bose's generals and the INA officers were tried, became landmark events. Initially, the British Government thought of a court-martial, but there was a countrywide protest against any kind of punishment. For common Indians, Axis and Allied powers hardly mattered, but they could not tolerate punishment of fellow countrymen who were fighting for freedom. The British Government was in no position to face open rebellion or mutiny and a general amnesty for INA soldiers was declared.

While Bose's approach to Indian freedom continues to generate heated debate in the Indian society today, there is no denying of his burning patriotism, his tireless efforts to free India from inside and outside and his reckless adventures in trying to reach his goals. His exploits later became a legend due to the many stories carried by the disbanded INA soldiers who came from every nook and corner of our great country. Had he lived, Subhash Chandra Bose could have given a new turn to Independent India's political history. But he lives on eternally in the Indian mind, more famous after his death.

4

NETAJI'S VISION FOR INDIA

THE FUNDAMENTAL PROBLEMS OF INDIA

Netaji addresses students of the Tokyo University in November 1944. I do not propose to speak to such a distinguished gathering on the commonplace things that you hear and read about India. I think it would be far better if I speak to you on the more fundamental problems of India. Having being a student of philosophy myself, I am naturally more interested in fundamental problems. I hope you will also agree with me that I should rather speak to you today on some of the fundamental problems that face my country, both in the present as well as in the future.

In my travels abroad, I have often found that people generally have a wrong and sometimes a rather funny idea about my country. For instance, among the people in Europe, the general idea about India is that it is a land in which three things can be found: Snakes, fakirs and maharajas. Among those who have been influenced by British propaganda, the general idea about India is that it is a country where people are always fighting among themselves, and where the strong hand of Britain is required in order to maintain peace and order among the people. If you approach the Orientalists in Europe, that is, the experts in Indology, you will find that they look upon India as a land of mystics and philosophers, a land which at one time produced a very rich philosophy, but which is today as dead as the ancient civilizations of Egypt and Babylon.

Now the question is, "what is India in reality?" No doubt we have a very ancient civilization, but unlike other ancient civilizations, such as Egypt or Babylon, Phoenicia or even Greece, the ancient culture and civilization of India is not dead. It still lives in the present. And we Indians of today think the same thoughts fundamentally, the same thoughts and have the same feelings, the same ideals of life, as our forefathers who lived 2,000 or 3,000 years ago. In other words, there is a continuity, historical and cultural continuity, extending from ancient times till the present day-which is in some ways a very remarkable thing in history. Now, in order to understand India, this fundamental fact should first be understood, namely, that the India of the past is not dead. India of the past lives in the present, and will live in the future.

Against this background, this ancient background, we see changes in our national life from age to age. During the last 3,000 years, people have come into India from outside with new ideas, some times with new cultures. All these new influences, ideas and cultures have been gradually absorbed into the national life of India, so that in spite of the fact that, fundamentally we have the same culture and civilization as we had several thousand years ago, we have nevertheless changed and moved with the times. Today, in spite of our ancient background, we are able to live in a modern world and adapt ourselves to that world. Those who have been influenced, whether consciously or unconsciously by British propaganda, have the impression that India was very easily conquered by the British and also that after the British conquest of India our country was for the first time politically unified. Both these notions are entirely wrong and without foundation.

In the first place, it is not true that India was easily conquered by the British. It took British 100 years, from 1757 to 1857, to finally subjugate India. Secondly, it is also an entirely wrong notion to think that India was politically unified by the British. The fact is that India was for the first time politically unified nearly 2,500 years ago under the Buddhist Emperor, Ashoka the Great. In reality, India of the time of Ashoka the Great was even larger than the India of today.

Ashoka's India included not only modern India, but also Afghanistan and a part of Persia.

After the time of Ashoka, India has gone through many ups and downs in her national life. There have been periods decay, followed by periods of progress and national upheaval. But through these ups and downs in our national life, we have been able, in the long run, to keep our progress. About 1000 years after Ashoka, India again reached the zenith of progress under the Gupta Emperors. This was followed by another glorious epoch in Indian history about nine hundred years later under the Mogul Emperors. Therefore, it is worth remembering that the British notion that we have been unified politically under British rule is entirely wrong. All that the British have tried to do is to divide the Indian people and to weaken, disarm and emasculate them.

I shall now present before you a problem which will interest scientists, and in particular students of sociology. The question is whether the Indian people have any right to live as a free nation. In other words, have they the strength and the vitality left in them to live and to develop themselves as a free nation? I personally hold the opinion that if a nation once loses its vitality, its inner vitality, then it has no right to exist. And even if it does continue to exist after loosing its vitality, that existence will have hardly any worth or value for mankind. The only reason why I stand for India's freedom and believe as a free nation we shall have a glorious future is that I believe that we have sufficient vitality left in us to live as free men and develop as a nation.

Now, if I have to answer this question as to whether sufficient vitality is left in us, I shall have to answer two questions: firstly, has our nation any creative faculty and secondly, is it prepared to fight and die in order to preserve its existence? These two tests have applied to India.

With regard to the first question, we have seen that in spite of the British rule in India, in spite of innumerable restrictions and disadvantages which follow from foreign rule, we have been able to give numerous proofs during the century that in different departments of our national life we still have creative power. The number of philosophers and thinkers produced in India under British rule, the number of writers and poets that enslaved India has produced, the artistic revival in India in spite of British rule, the scientific progress made by the Indian people in spite of so many difficulties in the way of their education, the standard already attained by our leading scientists as compared with scientists in different parts of the world, the industrial progress made by India as a result of her own effort and initiative and last but not the least, the distinction which we have attained in the field of sports, all these go to show that in spite of being politically subjugated the vitality of the nation has remained intact.

If under foreign rule and in spite of the obstacles and restrictions that follow from foreign rule, we could give so much proof of our creative faculty, then it stands to reason that when India is free and when the masses of the Indian people are afforded educational facilities, they will be able to give much better proof of their intellectual calibre and creative faculty in different walks of life.

I have just referred to the first test of a nation's vitality, namely, creative faculty. I shall now consider the second test, namely, as to whether the Indian people are able to fight and to die for the sake of freedom. On this point I should like to say, first of all, that, since the last great fight that they had with the British in 1857, the Indian people have not given up the struggle against the enemy, even for one day.

Unfortunately, owing to what I would call the folly of our forefathers, after our final defeat in 1857, the leaders in those days had allowed themselves to be disarmed. Whatever difficulty we have subsequently experienced in winning back our freedom has been due to largely our having been disarmed. But though owing to the mistake of the leaders the people were disarmed, nevertheless they continued to fight for their freedom in other ways. I shall not take up your time unnecessarily by giving a description of all the methods that have been used in India against the British. I will only say this, that all the methods that have been tried by revolutionists in different parts of the world for the achievement of their own independence have been tried in India. At the beginning of the century, particularly after the victory of Japan over Russia in 1904 and 1905, the freedom movement in India got a new impetus and since then, during the last 40 years, our revolutionaries have been studying very closely the methods of revolutionaries in other countries and they have tried to adopt as many of their methods as possible.

They have tried also to manufacture secretly arms and explosives for the achievement of independence. As a development of this struggle for freedom, India tried a new experiment-Civil Disobedience or Passive Resistance-of which the best exponent was Mahatma Gandhi. Though personally I believe that this method will not succeed in bringing us complete independence, there is no doubt that it has greatly helped to rouse and unify the Indian people and also to keep up a movement of resistance against the foreign government. I should, therefore, say that the fact that in spite of all the difficulties that result from foreign rule, a nation can produce a new method and practice that method with a large measure of success is also a proof of that nation's vitality. It shows that, that nation does not accept enslavement as a settled fact and is determined to struggle against it and to work out new methods for achieving independence.

I have, as a revolutionary, made a very close study of the revolutionary movements in other countries, and I can say without any exaggeration that since 1857 we have used every possible method of revolutionary struggle. In the course of this struggle, tremendous sacrifices have been made and many have given their lives. There was, however, one method that still remained for us to take up and that was the organization of a real modern national army.

That work we had not done up till recently because it was impossible to do that inside India under the eyes of the British army and the British police. But the moment this war gave the Indian people an opportunity of organizing a modern Indian national army outside India they at once seized it. As a result of that effort, and with the help of the Japanese Government and the armed forces of Japan, they have been able to build up this army. So my point is that throughout our revolutionary struggle against the British Government and their armed forces we have shown sufficient initiative, creative power and vitality and have made tremendous sacrifices. WE now hope that under the conditions, and with the advantages the war has given us, we shall be able, after all, to fulfil our national aspirations and win freedom for India.

Having replied to the question regarding the vitality of the Indian people and their right to live as a free nation, I shall now attempt a sociological analysis of modern India, you have to take note of the three important factors. The first factor is the ancient background, that is, the ancient culture and civilisation of India, of which the Indian people of today are conscious, and of which they feel proud. The second factor is the struggle which has gone on without any break or interruption since we were finally overpowered by the British. And the third factor consists of certain influences which have come into India from outside. Modern India is composed of its ancient background, the unbroken national struggle against Britain, and the impact of influences from abroad.

I shall now deal, in some detail with the influences which have reacted on India from outside and which have been responsible, to some extent, in making modern India what it is today. Among these outside influences, the first factor is the influence of Western thought which was crystallized in Liberalism, Constitutionalism and Democracy.

In other words, since 1857, modern liberal and democratic thought has been influencing the intellectuals of India to a large extent.

From the beginning of the present century, a new factor came into operation. After the victory of Japan over Russia in 1904-1905, the eyes of the Indian people were opened to a new movement in Asia—the movement for the revival of not merely of Japan-of other Asiatic countries. Since then, Indian thought has been greatly interested in Asiatic revival. During the last 40 years we have been thinking not merely of what was happening inside India, but also of what was happening in other parts of Asia.

Another important factor which had influenced our mind consisted of the struggles that have gone on in different parts of the world. Indian revolutionaries studied the Risorgimento Movement in Italy inder the leadership of Mazzini and Garibaldi and the struggle of the Irish people against their British oppressors. In Russia, before the last World War, there was, as you know, a movement against the Czar called Nihilist movement. That also was studied. And nearer India the new awakening of China under the leadership of Dr. Sun Yat-sen was also studied very closely and with great interest by the Indian revolutionaries.

Thus, Indian revolutionaries have been exceedingly receptive to the influences exerted by revolutionary struggles abroad. Then during the last World War, when the revolution broke out in Russia and, as a result of it, a new government-the Soviet Government-came into existence, the work of that Government was studied with great interest in our country.

People in India has not been interested so much in the Communist movement as in the work of reconstruction of Soviet Russia-in rapid industrialisation of that country and also in the way in which the Soviet Government solved the problems of the minorities. It is this constructive achievement of the Soviet Government which was studied with great interest by people in our country. As a matter of fact, intellectuals like our poet Tagore, who had no interest in Communism as such, were profoundly impressed when they visited Russia in the work of educational reconstruction in that country. Then there is another influence which came to India form outside in more recent times-I mean, the new movement in Europe headed by Italy and Germany called Fascism or National Socialism. This movement was also studied by our revolutionaries.

I have just dealt with some of the influences that have reached India form different parts of the world, form England, France, Japan, China, Russia, Germany and so on. I will now take up another question *viz.*, as to how we have reacted to these influences-how much we have accepted and how much we have rejected out of these outside influences. In dealing with this question of our reaction to these outside influences,

I must first point out that there is a big gulf between our generation and the last generation. As typical exponents of the last generation, I would like to mention Tagore and Gandhi. They represent for us the last generation, and between their thoughts and ideas and the thoughts and ideas of our generation there is a big gulf.

If you study the works of Tagore and Gandhi, you will find that all along there is a conflict in their minds as to what their reaction to the Western influence should be. So far as Mahatma Gandhi is concerned, he has never given us any clear solution this problem. He has left people in doubt as to what his attitude is toward the acceptance of Western ideas. Generally speaking, his attitude is one of antagonism. But in actual practice he has not always acted in accordance with his own ideas, the reason being that the rest of the countrie do not share that hostility or antagonism which Mahatma Gandhi personally has toward Western ideas and concepts.

You all know about Mahatma Gandhi's attitude on the question of violence of physical force. He does not advocate the use of arms, or the shedding of blood of the enemy for gaining one's freedom. This attitude towards violence or physical force is closely related to his general attitude toward foreign influence, particularly Western influence. Our generation has followed Mahatma Gandhi as the leader of a political struggle, but has not accepted his ideas on all these questions. Therefore, it would be a mistake to take Mahatma Gandhi as the exponent of the thoughts and ideas of the present generation in India.

Gandhi is in some ways a complex personality and I would like to analyze his personality, so that you may understand him better. In Gandhi, there are two aspects-Gandhi as a political leader and Gandhi as a philosopher. We have been following him in has capacity as a political leader, but we have not accepted his philosophy.

Now the question arises as to how we can separate the two aspects. Why, if we do not accept his philosophy, are we following him? Though Gandhi has his own philosophy of life, he is a practical politician and therefore, he does not force his own philosophy on the people. Consequently though we are following him in our political struggle, we are free to follow our own philosophy. If Gandhi had tried to thrust his philosophy on us, we would not have accepted him as a leader. But he has kept his philosophy separate from his political struggle.

I have mentioned as representatives and exponents of the last generation Tagore and Gandhi. Now let us compare their philosophies. There are some points in which they agree, but in some other points they do not. The points on which they agree are firstly, that they would like to see the national struggle being conducted with out the use of arms. In other words, on the question of physical force, they have the same views. On the question of industrialization of the country, they also have the same views. Both Tagore and Gandhi are against modern industrial civilisation. But in realm of culture, their views are not same. So far as thought, art and culture are concerned, Tagore is prepared to accept foreign influence. He believes that in the realm of culture there should be full cooperation between India and the rest of the World and there should be reciprocity. We should not be hostile or antagonistic to the culture or art or ideas of any other nation. In the realm of culture while Tagore advocates full cooperation between India and rest of the World, Gandhi's general attitude is antagonistic to foreign influence. We must however, remember that Mahatma Gandhi has nowhere given a very clear exposition of his views. I am only referring to his general attitude to this question.

I have previously remarked that there is a big gulf between the fundamental thoughts and ideas of the last generation and our generation. I will now explain what I meant thereby. As I have just said, this problem as to what our reaction should be toward foreign influence and toward industrial civilization troubled the leaders of the old generation all their lives and we see proofs of it in their actions. But, this problem does not exist for us. It does not exist for us, because our starting-point is that we want a modern India based of course on the past. We do not believe that India can achieve freedom with out the use of arms. Now once you take up this attitude, that for winning freedom we have to fight and use arms, it follows that we must have modern industries. What constituted the biggest problem for the old leaders constitutes our starting point. The problem for modern India is not our attitude toward modernism or foreign influence or industrialization, but how we are to solve our present-day problems.

I believe modern Japan will understand our generation much better than modern Japan understood the last generation in India. Our stand is virtually the same. We want to build up a new and modern nation on the basis of our old culture and civilization. For that we need modern industries, modern army and all those things necessary to preserve our existence and our freedom under modern conditions.

Having dealt with the fundamental standpoint of my generation. I will go on to discuss some of the detailed problems. For the present, of course, the biggest problem is how to fight and win this war. But that is a problem of which you are aware from what you have read in the papers or heard over the radio. I will now consider some of the problems of Free India. The moment India is free, the most important problem will be organizing of our national defence in order to safe guard our freedom in future. For that we shall have to build up modern war industries, so that we may produce the arms that we shall need for self-defence. This will mean a very big programme of industrialization.

After satisfying the needs of our nation in the matter of self-defence, the next problem in the degree of importance will be that of poverty and unemployment. India today is one of the poorest countries in the world, but India was not poor before we came under the British rule. In fact, it was the wealth of India which attracted the European nations to India. One cannot say that in the matter of national wealth or resources India is poor. We are rich in natural resources, but owing to British and foreign exploitation, the country has been impoverished. So our second most important problem will be how to give employment to the millions of unemployed in India and how to relieve the appalling poverty which now exists among the masses of the Indian people. The third problem in free India will be the problem of education. At present, under

British rule, about 90% of the people are illiterate. Our problem will be to give at least an elementary education to the Indian masses as soon as possible, and along with that to give more facilities to the intellectual classes in the matter of higher education.

Connected with the question of education is another problem which is important for India and that is the question of script. In India there are principally two scripts in vogue. One is the script known as Sanskrit (or Nagri) script and the other is Arabic (or Persian) script. Up till today in all national affairs and conferences we have been using both theses scripts. I must ad that in some provinces, there are scripts in vogue which are modifications of Sanskrit script. But fundamentally there are two scripts, and in all national affairs and conferences we have to use both these two scripts.

There is now a movement to solve this problem of scripts by using the Latin script. I personally am an advocate of the Latin script. Since we have to live in the modern world, we have to be in touch with other countries and whether we like it or not, we have to learn the Latin script. If we could make the Latin script the medium of writing throughout the country, that would solve our problem. Anyway that is my own view and the view of my closest friends and collaborators.

I have refereed to three important problems in Free India : National defence, how to remove poverty and how to give education to the people. If we are to solve these three important problems, how are we going to do it? Shall we leave it to private agency and private initiative or will the State take up the responsibility of solving these problems?

Well at present, public opinion in India is that we cannot leave it to private initiative to solve these national problems, especially the economic problem. If we leave it to private initiative to solve the problem of poverty and unemployment, for instance it will probably take centuries. Therefore, public opinion in India is in favour of some sort of socialist system, in which the initiative will not be left to private individuals, but the state will take over the responsibility for solving economic questions. Whether it is a question of industrializing the country or modernizing agriculture we want the State to step in and take over the responsibility and put through reforms within a short period, so that the Indian people could be put on their legs at a very early date. But in solving this problem we want to work in our own way. We will, naturally, study experiments made in other countries-but, after all, we have to solve our problems in an Indian way and under Indian conditions. Therefore, the system that we shall ultimately set up will be an Indian system to suit the needs of the Indian people.

Now if we do not tackle the economic question from the point of the view of the masses, the majority of who are poor, if we do not do that in India, we shall produce the same confusion or the same difficulties in our country, as we see in China today. You see in China today a split between Kuomintang and the Chinese Communist Party. Personally I do not see why this should have occurred or why, if Kuomintang Party has interests of Chinese masses at heart, there should be any need to have a separate party like the Communist Party under foreign influence.

Having learnt from experience, we do not want to repeat the mistake that China has made. We actually find today that because the nationalist movement in our generation has identified itself with the peasants who form more than 90% of the people, because we have their interests at heart, there is no raison d'etre for a separate party like the Communist Party. If the nationalists in India did not have the interests of the masses at heart, then you would have seen the same phenomenon as you see in China today.

Now we come to another question-namely, the political system or Government. If we are to have an economic structure of a socialistic character, then it follows that the political system must be such as to be able to carry out that economic programme un the best possible way. You can not have a so-called democratic system, if that system has to put through economic reforms on a socialistic basis. Therefore, we must have a political system-a State-of an authoritarian character. We have had some experience of democratic institutions in India and we have also studied the working of democratic institutions in countries like

France, England and the United States of America. And have come to the conclusion that with a democratic system we cannot solve the problems of a Free India. Therefore, modern progressive thought in India is in favour of a State of an authoritarian character, which will work as an organ, or as the servant of the masses, and not clique or of a few rich individuals.

That is our idea with regard to the political institution in Free India. We must have a government that will function as the servant of the people and will have full powers to put through new reforms concerning industry, education, defence, etc., in Free India.

Before I pass into the next problem, I should like to mention another point, namely the attitude of Free India toward religion and caste. This is a question that is frequently asked. India has several religions. Consequently, the Government of Free India must have an absolutely neutral and impartial attitude toward all religions and leave it to the choice of every individual to profess to follow a particular faith.

With regard to caste, that is now no problem for us, because caste, as it existed in the old times, does not exist today. Now, what is caste system? The caste system means that a community is divided into certain groups on a professional or vocational basis and marriage takes place within each group. In modern India there is no such caste distinction. A member of one caste is free to take up any other profession. So caste, in that sense does not exist today. Then there remains the question of marriage. In the old times, it was custom to marry within each caste. Nowadays, intermarriage between the different castes takes place freely. Hence caste is fast disappearing. As a matter of fact in the nationalist movement we never inquire as to what caste a man belongs to and we even do not know the caste of some of our closest collaborators, which shows that in our generation we do not think at all about caste. For Free India, therefore, caste is no problem at all.

In this connection, I should like to tell you that it was the British who created the impression throughout the world that we are a people quarrelling among ourselves, especially over religion. But that is an absolutely wrong picture of India. It may be that there are certain differences among the Indian people, but such differences you will find in every other country. If we take the so-called progressive countries of the world, *e.g.*, France before the outbreak of the present war, or Germany before Hitler and his Party came to power, you will find that there were acute differences among the people in these countries. Spain had even a first-class civil war.

But nobody ever says that, because the people in these countries had disputes and differences, they are not fit to rule themselves. It is only in case of India that the British say that, because there are certain differences among Indian people therefore they are not fit to be free. Again, the fact is that whatever differences there are among the Indian people are largely the creation of the British Government. There are hundreds of examples to show you that throughout the history of British rule, the British have tried by every possible means to divide the Indian people. After having done so much to artificially create differences among the Indian people the British turn around and say that we are not fit to be free.

I should also point out that if you take a modern power like Soviet Russia and see how heterogeneous the composition of the Soviet Union is, you will realise that if, in spite of this heterogeneous character, so many different races professing so many different religions could be unified in one political system and become such a strong Power, there is absolutely no reason why India which has much more homogeneity than the Soviet Union, should not be united as one nation. As a matter of fact, you will find that outside India, where there is no British influence, there are no differences among the Indian people. In the Independence Movement in East Asia and in the Indian National Army there is no question of religion or caste or class. It is just in India where the British have influence and control that you will find these differences.

On the question of National unity, I should like to give you a friendly warning that British propaganda tries to give the world the impression that the Muslims of India do not support the independence movement. This is wrong. Very often you read in the papers about certain organizations like the Muslim

League or the Hindu Mahasabha. The British boost these organizations, because they are in their policy pro-British and are against the Indian National Congress, and they try to make out that the Muslim League represents the Muslims of India. But that is British propaganda. The fact is that the Muslim League and its leader, Mr. Jinnah, represent only a minority of the Indian Muslims. The majority of the Indian Muslims are nationalists and they support the independence movement, as much as anyone else. The President of the Indian National Congress is a Muslim, and so are many other members of the congress, many of whom are in prison today. These facts are not known to the outside world and the outside world gets the impression that Mr. Jinnah represents all the Muslims of India and that they are not supporting the nationalist movement. So I would like to give out this warning about British propaganda.

I have already told you about the kind of economic and political system that we would like to have in Free India. Out of this, arises the problem as to what our political philosophy is. On this question, I gave my own views in a book I wrote about 10 years ago called "The Indian Struggle'. In that book I said that it would be our task in India to evolve a system that would be a synthesis of the systems in vogue in different parts of the world. For instance, if you take the conflict between Fascism (or what you might call National Socialism) on the one side and Communism on the other, I see no reason why we cannot work out a synthesis of the two systems that will embody the good points of both. It would be foolish for any one to say that any one system represents the last stage in human progress. As students of philosophy, you will admit that human progress can never stop and out of the past experience of the world we have to produce a new system. Therefore, we in India will try to work out a synthesis of the rival systems and try to embody the good points of both.

Now I would like to compare some of the good points of National Socialism and Communism. You will find some things common to both. Both are called anti-democratic or totalitarian. Both are anti-capitalistic. Nevertheless, in spite of these common points, they differ on other points. When we see National

Socialism in Europe today, what do we find? National Socialism has been able to create national unity and solidarity and too improve the condition of the masses. But it has not been able to radically reform the prevailing economic system which was built up on a capitalist basis.

On the other side, let us examine the Soviet experiment based on Communism. You will find one great achievement and that is planned economy. Where Communism is deficient is that it does not appreciate the value of national sentiment. What we in India would like to have is a progressive system which will fulfil the social needs of the whole people and will be based on national sentiment. In other words, it will be a synthesis of Nationalism and Socialism. This is some thing which has not been achieved by National Socialists in Germany today.

There are few points in which India does not follow Soviet Russia. Firstly, class conflict is some thing that is quite unnecessary in India. If the Government of free India begins to work as an organ of the masses, then there is no need for the class conflict. We can solve our problems by making the State the servant of the masses. There is another point which has been overemphasized by Soviet Russia and that is the problem of the working classes. India being predominantly a country of peasants, the problem of the peasants will be more important than the problem of the working classes.

Another point on which we do not fully agree is that, according to Marxism, too much importance is given to the economic factor in human life. We fully appreciate the importance of the economic factor which was formerly ignored, but it is not necessary to overemphasize it. To repeat once again our political philosophy should be a synthesis between National Socialism and Communism. The conflict between thesis and antithesis has to be resolved in a higher synthesis. This is what the law of the Dialectic demands. If this is not done, then human progress will come to an end. India will, therefore, try to move to the next stage of political and social evolution. I will now pass on the last point in my address, and that is our conception of an international order. On this point I have already spoken several times in Tokyo. I fully support the steps that have been taken through the Joint Declaration to create a new order in East Asia on the basis of freedom, justice and reciprocity. I have been personally greatly interested in international problems, having tried to work in several countries in order to get support for our movement and, in that connection; I also had the opportunity of studying the work of the League of Nations.

The experiment of the League of Nations has failed, and it is desirable and profitable for us to investigate as to why it failed. If I were to answer that I would say that it failed because the sponsor-nations were too selfish and short-sighted. The sponsor-nations were England, France and America. America dropped out of the League, so the Powers that controlled the League were England and France.

Now these two leading Powers, instead of setting an example of unselfishness, tried to use the League of Nations for their selfish interests and for their own benefit. The only basis on which we can set up an international order is freedom, justice and reciprocity. Therefore, the work in East Asia has commenced on the right lines and on the right basis. The only task that remains for us is to see that in actual work the principles embodied in the Joint Declaration are put into effect. If they are so put into effect, then the experiment will be a success. If not, then it will again prove to be a failure.

You must have seen in my speeches and press statements that I have been very enthusiastic about this Joint Declarations. There are several reasons. Firstly, it is on the right basis and on the right lines that the work has began. Secondly, if you want to set up an international order, it has to have a beginning in a particular region. If we make it a success in one region, it can gradually be expanded all over the world.

It is very difficult to set up a world order suddenly out of nothing and make it a success. But if you begin in one region where friendship and reciprocity between the nations can be developed, and if in that region you meet with success, then that example will be emulated by other nations in other parts of the world. So the method of setting up of a regional order is the only way in which a world order can gradually be built up.

The third reason is that I have found that this idea or plan find support among the mass of the people if this country, and especially among the youths. If I had found that this new order was being sponsored by a few politicians or leaders and that the rest of the nation was apathetic or indifferent, I should certainly not be optimistic. But it is because I have found that the people as a whole, and especially the youths are vitally interested in it and support it enthusiastically, that I believe that through the cooperation of the leaders and the people and the youths, it can be made a success. I should like to repeat that this undertaking is for the Government and the people of this country a very great responsibility. As you know, your Government was responsible for sponsoring this idea, so you are the sponsor-nation. The success of this experiment will depend on the example set by the sponsor-nation.

The League of Nations failed, because the sponsor-nations were selfish and short-sighted. This time if the nations that have joined together, and particularly the sponsor-nation, avoid a selfish and short-sighted policy and work on moral basis, then I see no reason why the experiment should not be a success.

I should like to emphasize again the tremendous responsibility which Japan has undertaken by becoming the sponsor-nation in this task. And when I talk of the responsibility of the nation, I want also to stress the responsibility of the youths. The youths of today will be the nation and leaders of tomorrow. An idea that is welcomed and supported by the youths will one day be supported by the whole nation. But an idea which does not find support among the youths will die a natural death. Therefore, their responsibility for making this new order a success devolves, in the last analysis, on the youths of this country. I hope and pray and trust that the youths and the students who are the future representatives of the nation will realise the tremendous moral responsibility which Japan has undertaken in initiating this new order.

There may be people who doubt whether a nation can rise to a high moral level, whether a nation can be farsighted and unselfish and undertake the work of establishing a new order. I have every faith in mankind. If it is possible for one individual to be unselfish, to live one's life at a high moral level, I see no reason why an entire nation cannot also rise to that level. In the history of the world we have seen examples in which a revolution has changed the mentality of a whole nation and made it rise to a high level of morality. Therefore, if anybody has any doubt whether an entire nation can rise to that level, then I do not share that doubt.

I repeat, in conclusion, that the sponsor-nation should realize the tremendous responsibility that it has undertaken. This is a task not only for the leaders and the politicians, but for the whole nation and especially for those who are the hopes of the nation-the youths and the students.

GLIMPSES OF NETAJI

Two questions which I am often asked about Netaji are, one about his personality and another about his life. The first question is, what was so exceptional in his ability which attracted and inspired those who came in touch with him? Whenever I am asked this question, I am reminded of the fable of "The Elephant and the blind men." Like one of those men I could not scan that great man Netaji Subhash Chandra Bose in totality. So before saying what I could perceive, let the reader allow me to look at him through the eyes of those who had better vision than I.

SA Ayer, Minister for Publicity and Propaganda of Azad Hind Government had this to say in his book *Unto him a witness*. "The title of Supreme Commander, if it truly fitted any commander on the battlefields of Europe or Asia, fitted Netaji most superbly. He looked supreme, every inch of him. The way he talked and moved with the soldiers on or off the war front was one of supreme dignity and self-confidence.

The word personality assumed a meaning when Netaji, in his Supreme Commander's Uniform, stepped on to the saluting base and faced the serried ranks of the INA. And yet, the uniform itself was the simplest in the world, no medals in a row, no shining leather belt or shoulder straps, nor a sword in its scabbard hanging from his waist, nor a horse ride. Whatever clothes he wore, he wore them smartly. Normally he wore khaki cotton clothes except when he visited Japan. There he had to use Khaki woollens as a protection against the severe cold weather. His forage cap with two tiny well polished brass buttons in the front sat majestically on his bright and broad forehead, the face beneath the cap of a rosy wheat complexion, now inscrutable. Immobile, dignified, now wreathed in a charming smile, now reminded one of the Bengal Tiger as when he roared an inspiring exhortation to soldiers or civilians at mammoth gatherings.

It was impossible to take one's eyes of his face whenever he ascended the platform; he held one spellbound by its compelling magnetism ...."

Now let me show another glimpse of Netaji's creative qualities when he drafted the Proclamation of the Provisional Government of Azad Hind. After a long busy day, a day just earlier to 21st October 1943, it was past midnight. This is what Ayer says:

> *"Then I witnessed a phenomenon. I had glimpse of the great man. He took hold of a bunch of quarter-sheets of blank paper, took pencil in hand and started writing, 'After their first defeat in the hands of the British in 1757 in Bengal ....'*

He did not lift his eyes from the paper in front of him, silently handed to me the first page as soon as he finished it, and I walked out of the room and sat at the type writer. Abid and Swami went to his room in turn and brought me the Proclamation manuscript, sheet after sheet, as Netaji finished it. What amazed me was that he never even once wanted to see any earlier pages that he had written. How he could remember every word that he had written in the preceding pages, how he could remember the sequence of the paragraphs? In the entire script there was not one word corrected or scored out, and the punctuation was complete.

That he wrote out the whole proclamation sheet after sheet without break and at one sitting was some measure of

Netaji's clear thinking, remarkable memory and grasp and facile pem! The entire historic proclamation was written with the ease with which a brief letter could be penned."

The proclamation shows Netaji's extraordinary grasp of history.

Alexander Werth, one of the important Liaison Officers at the Free India Centre, in Chapter Four, "Planning for Revolution-1941-1943", in the book, *A Beacon Across Asia*, edited by Sisir K Bose, Alexander Werth and SA Ayer (published by Orient Longman) has observed (page 127):

> *"Those who observed Bose during these years were all greatly impressed by the fact he succeeded so well in convincing all his co-workers-both Indian and German-about the great importance of the work they were doing and inspiring them with a sense of mission, common objectives and mutual cooperation. Whenever there were differences of opinion or misunderstanding or even quarrels amongst his colleagues, he showed his remarkable capacity of keeping the thread of all activities of his political, military and technical co-workers in his hands so that the over all control of the whole organisation remained with him. He was the driving spirit behind all activities of the Free India Center. He succeeded in doing so much inspite of the fact that the organisation that he built up was something between an official mission and a provisional government and no so fully recognized association of a group of exiles from India."*

Earlier, after his arrival in Berlin, Netaji went under the name of Orlando Mazzota for quite some time. He intended to remain in anonymity till he could bring round the Axis Powers to declare that the Independence of India was among their war aims. He also did not wish the British to know about his whereabouts. Without going into details of how difficult his task was, let me quote HN Pandit's work-*Netaji Subhash Chandra Bose from Kabul to Battle of Imphal* (Sterling Publishers Limited-Page 38):

For the whole story we have to turn to the narration of MR Vyas who was one of the first four associates of Netaji in Germany when Bose was still known as Orlando Mazzotta.

"It seems an emissary of the Foreign Office went to Badgastein (where Bose was staying) with the German Government's request for cooperation. Subhash thanked the German Government for the proposal and added that the collaboration would have to be based on a very well defined agreement. His terms were:

For all purpose of negotiation, India should be regarded as a completely sovereign state of which he would be the representative until such time as the Indian people could finally constitute their own Government on their own soil.

While India remained subjugation, he (Netaji) should have facilities for a separate free establishment of his own with the status of a diplomatic representative attached to the Head of a sovereign state.

For the finances of such a set up, the German Government should advance an interest free loan which would be repayable by India after the termination of hostilities.

The loan so granted must be without any condition and the expenditure for the same must be subject to diplomatic immunity.

Any broadcasts, any publications or any publicity to be carried on by the establishment so contemplated, must not be subject to any German censorship even though the same may have to be carried on from territories of Germany under her occupation.

Recruitment to any National Army to be raised would be made solely by Indians or representatives duly approved by the head of the state, i.e. Subhash Chandra Bose. The oath of allegiance by the members of the Army would be to Subhash Chandra Bose who as the Head of the Sovereign State of India, would also be the Commander-in-chief of all India armed forces.

Though apparent from above, still it must be specially agreed that the Indian forces, while operating in any joint sub-command, must not be deployed on any front other than against the British or other troops under the British command subject to any unforeseen military entanglements. While the free India establishment and its forces would support all anti British actions, it would not ipso facto consider itself at war with the other allies of Great Britain.

The Nazis were flabbergasted to see the terms. Were these conditions of a powerless one-man state for cooperation with the Reich? The man must be cut to size. The task was assigned to one of Ribbentrop's senior officers who came to meet Bose in the Foreign Office with an SS Colonel accompanying him in the mission. The following account of the conversation which took place has been given by Vyas:

> *"Your Excellency", Ribbentrop's officer began, "While we realise on many questions, don't you think that after your having come here, there could be no activity of any kind unless the German government voluntarily agrees to it?"*

Subhash Chandra Bose replied: "Do you mean that you could put me in prison if I do not agree to work on your terms?"

"Certainly not, Your Excellency", the SS Colonel interposed, "but you would be incapacitated and will have to remain inactive."

Bose: "If I wanted to remain inactive I would have remained in a British prison. But this war provides a unique chance for my country to be free. So I would rather go else where or even to India and fight from there, come what may."

The Foreign Office representative commented sarcastically, "But Your Excellency, even for leaving Germany, you will require our permission, isn't it?"

Apparently the officer bargained for more than he could afford, because the reply that came stunned him. : "Sir, I have heard a lot about your Gestapo. Probably the gentleman here is a representative of that body. But believe me, the British CID in India is no less efficient and ruthless. And if I have failed them and escaped, I shall do the same here. I have not come here to live the life of an exile. Gentleman, I think we shall leave it at that."

The meeting came to an end abruptly.

This happened in the second half of October 1941. For two days nothing happened. Then Ribbentrop (the Minister for Foreign affairs) had a meeting with Subhash Chandra Bose in a very friendly way. Shortly afterwards an official communication arrived that fuehrer (Hitler) had approved the civil parts of Netaji's terms from points 1 to 5. The decision on the military points too followed in due course of time with some minor modifications. Vyas says that although there was tough bargaining in the beginning, once the agreement was signed, the Germans honoured it in letter and spirit.

The Free India Center with the status of a diplomatic mission was established with its office in Lichtensteiner Allee, opposite to the Spanish Embassy in Berlin's diplomatic enclave. After having lived in various hotels, Subhash Chandra Bose was allotted a villa in the Charlottenburg area of Berlin. Before the out break of the war, this house was occupied by the military attache to the American Embassy.

The work of the Free India Center began with a few Indian Volunteers, mainly students. To start with, they were MR Vyas, NG Gunpulay, NG Swamy, Habib-ur-Rehman, Abid Hassan Safrani and one or two more. It can be said that more than a diplomatic mission, the Free India Center worked like the secretariat of a Government to be free. India movement came to be called Azad Hind, with its emblem of Tricolour with the springing tiger and Jana Gana Mana adopted Hindi words *Subh Sukh Chain Ki Barkha Barse*-without any alteration in the tune. Jai Hind was adopted as the greetings amongst the Indian nationals. It gave us a special identity as members of one nation irrespective of many religions and races. Our leader Subhash Chandra Bose was addressed by the members of the Azad Hind as Netaji. This title owes its introduction to the members of the Azad Hind Free India Centre. In Hindustani, 'Neta' means leader, the suffix 'Ji' is a common word of respect and courtesy used among equals and among the high and low alike. It sounds of closeness between the person addressed and the addresser in contrast to words like *Hazoor, Sahib, Janab, Nawab-e-Aala, Janab-e-Aali, Sahib Bahadur, Shriman, Sarkar, Alijab, Hukum*, etc. The word Netaji became so popular that it immediately reminds one of Netaji Subhash Chandra Bose. There have been 'netas', many of them will come and go but Netaji will remain only one and one only Netaji Subhash Chandra Bose.

BOSE IN TOKYO

About Netaji's early days in Tokyo, Dr. Joyce Lebra in her book, Jungle Alliance has this to say: "After several week on a submarine Bose was exhausted and in need of rest. But he had one aim in Tokyo, an obsession. He had to meet Premier Tojo. Yamamoto after a few days arranged meetings with Army Chief of Stuff Sugiyama, Foreign Minister Shigemitsu, Navy Minister Yonai, and various section chiefs of the Army, Navy and Foreign Ministers. Bose's opening words to Sugiyama took the Chief of Stuff by surprise. "The war will end in victory for Japan!" Bose boomed. Japan was in the midst of adverse circumstances in Guadacanal and the campaign was obviously not going well for Japan, perhaps Bose's statement was a material resource. Bose continued with out waiting for a response from the bemused Chief of Staff, "Will Japan send soldiers to India or not? We are going to fight our way to India step by step. If we don't push on with determination we won't be able to achieve Independence."

"The immediate reaction of Sugiyama was that Bose had none on the humility or reserve a Japanese would have shown in such an interview. But there was no doubting his sincerity of his aims. He was a known quantity, whatever Operations Bureau of IGHQ thought of his value to Japan. Sugiyama, despite his interest and sympathy derived from two year's experience in India, could only respond to Bose with a briefing about Japan's current military position. Bose, dissatisfied with Sugiyama's general discussion, explained with great fervour his hope of first taking Chittagong, then pushing on into Bengal. Sugiyama assured Bose of his sympathy with Bose's aspirations, and Bose's first interview in Tokyo ended more calmly than it had begun. But Bose was dissatisfied. He had to meet Tojo and get Japanese commitment. Yamamoto, meanwhile acting as a guide for Bose, for ten days escorted him through factories, schools and hospitals, trying to distract his attention from Tojo and keep him occupied. Bose was impressed with what he saw but not deterred from his object.

"Why was Tojo putting Bose off? In the first place, there were many other pressing military problems than India, and Tojo's please that he was too busy were not simply excuses. Secondly, there was group in the Operations Bureau of IGHQ which took a dim view of India and the INA. The INA had no direct relevance to military strategy and operations in Pacific or even Southeast Asia, and there was no proof of Bose's propaganda impact within India in any case. But the main reason for Tojo's reluctance to meet Bose was Tojo's own often formed opinion of a man before meeting him. The INA had been only a headache so far as Tojo was concerned. The trouble between Mohan Singh and Rash Behari Bose had disposed Tojo unfavourably towards the INA. And the demands in the Bangkok Resolution Tojo regarded as presumptuous. How could a small revolutionary group which did not even represent a government presume to make demands on the Imperial Government of Japan? There was no need for Tojo to meet another Indian, even if he had just come from Berlin.

"It was persuasion by Sugiyama and Shigemitsu which at length prevailed on Tojo to meet Bose. On 10th June the first of the two meetings took place. The magic of Bose enhanced Tojo immediately. It had been the same with Sugiyama, Shigemitsu and nearly everyone Bose met, whether Japanese or Indians. Apart from the impact of Bose's words and passionate devotion to Indian Independence, there was some thing about his face, his voice and his eyes that captured the minds and hearts of men. Tojo was enthralled.

The meeting was brief but fruitful exchange of views, between Bose and Tojo. Tojo explained Japan's ideas on the Greater East Asia Co-Prosperity Sphere. Bose, with his customary frankness, asked Tojo, "Can Japan give unconditional help to the Indian independence movement? I would like to confirm that there are no strings attached to Japanese aid." Tojo immediately gave Bose an affirmative reply. Bose continued, "Can the Japanese army push its operations into India proper?" This time there were complex military matters involved, and Tojo was unable to answer as decisively. But Bose had been favourably impressed and was grateful he had made a friend in Tojo. If Bose was to secure meaningful help from Japan for the INA, Tojo's sympathy and cooperation was the crucial point. In this Bose had succeeded admirably, and Tojo was ready to make public his official support to Bose and the INA.

On 16 June Bose visited the House of Peers in the 82nd Extraordinary Session of the Diet. Tojo made a historic address on the Greater East Asia Co-Prosperity Sphere which attracted attention outside Japan. Bose listened intently in the audience to interpreters as Tojo said, "India has been for centuries under cruel rule. We wish to express righteous indignation at their agony and sympathy for their aspirations for complete independence. We firmly resolve that Japan will do everything possible to help Indian independence, I am convinced the day of Indian freedom and prosperity is not far off..." Tojo spoke too of the emancipation of all of East Asia. This was not Tojo's first mention of India in the Diet. Early in 1942 he had spoken of the Pacific war as an opportunity for India to rise against British Rule. But, this time when Tojo promised aid and cooperation for Indian Independence Bose was listening in his audience and felt Tojo was making him a promise which he would follow through."

In the 11th Chapter of this treatise I narrated how cool, fearless and graceful was Netaji under fire. Now I wish to portray in General Shah Nawaz Khan's own words from his book, My Memories of INA & Its Netaji (Rajkamal Publications, Delhi-page 179) another picture of Netaji under fire. "He listened to me very calmly, because he knew that all that I said came from the very depths of my heart and was prompted by my extreme anxiety for his safety, he just smiled and said, "Shah Nawaz, it is no use pleading with me, I have made up my mind to go to Popa and I am going there. You don't have to worry about my safety, as I know England has not yet produced the bomb that can kill Subhash Chandra Bose." This last statement appeared particularly true, as Netaji seemed to lead a charmed life. That afternoon the place he was living in was heavily bombed by Sixty B-25. They caused terrible devastation all around, and it was difficult to imagine how Netaji escaped with out even a scratch. All of us had failed to persuade Netaji not to proceed any further, but once he had made up his mind no one could change it."

Dr. Ba Maw, the War time President of Myanmar wrote a paper which was read out on his behalf at Netaji Research Bureau, Calcutta on one of the Netaji's Birthdays. I reproduce some of the excerpts out of it as under:

> *"Taking a historical view now that the time has made it possible, Netaji is by any measure an Asian figure whose shadow stretched out across the whole of this part of the world during the last war and has remained there ever since. As one who was with him throughout most of the war years, I assure you that I what I have just said is true. I myself have seen it happen. I witnessed almost from the beginning to end Netaji's work and achievements during those years, how he moulded out of the rawest possible materials lying scattered throughout all Southeast Asia an Independent Indian State and Government and Army and made them a positive force in the World War. A single mind and will turned a dream into a reality. It purposed the Indian dream across half of the world, through the Middle East, and then into Russia and Germany, then to the furthest edge of Asia, and finally to Burma and or a few delirious weeks and his dream set aflame the hearts of three million of his countrymen who answered his call from every office and bazaar and workshop throughout Southeast Asia and gave him practically everything he asked for within an year of Bose's coming. Azad Hind was a full fledged state recognized by nine other states; it had acquired a large part of territory; its armies were*

fighting on eight sectors of Burma-India border and soon set foot on Indian soil, proudly planted the flag of free India on it and came within a few inches of winning a decisive victory there when all that really forged out of a single dream crashed together with half of the world."

Dr. Ba Maw goes on: "However to say something, I asked Netaji what he intended to do next. "Why", he replied calmly lighting a cigarette. "Start again and go on fighting when ready. What else can we do? The fight certainly has to go on." These were echoed my own thoughts so much that I nearly wept to hear them. In my case of course, with Burma and Burmese Army in the hand of the British and nothing ready in my hands I would not be able to do any thing, at least for some time. I explained that to Netaji and he understood completely. Later I heard that he told his men, "Now that Germany and Italy are out of the war, we must continue it with the Japanese as long as they are still in it; and if they too are knocked out we must fight on by ourselves." Those words spoken during the greatest crisis of his life sum up the essential spirit and character of the man. Time masses and powerful men in their day come and go, and a few of them, a very few, leave behind memories which live on and even grow by themselves with the years. Such men become part of the ultimate story of their people. There is every reason to believe that Subhash Chandra Bose is among those few men, I need not say more."

Netaji's personality appealed so much to us that he would ever remain and live as a superhuman hero in imagination of not only us who has the good luck to work with him but also in the imagination of our people. His spirit of patriotism is bound to manifest itself in the future generations and serve not only India and Asia but also the world. His very name commanded our subconscious mind without knowing and thus brought out the latent good lying deep down in and individual. Imagine a jawan having been awarded death punishment for committing heinous crime, i.e. rape and when given the option to appeal to Netaji against my award, the man cried out, "No sir, shoot me here rather than sending me to Netaji. Now I have no face which I can show him (ab main Netaji ko kya moonh dikhaunga?)

I am reminded of the man who when admonished by his Section Commander for exposing himself to the enemy fire, the raw recruit retorted, "How can I be killed today when Netaji himself has sent me a pair of boots?" It was that confidence in Netaji which made us face a enemy superior to us in all respects. In his book *Builders of Modern India-Subhash Chandra Bose* (Dr. Girija K Mookerjee (Publications Division, Ministry of Information and Broadcasting, Government of India) on page 104 says:

> *"The question to all of us is then: Will Subhash be remembered by the generations to come? I think he will. At least it was for this recompense that his restless soul traversed oceans and foreign lands in search of an answer to India's freedom. It is too horrible to think that he is no longer amongst us, to his colleagues he will remain ever alive, ever green and immoral. He imposed on them his vivid personality so well and they at least will not forger him so long as they live, but I hope those who will come after them will also gratefully remember this magnificent man, born to be a 'grand signeur' who lived and died so that India could be great and so that men and women of our race may have not to be born into this world with the stigma of being a subject people and not free and independent as we are today".*
>
> *Long back in the thirties, Rabindranath Tagore called Netaji* Deshnayak-*Leader of the Country. During the INA crisis when General Seizo Arisue, Second-in-Command of the Japanese Imperial Army General Staff invited Rash Bihari Bose in order to know his mind about Netaji's coming and discreetly asked, "Netaji is desirous of coming over here and I wonder how you would treat him." The old revolutionary quietly replied, "Netaji is a born leader of Leader's. I shall of course be quiet pleased to ask him to take over from me." I am also reminded of a conversation with General Fujiwara*

> *during my visit to Japan in Autumn 1974, we were passing along General Tojo's house reminiscing of the war days. I asked the General about Prime Minister Tojo's opinion about Netaji. Fujiwara replied that General Tojo was so much impressed by Netaji that he said, 'If there exists a man of the Century, he is one whom I met today." Fujiwara believed that if Netaji had arrived in the East earlier, we would have won the war.*

After citing the above impressions of some of the great men who happen to see Netaji from a close range, now I will try to sum up my answer to the questions as under:

> *Netaji practiced what he preached. There was never any difference in his words and deeds*-unki kathni aur karni mein koi farak na tha.

Netaji cared not only for the honour, welfare and comfort of his but also respected their feelings. He had a compassionate nature. He overwhelmed us with his concern for us individually and collectively, like sending a pair of boots to a sepoy with instructions to Regimental Commander to see personally that it fitted the man and report back to Netaji, offering a cigarette case to a veteran commander from Imphal, helping his own staff officers to wash hands, shedding tears with immediate steps to supply relief. Such spontaneous feelings coming out of his heart made him extraordinarily a rare leader of men in war. His men felt happy, proud and lucky to do and die under his command. It was this relationship which kept up our morale in spite of all our difficulties and deficiencies.

Netaji's knowledge of history of wars fought on different battlefields of the world could easily surpass the knowledge of any seasoned General. He read a lot and did his homework on the subject and he had to deal with. When we had to see anybody he would learn all about the person and his problems before the interview. The result was that the man could go back happy and contented that the Supreme Commander knew him intimately. An interview with Netaji went a long way in creating that confidence without which it is impossible to wage a revolutionary war. He had a gift of judging the character of a man which served him to put the right man at the right place at the right time in the right job. He picked up some of us from the dust and made heroes out of us.

He never failed to appreciate when appreciation was due. A good word from him made us to strive to do our job well. He had a very kind heart, so kind that he never punished anybody. He always gave a defaulter an advice so that the defaulter could improve himself.

He had remarkable power of observation and could predict any eventuality correctly. Once he wrote a small note to me on the margins of a routine order. It was scribbled in his own hand. He told me that as the mail was getting ready to be dispatched, he wanted to advice me that instead of expecting the enemy at a particular point which I had reported in my previous report, I should also watch at a point. He gave 6 figured map reference. The note was written in Rangoon about 500 kms away from me. When I received it I was surprised at the accuracy of Netaji's judgment. I was already facing the enemy where he had told me to watch. This was measure of Netaji's skill at generalship. Again, I am reminded of my conversation with him when he gave me the command of The Nehru Brigade-4, the Guerrilla Regiment. I said, 'Netaji, may I know how long will it take me to get in touch with the enemy?"

Netaji's reply was, "Well, you are already on the foremost defended locality. There are no positions held between you and the enemy. It all depends on how long the enemy takes to reach the Irrawaddy. The initiative lies with them. You may be lucky to get sixty or seventy days before you are attacked, I guess."

Netaji's guess was accurate. I took my command in mid November 1944. I got to grips with the enemy in February 1945. Another example of Netaji's military foresight is when in March 1939 during the annual session, he proposed that the Congress should at once send ultimatum to the British Government demanding independence with in six months and should prepare immediately for a national struggle. The proposal was opposed by the rightist leaders. Netaji's proposal was based on appreciation of the European situation which was some thing beyond the understanding of our political leaders. But Netaji's prediction turned out to be correct.

The war did break out within six months on 3rd September 1939. Similarly Netaji's of repeated statement, "There is no power on earth that can keep India enslaved. India shall be free and before long." The enemy officers used to mock at the statement which they thought was illusory and face-saving device. Actually Netaji had a plan which was beyond the comprehension of professional soldiers. He kept the INA in the field even in the face of defeat. He wanted us to pay the price of liberty not only when we were on advance but also during the retreat while going away from India not to win a territory but to continue fighting against the British forces who were holding India in perpetual bondage. These forces consisted of a greater number of the Indian soldiers who paused and pondered as to why the INA with their poor strength and poorer equipment yet higher spirit were fighting against the British. It created a psychological revolution. The war ended and with it ended the slavish mentality of the Indian soldier. When the British started the INA trials in the Red Fort they thought that the Indian people, especially the soldiers would appreciate the British action against the INA officers. Reverse was the case.

As soon as the first INA trial of the three front line commanders started on 5th November 1945, within a week disturbances broke out in Lahore, then in Lucknow and in Calcutta where hundreds of demonstrators were injured and twenty killed by the police firing. Even after the first INA trial in which the three accused officers were released by the Commander in Chief, the public demand to stop the future INA trials continued. Anti British Raj feelings kept on rising unabated. The climax came with the mutiny of the Royal Indian Navy in Bombay during February 1946. There were further disturbances in Royal Indian Air Force in Karachi and certain units of the Armed forces in Jabalpore. The British Top brass were for a strict action. The British were however lucky that Field Marshal Sir Claude Auchinleck, the Commander in Chief in India could read the writing in the wall. Netaji's stratagem had transformed the British Indian Army into the Indian Army. The days of the British Raj in India were close to their end.

Having shown Netaji's powers of Generalship which turned the defeat of the INA into the defeat of the British Raj, let me record that another great asset in Netaji's being was that he was at once secular. Whatever our religion and the area or the situation of our birth, we had full confidence that we would get absolute justice from him and his Government-the forerunner of our Government today. To show how his mind worked in this direction, his brief but an all-embracing idea of independence is shown in distilled form in the last but one para of the Proclamation of the Provisional Government of Azad Hind :

> *" The provisional Government is entitled to, and hereby claim the allegiance of every Indian. It guarantees religious liberty, as well as equal rights and equal opportunities to all its citizens. It declares its firm resolve to pursue the happiness and prosperity of the whole nation and all its parts, cherishing all the children of the nation equally and transcending all the differences cunningly fostered by an alien government in the past."*
>
> *JAI HIND*

Netaji-The Leader with a Mission

Writing about Netaji Subhash Chandra Bose is a journey down memory lanes, a journey that's both painful and exhilarating: painful in the way he was taken away from us before he could see his dreams come true and I am filled with an overwhelming feeling of sadness because he is still being missed today; exhilarating in the way my admiration for this great man grows day by day.

He certainly had an extraordinary aura that was difficult to ignore. He touched the lives of thousands of Indians in the manner in which he lived. To me, Netaji has been a source of great inspiration, a way to live life sans fear. He personified the courage never to yield. He had the mettle to swim against the tide. He won people's hearts by the sheer force of his personality and he commanded energies beyond the average I have never known anybody with his strength of will. He was formidable in so many ways: as a reformer, a revolutionary leader, and administrator, a statesman, an ambassador, a planner...How many talent is it fair for one man to have! I remember Netaji as a man of magnetic charm, a man of iron will, determination, dedication, discipline, immense stamina and a proclivity for hard work. He acquired the reputation of being different. And more importantly he was a man who possessed that elusive quality-strength of character.

Character is about deciding the course of your life and staying by it, no matter what comes in the way. It was well known that he revolted against anything that was not fair to human. As a student in the Presidency College, be became involved in beating up of Professor Oaten who had apparently mishandled a student. Whether young Bose was directly involved or not is not known, but his leadership was taken for granted and he was expelled form College in 1916. This incident had an everlasting impact in the mind of this proud under graduate: in his own eyes he became a victim of racial prejudice. Racial hatred ate into his soul and he made it his mission to show himself and India superior to the white-faced foreigner.

A year later he joined the Scottish Church Collage and took to studies with a new zest. He joined the University unit of the Territorial Army and put on a soldiers uniform. His military training was to stand him in a good stead when 25 years later he led an armed revolt against the British. It can be safely said that the Scottish Church College has done much in producing a person of his calibre.

Again when he decided to give up the coveted ICS service and dedicate himself to the service of the Motherland, he knew he was taking a major decision of his lifetime. He said, "I must either chuck this rotten service and dedicate myself wholeheartedly to the country's cause, or I must bid adieu to all my ideas and aspirations." To the Under-Secretary of State of India he said, "...I did not think that one could be loyal to the British Raj and yet serve India honestly, heart and soul." The bell rang in his heart, India calling. And the rest is history.

Later in life when Netaji arrived on the Indian scene, the going was tough and those who appeared though couldn't get going. He brought in a different mind set altogether. When the whole nation was singing hosannas of Gandhiji and his doctrine of Ahimsa, Netaji was marching to the beat of a different drum-armed combat. He had a little or no faith in the idea of nonviolence. He felt that the British would understand only the language of the sword and any inaction on the part of the Indians would be inferred as weakness, as a sign of subordination. He had seen what revolution had accomplished in the other parts of the world. He sought to instil this fighting sprit among all Indians. He was dreamy. He was unconventional. The masses sensed the mood. Scepticism turned to admiration, criticism lost out to felicitations. He no longer looked ordinary. He looked different. In Netaji there were courage and mission: he possessed one and pursued the other. That's a powerful combination. His perseverance paid of. It was the beginning of a new dawn.

Character is about staying calm in the face of adverse crisis. Whatever the danger, Netaji was always a picture of calm and control. He missed death by inches several times and yet remained unperturbed. Once when he along with Major Abid Hassan was travelling by submarine from Germany to Japan, they were attacked by Allied submarines several times and at times the danger was great but Netaji remained a picture of calm. He coolly turned to Abid Hassan to whom he was dictating a letter and asked him, "... Hassan Sahib, what is the last word you have taken down...". Such control is indeed rare to find. Physically her was weak but his mental stamina proved to be his major strength.

Character is about hanging in there and taking your chances. He took the chance on things other people won't. This proved to be his forte. Look at the way he escaped from India in 1941. When the Second World War broke out, he decided to make his move. The long wait had been worth the while, for Netaji sent out the unequivocal message that he was indeed a man of thought and action, that he meant business which for the British implied that their days in India were numbered. The breakthroughs, the things that save countless lives and change history have never come from conventional wisdom.

They have never come from playing safe. His escape was bold, daring and risky, dramatic and high voltage. Everything planned to the smallest detail. Netaji took his chance when it came and won the game.

Character is about being humane. The touchingly human side of this great man shines through small incidents. The way in which he would care for us, the INA Tokyo cadets, is still fresh in my mind. He would give us his share of food because he knew that it was in short supply and also because he thought we needed it more. In his letters to us, each word that he wrote touched a chord in our hearts and we wept with joy and love for this great leader of ours. This compassionate concern shown by Netaji drew us even closer to him, so much so that we were willing to gamble with our lives at his demand. During the war when the INA soldiers were given the option of surrendering, they embraced death with a smile and with cries of Jai Hind! There were some who wouldn't allow their wounds to be attended to because they recalled Netaji's promise, "Give me blood and I shall give you freedom...!" these men believed that by bleeding to death, they were being of service to Mother India. Such unshakable faith in their leader!

In today's times, forget following you leader, we don't even have an iota of respect for them. Our ancestors handed down a legacy of knowledge and wisdom, character and integrity, values they had imbedded form their forefathers, thinkers, sages scholars. We, the present generation, have wasted away all those primary values that are imperative for the growth of any nation. We have squandered the lessons that Netaji wanted to teach us. Lessons of valour, Lessons of self-discipline, Lessons of patriotism, Lessons of self-service. This he learnt form the great Swami Vivekananda. He was greatly influenced by the writings of the Swami who propagated salvation through service to humanity. How selflessly he did service to Mother India is evident in all his actions. Vivekananda's teachings also helped him in his years of imprisonment where he learnt to think and not to brood.

He was truly a unique phenomenon. A man who aroused thousands of Indians with his one resounding battle-cry of

'Delhi Chalo". There was something in his words that went beyond mere words. There was passion. There was sincerity. There was confidence. He was the true Neta, one who was able to command the respect of his men. In his speech of the INA in Singapore of 5th July 1943, he said, "For the present, I can offer you nothing except hunger, thirst, privation, forced marches and death. But if you follow me in life and death...I shall lead you to victory and freedom." To this great man we must give due credit for he made heroes out of ordinary men, students, shopkeepers the common man. He formed the Balak Sena comprising of young boys and inculcated in them the sprit of patriotism, discipline and pride of being Indian.

His respect and belief in the womenfolk of our country led to the formation of woman's regiment-The Rani of Jhansi Regiment-and it played an active part in the war. He told them, "...When I express my confidence that you are today prepared to fight and suffer for the sake of your mother land, I do not mean only to cajole you with empty words. I know the capabilities of our womanhood well. I can, therefore, say with certainty that there is no task which our women cannot undertake and no sacrifice and suffering which our women cannot undergo...". Under him the women never lagged behind anybody and along with the men folk they also faced lathi charge by the merciless British Police and faced privations of prison life, torture and humiliations. This army did the services of Florence Nightingale and fought fearlessly like the famous Joan of Arc.

Netaji also formed the Reconstruction Brigade where he hired doctors, lawyers, administrators and engineers and involved them in all activities in the freedom movement. He made arrangements with the Japanese authorities to send students to Japan for further training. I was among the 45 students selected by Netaji himself for the training. Till this day I treasure the moments spent with Netaji and my souvenirs include letters written by Netaji to us. He was able to mobilize not just resources but total involvement of all Indians. Such was his charisma. He was also able to restore the lost confidence of 40,000 demoralised soldiers who had surrendered to Japan. He found in them a wealth of conscience and in his own way prepared them for the ultimate sacrifice for the prestige of our country. They fought many heroic battle for which the present generation should be proud of.

He was very clear in his mind that the path he had adopted was strewn with difficulties and even death. He said, "...It does not matter who among us will live to see India Free. It is enough that India shall be free and that we shall give our all to make her free...". While the army could not march to Delhi victorious, it had succeeded in its intent of arousing the sentiments of the Indians in India and more important, the Indian soldiers in the British Indian Army. These men met their own countrymen in the battle field but on opposite sides. Seeing the courage and the spirit of sacrifice of the INA men, the Indian soldiers had a change of heart. They, who so far had pledged their allegiance to the British, now rose up in revolt. When these two and a half million Indian soldiers revolted, the British Army was thrown out of gear. Netaji's giant suicide squad had done what it had set out for. While the INA had lost the war, they had won a moral victory. This revolt of the soldiers was followed by the RIN mutiny lead by courageous Punnu Khan. And then there was the public trial of the INA men at the Red Fort-an episode that spelled doom for the British. It was a disaster waiting to happen. The trial inflamed the passion of all Indians and the British realised, albeit late, that they had lost.

Netaji is truly one of the greatest leaders that India has ever produced. He was a man who was focused. India's freedom was uppermost in his mind and nothing, absolutely nothing could come in between him and his cause. Not even his failing health or the fear of death. His single minded devotion to the cause of India's liberation is truly a lesson for all of us to learn. He said, "...Let us all stand shoulder to shoulder and say with one heart and with one voice that our motto is, as Tennyson said through Ulysses, to strive, to seek, to find and not to yield." This became his credo. And it was this faith that he was able to instil into his men. He told them, "From today you are the soldiers of the Indian national Army of Free India. You have volunteered to shoulder the responsibility of 40 crore of Indians.

Form today your mind, might and money belongs to the Indian nation."

He again said, "...Your names will be written in golden letters in the history if free India. Every soldier who is martyred in this holy war will have a monument in free India. The coming generations will shower flowers on those monuments. You are very fortunate that you have got this valuable opportunity to serve the mother land..." Well this was the way Netaji thought we Indians will remember those martyrs. But no, those brave soldiers who died fighting for the freedom of our motherland are today forgotten. Their sacrifices have been sidelined. It is tragic that even our leader Netaji has not been given his due place in the history. His life has been a chronicle of continuous endeavours and relentless toil.

He was truly an extraordinary may whose only burning desire was to shake off the shackles of colonial rule. This worthy man shed his blood, suffered immensely and died for our freedom, our prosperity and our well being. It is almost as if he said to his future children: here's my gift for you. But look at the condition that India is in today. In his address to an independence day meeting in Berlin on 26th January, 1943 he said, "... And India is a country where the past has not been forgotten, but where our past history and tradition live in our blood and the marrow of our bones. It is because of this national self-consciousness that neither political domination nor economic impoverishments have been able to kill our soul..." Such sterling words form this great man. He was one leader whose style of functioning was worth imitating, whose ideas worth adopting and whose examples worth following. But today we have buried our past. We have not made use of the wisdom of the past.

Netaji's skills as a diplomat left many of his contemporaries astounded. The manner in which he dealt with Hitler-even while requesting for help from Germany he minced no words in telling Hitler that he did not approve of his treatment of Jews-leaves one with no doubt of his courage and abilities as a diplomat. The Japanese Prime Minister Tojo was so enamoured by his engaging personality and sincerity that he granted him all his requests including the formation of the Provisional

Government of Free India and handing over Andaman and Nicobar Islands to the Government. He maintained complete autonomy in dealings with the leaders and equalled them in more ways than one.

Much has been said and written about Netaji's conflict with Gandhiji. The conflict was only on ideology. Nonviolence was the lifelong creed of Gandhi but Netaji saw this as, a "temporary tactic, a tactic which is temporarily useful." It wasn't as if he didn't believe in the civil disobedience movement of Gandhi but as he said, "India will get freedom through an armed struggle coupled with a civil disobedience movement. But civil disobedience movement alone will not be enough .... As the British Government relies on the strength of bayonets, we too should use bayonets in order to defeat them decisively. As the enemy stands before us with the drawn sword, we should fight him only with the aid of the sword." The impossible is always absurd until it's done. Then it is possible.

The British never for a moment believed that Indians had the strength to pick up arms and fight them but Netaji made this possible. And history is a witness to the truth that India got her independence only by revolutionary stand taken by Netaji and in the words of Lord Attlee, the role of Gandhi was "minimal". When Gandhi commended his non-cooperation programme to the Indian nation at the annual session of the Congress at Nagpur on 1920 he said, "If India had the sword today, she would have drawn the sword." So it was not as if Gandhi was opposed to the armed combat but was forced to believe that his country men lacked the capacity to militarily fight the enemy, and a much better equipped one at that. Hence Satyagraha was the only viable weapon he had at hand and one that proved to be highly successful in demonstrating to the British that Indians were capable of organizing themselves into a united front.

All said and done the respect that Netaji had for Gandhi was unquestionable. It was Netaji who gave him the title of Father of the Nation. He said, "...The service which Mahatma Gandhi had rendered to India and to the cause of India's freedom is so unique and unparalleled that his name will be written in letters of gold in our national history for all time." Well, the tragic and some times disturbing fact is that Netaji and his contribution to India's freedom has been relegated to the background. Today a child in school is being given a very distorted picture of history. I sincerely hope this situation is rectified soon for otherwise the damage done will be dreadful. But sadly, we aren't even looking in this direction. Our minds are preoccupied with other issues.

How little it takes to make our lives unbearable...the broken top button of the shirt, a traffic jam, a tyre puncture, Indian team performing badly .... Everything slightly inconvenient makes us look up to the God and complain, crib, curse. We waste time in trivialities like the protest against the Miss World pageant which was appalling to say the least. We seem to ignore larger issues that are facing us in the eye. Issues like bride burning, child marriages, sati, female infanticide which have debauched our society. Issues like corruption are staggering. But what is even more shocking is out total indifference to the situation. For long we have been swallowing our anger with our pride that we have begun to get used to its taste. Injustice is to us, second nature. We thrive on it and let others thrive on it.

Post independent India has been through some really rough weather. Today our hard-earned freedom for which countless men and women laid down their lives is being threatened by various foes. Why have we not been able to learn form the experiences of our past leaders, sages, thinkers and scholars? Our forefathers showed us that courage and sacrifice can triumph against overwhelming odds. Netaji said, "... I would like to remind you that a revolutionary is one who believes in the justice of a cause, and who believes that the cause is bound to prevail in the long run. He who gets depressed over failures is no revolutionary. The motto for a revolutionary is: Hope for the best, but be prepared for the worst...Hope is a quality we share with the spider. He makes us feel positive. Hope makes us forget failures. Hope brings hope. But for a leader, hope takes much more. It takes more than just waiting to make hope arrive on the horizon. He has to pledge his life. Netaji was hopeful. Still believing that his tomorrow can be bright. If the spider wouldn't give up, why should we? The spirit of our past leaders knew no fatigue or death and by their abiding faith in India and their mission, they had shaped the destiny of future India. The optimist that he was, he said, "...And if we fail in that too (attaining independence) then there will indeed be World War III to give us another opportunity to strike for our freedom." Let us drive inspiration form the pages of his life. Fortunately for posterity, he was also a prolific writer and his own letters have survived.

For a whole section of Indians then, Netaji was a lighthouse of hope. Fifty years of Independence and we have done all that we could to extinguish that flicker of hope. We have allowed his sufferings and those countless soldiers to be diluted. Where are all those men who should have been worthy successors of our priceless heritage? Where all those modern crusaders who were are suppose to finish the task left behind by our forefathers? They paid the price for the kind of mission they had embarked upon. After all nothing can be got free, a price has to be paid for everything. With our any expectation of a miracle, this country must do all it can to see that the current scenario is corrected. Society is full of issues to fight and the least we can expect from our leaders is concrete evidence that these issues are being talked. Let our youth take charge for this is their country and they are its future.

We are not mere syncopates. We believed in Netaji. We identified with his mission. We shared his dreams. We were his partners in his fight for liberation who contributed our bit, suffered and sacrificed for our country. To the youth I seek their attention. For on their shoulders rest the future of India.

Netaji taught us to stand up and be counted for values that count-discipline, sacrifice, patriotism and good old hard work. Fifty years after independence and these fundamental values still count. His efforts are testimonials of his determination to succeed, come what may.

... He spread his wings and gave his country the opportunity to test untried waters. The results did not matter. The fact that the chance did. He made the world envious of him, envious of

India and her achievements. Truly, only Netaji could have done that! Let our youth take over form where Netaji had left. We are hopefully moving into the 21st century. The young must wake up to that. And with the confidence of a winner say, *Hum honge kamayab*.

SYMBOL OF NATIONAL INTEGRATION

India is more than a country. It is a continent comprising of people who speak different languages, look different and dress differently. It is a country where religion has a very strong base and where followers of perhaps all known religions live and practice their faith in their respective manner.

India has not only almost 850 million people but also has a great diversity of culture. For example, let us take a person from Ladak or the Kashmir Valley in the north and compare him with someone in Kanyakumari in the South or, for that matter, with someone in Rajasthan or Gujarat in the West or Nagaland and Manipur in the East. What have they in common? They do not look alike for their climatic conditions are very different. In fact they can not even converse with one another because they speak completely different languages. Yet each is an Indian. Often they quarrel among themselves, but in time of crisis or danger, they become one. There is some thing which holds them together. It is a fine line but the bond is very strong. It is difficult to find words to describe this. I call it Indianness or being an Indian-the pride of belonging to India, the land which has given them birth and where they shall return ultimately after death or where they shall return ultimately after death or where the ashes of their mortal remains will mingle and become one with the waters of the rivers which flow through the country's length and breadth.

In order to keep this vast and varied multitude of people together, the country needs a leader of the caliber of Netaji Subhash Chandra Bose. He believed passionately that all Indians, irrespective of the region they come from or language they spoke or religious faith they practiced, were members of the same family. He gave his belief practical shape and convinced all those who came in contact with him that unless this basic fact was accepted without hesitation, there was no future for India.

Netaji as Subhash Babu in his early days was a symbol of the restlessness of Indian youth, who dreamed of a great and free India. As Netaji Subhash Chandra Bose, he was the colossus who strode across East Asia and organized and led an army of liberation against the British Empire, entrenched in India for almost 200 years. In the two years when he led the Indian independence movement, he lived a dream-a dream that the dedicated and the restless youths of India had dreamt for decades and for daring to make that dream into a reality, several had gone to gallows with a smile on their faces.

I came in contact with this great man and, in the opinion of many of us, the greatest Indian leader of his time, when I was only 23, a very impressionable age. Netaji opened our eyes, so to say. He made us see Indian through the eyes of an Indian. His call was "Give me blood and I promise you freedom". Indians all over South-East Asia and Burma flocked to him in their thousands, offering all their worldly possessions and their own lives in the service of the nation. He had the knack of getting the best of every person. There was absolutely no distinction about which part of the country he or she came from, or which religious faith he or she followed or which language he or she spoke. It was pleasure and privilege to be an Indian at that time. Many, and I repeat many, of us wanted to become martyrs in the service of our country for a martyr never dies; he becomes immoral and lives forever in the hearts, memory and the history of his country.

Let me now conclude by giving the Azad Hind Government national Anthem. Here the spirit of every freedom fighter of the INA is completely and adequately expressed.

National Anthem

Subh Sukh Chain ki barkha barse; Bharat bhag hai jaga

Punjab, Sind, Gujrat, Maratha, Dravid, Utkal, Banga

Chanchal Sagar Vindh Himala; Nila Jamuna Ganga

Tere nit gun gayen; tujh se jiwan paen;

Sab tan paye asha.

Suraj ban kar jag par chamke, Bharat nam subhaga

Jaya ho, Jaya ho, Jaya ho, Jaya, Jaya, Jaya, Jaya ho,

Sab ke dil men prit basae; teri mithi bani

Har sub eke rahne wale; har mazhab ke prani

Sab bhed aur farak mita ke; sab god me teri ake,

Goondhe prem ki mala

Suraj ban kar jag par chamke, Bharat nam subhaga

Jaya ho, Jaya ho, Jaya ho, Jaya, Jaya, Jaya, Jaya ho,

Bharat naam Subhaga

Subh savere pankh pakharu; tere hi gun gayen

Bas bhari bharpur hawaen; jiwan men rut layen

Sab mil kar Hind pukaren; Jai Azad Hind ke nare

Piara desh hamara

Suraj ban kar jag par chamke, Bharat nam subhaga

Jaya ho, Jaya ho, Jaya ho, Jaya, Jaya, Jaya, Jaya ho,

Bharat naam Subhaga.

Jai Hind.

BOSE AND NATIONAL INTEGRATION

Netaji uttered a note of caution to his army that the partition of the country would solve no old or outstanding problem, but would give rise to fresh ones instead. He could bear out through his INA experiment that despite disparities in religion, language and ethnicity, there was some thing of an underlying unity in the midst of diversity in our people. Bound by a common goal. A common subjectivity and action programme as it was, the INA could live down at the operational level, all manner of differences of religion, language, caste and the rest of it.

Throughout his political career Bose crusaded for unity in action and unity of faith. He never agreed to a unity of sorts for the sheer purpose of temporizing, rather he did encourage a genuine respect for all the religions and communities in his INA. He made sure that religion was treated purely a personal affair. A common greeting, a common but simple lingua franca and a National Anthem were all devised to work as cementing forces in the conduct of the INA affairs.

Not only were the INA soldiers united in their implicit allegiance to their leader and government but also they were deeply animated by a spirit of national integration. Incidentally Bose himself was a religious man in personal life, there was no place for any communal or sectarian consideration in his political ideology.

He never shied away, throughout his political life, form and insistence on complete separation of religion from the nationalist politics of the day. His ideas in regard to communal harmony found an almost complete expression and in perfect implementation in the INA. He saw to it that INA was rendered free from all political influences which the British Raj encouraged to maintain in India as a dependency. His spirit of secularism moved and gripped the INA as a whole, much though every soldier in it had perfect liberty to practice his own religion privately. The lesson was brought home to them by Bose, that the communal divide was just a sample of British propaganda.

Nataji was quite alive to the problem of national unity since the inception of his rather short but eventful political career. His approach to this problem was both incisive and positive. He always endeavoured to persuade the Muslims of India to join the main stream of the struggle for the emancipation of India. The Pakistan idea was never his cup of tea. Indeed through his INA and Azad Hind Government, Netaji showed us at a critical moment of our history how to forge national will in a concrete, resolute action. He fervently tried to give rise to a cultural organization in South East Asia, through which the various races and religions would be enabled to converge our Indian foundation. In his first platoon lecture to the Fauz entitled "Unity of India, past and present", he dealt with the insidious British propaganda to the world regarding our so-called manifold differences.

As early as August 1942, he raised the issue of national integration in India in the columns of a German paper. He also arranged for a committee to be set upon our national integration when the Andaman and the Nicobr Islands were occupied by the INA Government. The speech he delivered on the same subject at the Chettiar temple is one to reckon with. He facilitated the entry of men of other religions as well in the temple in the face of vehement resistance from the keepers of the temple. More than that, the pledge the INA soldiers had to sign the highlights the commitment of the army to the ideals of unity, secularism and democracy.

For the growth of a genuine national spirit in the Army, Bose waged a relentless struggle against the splitters and opportunists both in the country and outside. He made the remarkable prophecy that India freed form the British was destined to develop a strong nation. In his opinion only a truly national government could implement a meaningful programme of unity of our people and only a genuine patriotic army could bring about our unity at the barricades.

He claimed he could bring about a measure of communal unity in his ranks simply because the Britishers were not there. Apart form this he initiated a scheme of secular and scientific education through his government and started a sustained propaganda on its behalf to fight out all divisive forces. He felt that India must reject the Wavell plan which really meant parcel our country, a similar plan the British tried in Ireland and Palestine too. The prime item on his agenda was the removal or religious intolerance and fanaticism through intensive and ceaseless propaganda. In his famous Tokyo speech of 1944, he touched upon India's basic unity, a model which could be served to the people with in India through his INA.

For one thing the INA proved to be a living example of national unity and Gandhi was all praise for the way in which Bose infused the spirit of unity amongst his men. In fact the INA trial virtually shook the unfree and undivided Indians form their long deep slumber. Hindus, Muslims, Sikhs and Christians were evenly represented in the Government and the Army and they all unitedly posed from outside a serious challenge to the separatist forces set work in the homeland. The Indian National Army became a dramatic symbol of national unity as the trials of a Hindu, a Sikh and a Muslim INA officers proved to the hilt.

A Muslim accompanied Bose in his perilous submarine journey and another Muslim sent him off for the last time at the airport. Some of his brigades were led by Muslim officers exclusively and some were named after the living Indian nationalists leaders. The INA trials followed up by the RIN revolt represented a turning of the tide as far as the prospects of the secularism were concerned.

Netaji Subhash assembled different scattered forces in East Asia and formed an army with the help of youths of different areas and communities in India. He mobalised the a-political forces in South East Asia in order to fight the last war of liberation for a United India. Indeed he and his INA served to hold up the dropping spirits of all sections of Indian people and example of rare unity and patriotism. He infused into his men a certain non-communal spirit, and inspired them to feel proud of their Indian identity. He inspired his men, in his own inimitable way to identify themselves not as Hindus or Muslims but as the sons and daughters of India. He succeeded in installing in them a kind of cultured sensitivity and a secular passion.

He succeeded in rousing a mighty army unified in spirit and committed ideologically to work for a free and united India. He almost fully carried out his ideas on national unity in the formation of the INA which consisted of more than sixty percent of Muslims. He could persuade his associates to shed their religious superstitions about food and the practice of denominational faith. He forge an emotional relationship among the diverse ethnicities that came to serve in his army on their own accord. In fact the INA became a paradigm of national and emotional integration. However, it is not enough to recapitulate the INA saga but it is peremptory to take lessons form it, now more than ever, particularly when we have to tackle the problem of disintegration that threatens us today, when the whole nation is faced with a crisis of leadership of conviction and general sense of direction.

TRANSPARENCY

What reminds me of Netaji Subhash Chandra Bose the most are those words which he spoke to us on various occasions, when we had the good luck to wage a regular war for the Independence of India under his command from 1943 to 1945. Apart from the clarity of his vision, spontaneity of speech, serenity and uniformity of thought, with which he explained with perfect ease various problems of our struggle and his plans, was the expression on his face which served as a window through which we could see where he was leading us to. So transparent were his dealings with us!

A communication with him always left us more enlightened and responsible. It gave us confidence in the righteousness of our cause, in his ability to lead us and our nation to victory and freedom. We gained so much self-confidence that we felt that the very destiny was in our hands.

"Let me show a sample of his oration when he addressed us, the soldiers of the Indian National Army, for the first time after receiving our parade at Singapore on July the 5th 1943. His concluding words were :

"I have said that today is the proudest day of my life. For an enslaved people, there can be no greater pride, no higher honour, than to be the first soldier in the Army of Liberation. But this honour carries with it a corresponding responsibility and I am deeply conscious of it.

I assure you that I shall be with you in darkness and in sunshine, in sorrow and in joy, in suffering and in victory. For the present, I can offer you nothing except hunger, thirst, privation, forced marches and death. But if you follow me in life and in death, as I am confident you will, I shall lead you to victory and freedom. It does not matter who among us will live to see India free. It is enough that India shall be free and that we shall give our all to make her free. May God bless our Army and grant us victory in the coming fight.

Inquilab Zindabad!

Azad Hind Zindabad!"

Above words coming strait from the heart of the man of the splendours of Netaji Subhash went straight into our hearts. Those words left us honoured and proud of being in the INA. We felt we were important and responsible beings. Netaji's achievements and sacrifices were already so great that no further decoration could enhance his majesty. On the contrary his being first amongst us was much needed recognition for us. He placed his confidence in us. Confidence is a great morale booster. It invigorated our spirits. Our chests expanded, with heads held high and feet dug deep into ground with the battle cry-CHALO Delhi on our lips, we followed the fluttering TRICOLOUR. And we sang :

Kadam kadam Bharaey ja

Khushi Ke geet gaye ja

Ye Zindegi hai Qaum ki

Tu Waum par lutaey ja.

Within a few days of his arrival in the East, Netaji gave us Vanguard-the Rani Jhansi Regiment. We felt that the valour of the Goddess Durga had reincarnated in the daughters of Mother India. They manifested the blessings of the Goddess and power of her Shakti.

With our allies the Japanese our armies advanced against the armies of Great Britain and their allies who were in occupation of the Indian Subcontinent. Some of the bloodiest battles of the Second World War were fought in the spring of 1944 on the battle fields of Akyab, Arakan, Manipur, Imphal, Nagaland, Kohima and Red Hill. India's Tricolour was planted on the liberated territory of India at Moirang in Manipur.

Victory was a matter of touch and go. Then came rains. Our supply lines were cut off. Tables turned. Having lost one hundred thousand lives, we and our valiant allies the Japanese withdrew to the Irrawaddy line. Initiative passed on to opponent's hands. Delhi started getting out of our reach. The Allies were winning everywhere. We had practically lost the War. When Netaji was asked, "Now what is left for us to fight for?" his prompt reply was, "To pay the price of India's Liberty."

We continued our fight on the banks of the Irrawaddy at Nyaungu and Bagan, Mount Popa and Kyauk padaung, Magwe and so on, towards Prome and Pegu on the way to Rangoon. We fought against odds. What to talk about weapons and rations, even water was scarce.

So what? Wasn't it one of the things offered to us by Netaji during his very first address on 5th July.1943. His oft-repeated words, "There is no power on earth which can keep India enslaved any longer. India shall be free and before long." His prophetic words sustained our spirits. His appreciations of our actions on the battle fields kept up our morale. The fight was kept on.

Eventually we did reach Delhi-our destination-not as free persons but as prisoners. We were vanquished and the British were the victor. Dungeons of the Red Fort were our abode. Our trial was held from 5th November to 31st December 1945. The autumn of that year was one of the gloomiest the Indian nation ever had. The people did not light their homes on Diwali-The Festival of lights. The charge against us was of waging war against the King and of murder and abetment of murder. The trial was held in the dormitory of a British Barrack on the Red Fort of Delhi. According to the law death appeared to be the just punishment for us.

The British Government were determined to set an example, so as to teach the Indian soldier a lesson never to dare to take up arms against the King. They had not won the World War to liquidate the British Empire. But for us it was the last chance to pay the price of India's liberty. During the War the British had succeeded in keeping the INA actions and even the name of the Indian National Army a well guarded secret. They could not keep that secret anymore. Soldiers coming home after the War had gone through a complete psychological revolution when the brother did shed brother's blood on either side in the battle-field on lands abroad.

The Indian soldier had seen the INA fight against the British guns with rifles, and tanks with bullock carts and the aircrafts with empty stomachs in tattered uniforms. As if that was not enough, the British victorious officers and men in towns of Singapore, Malaya, Thailand and Burma, were greeted with "JAI HIND" by boys and girls of Balak Sena. Greetings of "JAI HIND" meaning "Victory to India" made soldiers of Indian Army pause and ponder as to what did they fight for?

For their bread or for the British? Thus when we, the soldiers of the INA., were prisoners behind the gates of carious jails and detention camps tiny tots of Netaji's Balak Sena were still in the field shouting JAI HIND. The British had no weapon which could be used against the Balak Sena.

Under those circumstances the British Government's decision to put on trial three INA officers-a Muslim, a Hindu and a Sikh, was a blunder. The Indian public were yet in the dark about us and our actions. Actions which were noble, nationalist, according to civilized rules of International war, and for the liberation of our motherland.

The British were determined to teach us a lesson and we were determined with unity and faith to sacrifice our life to pay the price for India's liberty. In a situation like that no enemy could ever favour her archenemies by providing such a grand (nor a better) stage than the historic Red Fort of Delhi. We were further favoured by our own people who united as a man to defend us during the trial.

Tallest of the tall legal luminaries of India got together with Shri Bhulabhai Desai as their chief Counsel to defend the accused officers of the INA. In his historic address Mr. Desai explained, that it was the right of a subject race to wage war for their liberty. Desai's address awakened the whole nation.

How apply the British Commander in chief in India, General Sir Claud Auchinleck, who had spent all his life in the Indian Army and known the soldiers' mind well, did assess the situation then prevailing is apparent through his letter to Army Commanders dated 12th February, 1946. The letter is marked STRICTLY PERSONAL AND SECRET: NOT TO BE PASSED THROUGH ANY OFFICE.

It is a long letter in which Sir Auchinleck laboured hard to explain to his Army Commanders the effect of the action taken in respect of the first INA trial on the Indian Army as a whole. I quote just an excerpt form his letter. It is most important that we should study and analyse carefully these effects, as they may influence very greatly our ability, to maintain the solidarity and reliability of the Indian Army in the difficult times which undoubtedly lie ahead of us. It is for this reason that I am writing this letter to you. I have considered the desirability of making a personal public statement in explanation of my action in commuting the sentences of transportation passed by the Court on the first three accused, but I have decided that this would not be in the best of interest of discipline of the maintenance of my influence and authority as Commander-in-Chief.

I feel however, that we should do all we can to remove the feelings of doubt, resentment and even disgust which appear to exist in the minds of quite a number of British Officers, who have not the knowledge or the imagination to be able to view the situation as a whole, or to understand present state of feeling in India. As I see it, the communication of the sentences of transportation on Shah Nawaz, Dhillon and Sehgal has had the following effects in India:

(a) On the general public, moderate as well as extremist, Muslim as well Hindu. Pleasure and intense relief born of the conviction that confirmation of the Sentences would have resulted in violent internal effect.

(b) This feeling does not, in my opinion, spring universally from the idea that the convicted officers were trying to rid India of the British and therefore, to be applauded, whatever crimes they might commit, but from a generally genuine feeling that they were patriots and nationalists and that, therefore, even if they were misled they should be treated with clemency, as true sons of India. In this connection, it should be remembered, I think, that every Indian worthy of the name today a "Nationalist", though this does not mean that he is necessarily "anti-British." All the same, where India and her independence is concerned, there are no "Pro-British Indians."

Netaji's contributions in the making of India are unique. What to talk of INA, Netaji inspired not only the Indians as a whole, but also the nationals of those countries who where still not independent.

The actions of the Royal Indian Navy and certain personnel of all the three Military Services at Bombay, Karachi and other places in the name of Netaji were like the last straw which broke the back of the mighty British Colonial Empire on whom the Sun never used to set. According to Netaji's oft-repeated words, "India shall be free and before long", we did attain freedom of which we are celebrating the Golden Jubilee today along with Netaji along with Netaji Subhash Chandra Bose's Birthday when he completes a century and enters the new one.

I wish Netaji was here today to see us free. He was the only leader who could keep India united. But when the partition of the subcontinent is an established fact, let us wish all the offsprings of Hindustan, Bangladesh and Pakistan, happiness, peace, plenty and glory.

PROCLAMATION OF THE PROVISIONAL GOVERNMENT OF AZAD HIND

After their first defeat at the hands of the British in 1757 in Bengal, the Indian people fought an uninterrupted series of hard and bitter battles over a stretch of one hundred years. The history of this period teems with examples of unparalleled heroism and self-sacrifice. And, in the pages of that history, the names of Sirajuddaula and Mohanlal of Bengal, Haider Ali, Tippu Sultan and Velu Tampi of South India, Appa Sahib Bhonsle and Peshwa Baji Rao of Maharashtra, the Begums of Oudh, Sardar Shyam Singh Atariwala of Punjab and last, but not the least, Rani Laxmibai of Jhansi, Tantia Tope, Maharaja Kunwar Singh of Dumraon and Nana Sahib-among others-the names of all these warriors are for ever engraved in letters of gold. Unfortunately for us, our forefathers did not at first realize that the British constituted a grave threat to the whole of India, and they did not therefore put up a united front against the enemy.

Ultimately, when the Indian people were roused to the reality of the situation, they made a concerted move and under the flag of Bahadur Shah in 1857, they fought there last war as free men. In spite of a series of brilliant victories in the early stages of this war, ill-luck and faulty leadership gradually brought about their final collapse and subjugation. Nevertheless, such heroes as the Rani of Jhansi, Tantia Tope, Kunwar Singh and Nana Sahib live like eternal stars in the nation's memory to inspire us to greater deeds of sacrifice and valour.

Forcibly disarmed by the British after 1857 and subjected to terror and brutality, the Indian people lay prostrate for a while-but with the rebirth of the Indian National Congress in 1885, there came a new awakening.

From 1885, until the end of the last World War, the Indian people in their endeavour to recover their lost liberty, tried all possible methods-namely agitation and propaganda, boycott of British goods, terrorism and sabotage-and finally armed revolution. But all these efforts failed for a time. Ultimately in 1920, when the Indian people haunted by a sense of failure, were groping for a new method, Mahatma Gandhi came forward with the new weapon of non-cooperation and civil disobedience.

For two decades thereafter, the Indian people went through a phase of intense patriotic activity. The message of freedom was carried to every Indian home. Through personal example, people were taught to suffer, to sacrifice and to die in the cause of freedom. From the centre of the remotest villages, the people were knit together into one political organization.

Thus the Indian people not only recovered their political consciousness but became a political entity once again. They could now speak with one voice and strive with one will for one common goal. From 1937 to 1939, through the work of the Congress Ministers in eight provinces, they gave proof of the readiness and their capacity to administer their own affairs.

Thus, on the eve of the present World War, the stage was set for the final struggle for India's liberation. During the course of this war, Germany with the help of her allies has dealt shattering blows to our enemy in Europe-while Nippon, with the help of her allies, has inflicted a knockout blow to our enemy in East Asia. Favoured by a most happy combination of circumstances, the Indian people today have a wonderful opportunity for achieving their national emancipation. For the first time in recent history, Indians abroad have also been politically roused and united in one organization. They are not only thinking and feeling in tune with their countrymen at home, but are also marching in step with them along the path to freedom.

In East Asia, in particular, over two million Indians are now organized as one solid phalanx, inspired by the slogan of 'Total Mobilisation'. And in front of them stand the salaried ranks of India's Army of Liberation, with the slogan 'Onward to Delhi', on their lips.

Having goaded Indians to desperation by its hypocrisy and having driven them to starvation and death by plunder and loot, British rule in India has forfeited the goodwill of the Indian people altogether and is now living a precarious existence. It needs but a flame to destroy the last vestige of that happy rule. To light that flame is the task of India's Army of Liberation. Assured of enthusiastic support of the civil population at home and also of large sections of Britain's Indian Army, and backed by gallant and invincible allies abroad-but relying in the first instance on its own strength, India's Army of Liberation is confident of fulfilling its historic role.

Now that the dawn of freedom is at hand, it is the duty of the Indian people to set up a provisional Government of their own and launch the last struggle under the banner of the Government. But with all the Indian Leaders in prison and the people at home totally disarmed, it is not possible to set up a Provisional Government.

It is therefore the duty of the Indian Independence League in East Asia, supported by all patriotic Indians at home and abroad, to undertake this task-the task of setting up a Provisional Government of Azad Hind (Free India) and of conducting the last fight for freedom, with the help of the Army of Liberation, (that is, the Azad Hind Fauj or the Indian National Army) organized by the League.

Having been constituted as the Provisional Government of Azad Hind by the Indian Independence League in East Asia, we enter upon our duties with full sense of responsibility that has devolved on us. We pray that the province may bless our work and struggle for the emancipation of our Motherland. And we hereby pledge our lives for our comrades in arms to the cause of her freedom, of her welfare and her exaltation among the nations of the world.

It will be the task of the Provisional Government to launch and to conduct the struggle that will bring about the expulsion of the British and their allies from the soil of India. It will then be the task of the Provisional Government to bring about the establishment of a permanent National Government of Azad Hind constituted in accordance with the will of the Indian people and enjoying their confidence. After the British and their allies are overthrown and until a permanent National Government of Azad Hind is set up on Indian soil, the Provisional Government will administer the affairs of the country in trust for the Indian people.

The provisional Government is entitled to, and hereby claims, the allegiance of every Indian. It guarantees religious liberty, as well as equal rights and equal opportunities to all its citizens. It declares its firm resolves to pursue the happiness and prosperity of the whole nation and of its parts, cherishing all the children of the nation equally and transcending all the differences cunningly fostered by an alien government in the past.

In the name of God, in the name of bygone generations who have welded the Indian people into one nation, and in the dead heroes who have bequeathed to us a tradition of heroism and self-sacrifice-we call upon the Indian people to rally round our banner and strike for India's freedom. We call upon them to launch the final struggle (against the British and all their allies in India and prosecute that struggle) with valour and perseverance in full faith in final victory-until the enemy is expelled from Indian soil and the Indian people are once again a free nation.

5

WHAT HAPPENED TO NETAJI?

The year 1978 brought with it so much hope and happiness. A people's movement under the leadership of Loknayak Jayaprakash Narayan himself and one and a half lakh activists caught up by the one and a half years of Emergency rule. Except the very old Acharya Kripalani and the leaders of Left Front, all other opposition leaders were in the prisons of Indira Gandhi. The magnitude which this people's movement against the government of Indira Gandhi took as soon as Emergency was declared, has not been seen after the freedom struggle. Towards the end of 1976, Indira Gandhi lifted the Emergency and declared general elections. Both Indira and Congress were defeated in the elections. A Janata government was established under the leadership of Morarji Desai in 1977.

A new era of state authority was ushered in. I entered the lobby of the Lok Sabha with the excitement of a joyous mind. Seeing me H M Patel and Nanaji Deshmukh came forward eagerly. They told me that the new council of ministers will be sworn in tomorrow. Morarji Bhai has asked me to be ready for swearing in. Immediately I said, "No, I am not interested. Please tell Morarji bhai."

Both of them stared at me incredulously. I was then the leader of the Socialist Party in Lok Sabha. It was natural that my name would come up first for joining the council of ministers from the party.

I had decided as soon as the results of the election were declared that I would not join the ministry even if I am requested to. In order to prevent any weakness for becoming a minister,

I had openly declared in a public meeting at Calcutta that I would not be trapped in any ministry even if I am asked to join the Government. I would strive to utilize the opportunity in the form of Janata Party rule to do whatever I can to undo the injustice that has been done and still being done towards Netaji. There were two more speakers in this public meeting at Maidan-Janata Party leader Prafulla Chandra Sen and Communist Party leader Jyoti Basu. That was a time of Janata-Communist understanding. My relatives, as well as friends in the Socialist Party were surprised and aggrieved to hear my intentions.

Janata Party was formed in Delhi after the elections by the merger of Congress (O), Charan Singh's party, Jana Sangh and Socialist Party. Babu Jagjivan Ram's party also joined this combine after the elections. Why did I not feel like joining the council of ministers? Can't one serve the country if he becomes a minister? Of course he can! But the injustice meted out, the indifference showed to the Maha-Kshatriya whose Azad Hind revolution dealt the last blow to the empire, forcing the British to quit India must be protested. Whatever little is possible must be done to justice. The conspiracy of Nehru Raj towards Netaji must be brought to an end. That was my resolution in those days.

At the end of the war stories of the heroic deeds of the Azad Hind revolution flooded the public life in India churning up the nationalist sentiment to its greatest heights. All separatist feelings originating from caste, creed, sect, religion and regions were washed away. The air in the country was filled with the rending roar of 'Jai Hind,' 'Netaji Zindabad,' and 'Azad Hind Zindabad.' Such national unity, national upheaval for freedom were unprecedented. The slogans were heard even at Gandhiji's prayer meetings. People also shouted 'Gandhiji Zindabad,' but alas, only after raising slogans on Netaji. Many soldiers in the British Raj met Gandhiji, Sardar Patel and Maulana Azad telling them that if they took the moral responsibility, the soldiers will rise up in revolt and bring the Indian leaders to power. The fire of a national upheaval lighted by Netaji had set on fire the spirit of revolt too. The Indian Army of the British Raj was feverish with the emotions of freedom for the country. Whether anyone else understood it or not, Gandhiji knew full well what effect the fiery tales of Netaji's epic revolutionary heroism had on the mind of the Indians. In his inimitable style he gave expression to this explosive public spirit in his Harijan, "Hypnotism of INA has cast spell on us. Netaji's name is one to conjure with. His bravery shines through all his actions."

But what happened to such a personality who made history? Not only Pandit Jawaharlal, who secured his place after the transfer of power from the British Raj, the entire official authority of the new Indian State totally forgot Netaji and his INA. Pandit Nehru couldn't remember showing the slightest of state honours to Netaji. Netaji was wiped out of the mind space of the Indian state power.

In 1945-46, no leader in India believed the story of Netaji's death in air crash at Taihoku. Gandhiji, Pandit Nehru, Maulana Azad said in unison that the story of Netaji's death is just that-a story. It is a rumour. Even the Governor General Lord Wavell did not believe in the news. Wavell sent a secret report to the Prime Minister Attlee on what can be done with Subhash if he is caught. This was first published in the sixth volume of the book 'Transfer of Power' in 1975.

In 1945, Nehru said repeatedly that he did not believe in the news of Netaji's death. Gandhiji said, "I will not believe that Subhash is dead even if someone shows me the ashes. He is alive and must be hiding somewhere." Gandhiji said this many times.

After knowing so much and saying so much what did Nehru do after he became the Prime Minister?

The loquacious Pandit Nehru all of a sudden became mum after February 1946. Let alone investigating the issue, the Government of India did not even try to know about or publish the investigation reports of the allied powers-as soon as the air crash was announced in 1945, Douglas MacArthur, the Supreme Commander of the allied forces in the Southwest Pacific as well as Louis Mountbatten, Supreme Allied Commander of Southeast Asia had ordered inquiries. Nehru did not even try to know about the inquiry that his once-upon-a-time-friend Chiang-Kai shek conducted as soon as he took over Formosa. Pandit Nehru was both the Prime Minister and the Foreign Minister of the country. If he had only written a letter he would have got all these reports. Why did he not do that? Pandit Nehru's intimate friend Mountbatten was India's Governor General before and after partition of the country. It is not known whether Nehru was familiar with his investigation. Pandit Nehru's immediate national duty after India's freedom was to investigate in every possible way what happened to Netaji.

It is learnt from official documents of that time that the British Intelligence came to know that in a secret message from Russia, Netaji requested Nehru to arrange for his return to the country. But Pandit Nehru did do any such thing-he never conducted a proper investigation to know what really happened to Netaji. As soon as he became the Prime Minister, he entered a zone of silence and indifference regarding Netaji. The official policy of the Government of India regarding Netaji was total silence, indifference, apathy, coldness. Netaji's role in the freedom struggle of India is unrecognized and ignored.

Why did Pandit Nehru follow such an official policy of ungratefulness? Some information regarding this is available from the speeches and writings of late Amritlal Seth, the former editor of the Gujarat daily, Janmabhoomi. In February 1946 Congress leader Pandit Jawaharlal Nehru went to Singapore on the invitation of Admiral Mountbatten. The ex-soldiers of INA gave a warm welcome to Pandit Nehru at the airport. They informed Nehru that the memorial for the INA martyrs that Netaji had got erected at Singapore before he left the place was destroyed by the orders of Mountbatten. The resident Indians of Singapore along with the INA soldiers of Singapore and Malaya earnestly requested Panditji to pay floral tributes to the ruins of the memorial. Panditji agreed. It was decided that he would join the ceremony the next morning.

But when the Indian representatives went to bring Panditji from Mountbatten's house, he rudely refused the decided programme. Why did Pandit Nehru behave in such ungainly manner? Wasn't this the same person who put on the barrister's gown along with Bhulabhai Desai to defend the INA soldiers? He said that the trial was not an ordinary one-it was 'India vs England.' Didn't he go around the country talking about the INA in order to become a part of its unprecedented revolutionary legacy? How did the same Nehru act in this way, going against national honour?

The answers to this question are available from the then editor of Janmabhoomi, Amritlal Seth. A few Indian journalists went with Nehru on his trip to Singapore to meet Mountbatten. Seth was one of them.

On his return from Singapore, Seth went straight to meet Sarat Chandra Bose in Calcutta. He told Netaji's elder brother that Mountbatten warned Nehru on hearing that he was planning to pay floral tributes to the destroyed INA memorial. He told Panditji, "According to our report, Subhash Chandra Bose did not die in the reported air crash at Taihoku. He has escaped. If you play up Bose or his INA, you will be taking the risk of presenting India on a platter to Bose when he reappears."

Mountbatten was the Supreme Commander of the Allied forces in Southeast Asia. This British admiral started investigating the story of death in air crash soon after it was announced. The story of how this man from the royal family of Britain and his wife cast their influence over Nehru to make him accept the proposal for dividing India is not unknown. A grateful Nehru decided to remain within the Commonwealth after the division of the country and India, like Australia and Canada, was a dominion of the British Commonwealth for two and a half years even after the so-called independence. The same Mountbatten wrote in a letter to the Indian High Commissioner N G Goray in March 1978 that "There is no official record of Shri Subhash Chandra Bose's death in the archives."

It was only due to the warning of Mountbatten that Nehru made a volte-face even after giving his word to pay tributes to the destroy INA memorial. Yes, from this very day the spectre of Netaji's reappearance clouded Nehru's mind. From that day he deliberately became oblivious of Subhash who had once upon a time addressed him as elder brother. He forgot the heroism of the INA, he forgot the responsibility of the Indian Government towards the INA soldiers. Not only that, Nehru did something more treacherous to Netaji. It was known from official documents in 1956 that in 1946 the British intelligence sent a secret message to Wavell that they had come to know that Bose was in Russia and he has secretly contacted Nehru to make arrangements for coming back to India.

Shamlal Jain of Meerut gave a mind boggling witness account to the Khosla Commission in this regard. Jain was the stenographer of Asaf Ali, the secretary of the INA defence committee during the INA trials in Red Fort. Jain stated that after receiving a secret message from Netaji, Nehru wrote a letter to the British Prime Minister Attlee. This letter was typed by Jain. In that letter, Pandit Nehru wrote:

Dear Mr Attlee,

I understand from a reliable source that Subhash Chandra Bose, your war criminal, has been allowed to enter Russian territory by Stalin. This is a clear treachery and betrayal of faith by the Russians. As Russia has been an Ally of the British-Americans it should not have been done. Please take note of it and do what you consider proper and fit.

Yours sincerely

Jawaharlal Nehru

Why did Nehru commit such an unbelievable act of betrayal towards Netaji? The evidence from the trials of the German and Japanese war criminals clearly explains the implications of marking Netaji as a war criminal to Attlee. Nehru was not ignorant about what it meant to give out to the British Government the secret about Netaji, who was considered as the enemy number one of the empire. Nehru was a patriot and one of the leaders of the freedom struggle. His multifaceted talents were also universally acknowledged. But he could never imagine putting himself at the second position in the ranking of Indian leaders unless the first person concerned was Gandhi. He knew very well that Gandhiji would never sit on the throne of State power. Even with all his outstanding intellect Nehru was blind in his desire to become established as the icon of the highest

State authority. He could never tolerate any challenge to this dream of his.

In the final stages of the debate over the formation of Pakistan, Gandhiji made a desperate bid to protect the historical and national unity of India. He proposed to Mountbatten that Jinnah be made the Prime Minister of India after transfer of India. Jinnah too started showing signs of agreement to this proposal. But Nehru exploded in anger when this proposal was placed in the meeting of Congress leaders. He was dead against it. As a result the last efforts of Gandhiji to stop India's division failed.

Pandit Nehru was ruthless in case of any power struggle or at the possibility of any opposition. He accepted Mountbatten's warning, that if Subhash Bose comes back no one will be able to stop him from being the supreme leader of the country, as the sterling truth. All Congress leaders, including Gandhiji, knew this well. The Indian public at that time was mesmerized by Netaji. Morarji Desai, a Gandhian, was always a political opponent of Bose during the days of freedom struggle. The same Morarji Bhai said to me in 1978, "Samar Guha, why are you saying Subhash Babu is alive? If he had returned to the country in 1946, he would have become all-in-all. There would have been no Nehru, none from the Nehru family. Subhash Babu would have been all-in-all."

Another fact regarding this became available in 1989. On Gandhiji's instruction his trusted disciple and secretary Smt. Khurshed Naoroji wrote a secret letter on 22 July 1946 to the American journalist Louis Fischer who was very close to Gandhiji. Informing Fischer about the state of opinion amongst the public and the British Indian Army, she wrote, "At heart the Indian Army is sympathetic to the Indian National Army. If Bose comes with the help of Russia neither Gandhiji nor the Congress will be able to reason with the country."

Nehru also knew that if Netaji came back to India, he would become all-in-all. Even the though of such a scenario was intolerable to him. Thus, the murky power struggles that has happened in history all over the world, was repeated just before the transfer of power in India. Not only did Nehru, out of his fear of being thrown out of power, make arrangements to keep Netaji in exile despite knowing he was in Russia, he did not hesitate to formulate a national policy of giving the living Netaji a political burial. He never spoke about Netaji on his own after he came to power. Neither did he care about the demands of the nation to find the truth about Netaji. The subsequent governments too have followed the same policy of cruel silence, indifference and efforts to put a veil on the Azad Hind Revolution and the life of its Supreme Commander.

Shastri Wanted Probe into Netaji's Fate

In the records of Khosla Commission, still held classified by the Government, there are testimonies underlining the fact that the controversy about the fate of Subhash Chandra Bose pricked the conscience of even the members of the party that turned one of the greatest Indians ever into a persona non granta. In recent times we have seen the likes of Priya Ranjan Dasmunshi, Ambika Soni, Renuka Chowdhury and Abrar Ahmed expressing subdued concern, but in the good old days people were somewhat more forthcoming.

A good example was that of late Jagdish Kodesia, a former Delhi Congress chief who appeared before GD Khosla on March 1, 1971. Kodesia had spent his lifetime in the corridors of power—an experience that made him rub shoulders with high and mighty. "All my knowledge is based on my political connection with the high-ups and high leaders of the country, and working as special representative of the All India Congress Committee from 1954 to 1969," he told the commission. Kodesia confided in that he enjoyed close personal relations with Home Minister and then Prime Minister Lal Bahadur Shastri. He said he knew what Shastri knew, but added the rider that "If something was known to Shastriji and in confidence I have come to know of it, I am not supposed to reveal the secrets ...(due to) the oath which Shastriji had taken." "I will only tell what I have known personally. I will not make hearsay reports. There are so many whispers," Kodesia stressed.

Several times during his on-oath deposition, Kodesia stated that "Shastriji was one person" who did not believe in Netaji's death in the plane crash. According to Kodesia, Shastri's suspicion had been aroused due to the "obvious reason that the commission (Shah Nawaz Committee) did not visit the place of the accident (Taipei) itself". "When he became Home Minister ... he wanted to know the truth whether Subhash Bose was alive or not. In the whole Cabinet he was the only man who was very much interested."

Going down the memory lane, Kodesia recapitulated many of his experiences across the world. Sample these nuggets:

- The All India Congress Committee, of which Netaji Subhash Chandra Bose was the President twice, never passed a resolution condoling his death. The reasons are best known to the leaders of the Congress.
- From the records of Parliament it was seen that always a stereotyped reply was coming when questions were put about Netaji.
- The feeling among the various Congress leaders was that Panditji had an aversion for Netaji and he did not want Netaji's name to be highlighted.

More noteworthy was the Congressman's total recall of his 1954 meeting in Tokyo with the Indian Ambassador Mohammad Rauf, an Allahabadi like Kodesia. At lunch with Ambassador, Kodesia expressed desire to visit Renkoji temple, where Netaji Bose's alleged ashes were said to have been preserved. Rauf shocked Kodesia, telling him point-blank: "Why waste your time. They are not the ashes of Netaji. Whether they were ashes or not is also not sure. But definitely, don't waste your time." More shock was in store for shell-shocked Kodesia when he returned to Delhi. "When I came back, Sir, I gave this information to Shri Lal Bahadur Shastri and Pandit Jawaharlal Nehru. Shastriji was slightly inclined to listen to me patiently. But Panditji simply laughed at what I said," Kodesia told GD Khosla.

And what must have sent shivers down the spines was this disclosure: Kodesia felt that "after he became the Prime Minister ... (Shastri) was emphatically working that there should be a fresh probe into Netaji's disappearance."

"One thing is there that Shastri definitely wanted that there should be another inquiry Commission. If he would have lived longer, he must have seen to that...."

GD Khosla, a good friend of former Prime Minister Jawaharlal Nehru, made no mention of Kodesia's testimony in his fraudulent report.

Nonviolent Murder

KF Nariman was the president of Bombay Provincial Congress Committee and a former mayor of Mumbai. He wrote this on February, 28th 1941. Many followers and admirers of Subhash Babu will be perturbed by the publication of the last correspondence between him and Gandhiji, wherein Gandhiji had once again rejected Subhash Babu's generous and patriotic offer of cooperation in Satyagrah movement, in spite of his strong differences with him; some will be inclined even to attribute motives, and criticise this rejection as exhibiting pettishness and ill-will, unworthy of a Mahatma.

But I feel constrained to state that Gandhiji's rejection of that offer was plausibly justified on the ground of fundamental and vital differences, not only in the outlook but also in the ideology and mentality of these two leaders.

Whereas to Subhash Babu and to the rest of his followers, including the humble writer, nonviolence is only a political expediency, and mass satyagraha a suitable political weapon, to carry on the struggle for independence. In other words, both nonviolence and satyagraha are means to an end, to be adjusted and altered, as the exigencies and expediency demand. Gandhiji will adhere to that ideal of highest standard of nonviolence, even if the pursuit means sacrificing and giving up the political goal of Swaraj, whereas the other national group being essentially political, will rather alter and adjust the means than give up the goal.

Thus it is obvious that the differences between the two ideologies and mentalities are psychological and fundamental, and hence Gandhiji's rejection of Subhash Babu's offer looked at from that higher point of view seems apparently justified.

But the compliant is that there is no difference at all between Subhash Babu's "nonviolence" and the "nonviolence" of Gandhiji's numerous so-called followers who have nevertheless signed Satyagraha pledges with easy and accommodating conscience, and have been accepted by Gandhiji, though they too feel and believe exactly like Subhash Babu.

If Gandhiji was logical and consistent, he should have rejected one and all, on the same ground on which he has rejected Subhash Babu's offer, with few exceptions, perhaps of the first one or two genuine Satyagrahis like Vinoba Bave and Brahma Dutt; the whole of the rest, if judged by the same standard, deserved to be tarred by the same brush and swept off by the same broom, so far as their belief in faith in nonviolence is concerned. It is this discrimination in treatment that is not galling and against which we have made repeated complaints.

The only difference is that the Protestants like Subhash Babu and his friends are honest enough and declare their opinion whereas Gandhiji's followers, for obvious reasons, suppress their "inner voice". The result is that Subhas's group is disqualified and rejected for its frankness and sincerity, whereas the obedient and blind-folded "herd" is patronised and accepted in spite of transparent duplicity and hypocrisy. I challenge any one, including the Mahatma, to prove that Subhash Babu, in the above political sense, is less nonviolent than any of the patronised selected pets, from Maulana (Abul Kalam Azad) downwards. Maulana Sahib had even confessed his limitations. But what is the use of all these protests and challenges? Just as in the British constitution, the King can do no wrong, so in the present Congress the Mahatma can never be in the wrong. The oracle has spoken and that is the last word.

Incidentally, this correspondence also throws a lucid light on Subhash Babu's sudden disappearance; evidently this was the last straw that has broken even a tough back of that "Bengal Lion".

No only the places, patronage and power but even the privilege and honour of offering sacrifice for the country, is to be reserved for the favoured few, and sincere patriots like Subhash Babu must be hounded out, not only from the Presidential Gadi but also from the field of service. That is the nonviolent way of killing with kindness and murdering brilliant political careers. This position and attitude becomes more clear when we consider the latest Fascist pronouncement from the new Congress Bugler—Mr Kriplani, who recently in a public meeting at Madras announced "that those who do not go with Gandhiji are politically dead". It would be more correct to say "are politically murdered" and Subhash Babu is the latest and the greatest victim. That is how opposition is silenced, criticism is stifled, and mass hypocrisy is encouraged in the sacred name of truth and nonviolence.

Subhash Bose on Clash with Mahatma Gandhi

In December, 1937, the writer (Netaji) paid another visit to his favourite health-resort, Badgastein, in Austria, and from there he visited England. While in England, in January, 1938, he received news that he had been unanimously elected President of the Congress. During the course of this visit, he met members of the British Cabinet, like Lord Halifax and Lord Zetland, as well as prominent members of the Labour and Liberal parties who then professed sympathy for India, *e.g.* Mr Attlee, Mr Arthur Greenwood, Mr Bevin, Sir Stafford Cripps, Mr Harold Laski, Lord Allen, etc.

As Congress President, the writer did his best to stiffen the opposition of the Congress Party to any compromise with Britain and this caused annoyance in Gandhian circles who were then looking forward to an understanding with the British Government. Later in the year 1938, he launched the National Planning Committee for drawing up a comprehensive plan of industrialisation and of national development. This caused further annoyance to Mahatma Gandhi who was opposed to industrialisation. After the Munich Pact, In September, 1938, the writer began an open propaganda throughout India in order to prepare the Indian people for a national struggle, which should synchronise with the coming war in Europe. This move, through popular among the people in general, was resented by the Gandhites who did not want to be disturbed in their ministerial and parliamentary work and who were at that time opposed to any national struggle.

The breach between the writer and the Gandhi Wing was now wide, though not visible to the public. At the Presidential election in January, 1939, he was therefore vigorously opposed by the Gandhi Wing as well as by Pandit Nehru. Nevertheless, he was victorious with a comfortable majority. This was the first time since 1923-24 that the Mahatma suffered a public defeat and in his weekly paper, *Harijan*, he openly acknowledged this defeat. The election had served to show the wide and influential following that the writer had, throughout the country, in open opposition to both Gandhi and Nehru.

In March, 1939, at the annual session of the Congress, the writer who presided made a clear proposal that the Indian National Congress should immediately send an ultimatum to the British government demanding Independence within six months and should simultaneously prepare for a national struggle. This proposal was opposed by the Gandhi Wing and by Nehru and was thrown out. This situation arose in which though the writer was the President of the Congress, his lead was not accepted by that body. Moreover, it was seen that on every conceivable occasion, the Gandhi Wing was opposing the President with a view to making it impossible for him to function. A complete deadlock within the Congress was the result. There were two ways of removing this deadlock—either the Gandhi Wing should give up its obstructionist policy, or the President should submit to the Gandhi Wing.

With a view to finding a possible compromise, direct negotiations between Mahatma Gandhi and the writer took place, but they proved to be abortive. Under the Constitution of the Congress, the President was entitled to appoint the Executive (Working Committee) for the coming year, but it was clear that the Gandhi Wing would continue to obstruct, if the Executive was not appointed according to its choice. And the position of the Gandhi Wing within the Congress was such that determined obstruction on its part would render its virtually impossible for the President to function in an independent manner.

The Gandhi Wing was determined neither to accept the lead of the writer, nor to allow him control the machinery of the Congress, and it would tolerate him only as a puppet President. The Gandhi Wing had, moreover, this tactical advantage that it was the organised party within the Congress, acting under a centralised leadership. The Left Wing or the radical elements in the Congress who were responsible for the writer's re-election as President in January, 1939, were numerically in a majority—but they were at a disadvantage, because they were not organised under one leadership, as the Gandhi was. There was, till then, no party or group commanding the confidence of the entire Left Wing. Though at that time the Congress Socialist Party was the most important party in the Left Wing, its influence was limited. Moreover, when the fight between the Gandhi Wing and the writer began, even the Congress Socialist Party began to vacillate. Thus, in the absence of an organised and disciplined Left Wing, it was impossible for the writer to fight the Gandhi Wing. Consequently, India's primary political need in 1939 was an organsied and disciplined Left Wing Party in the Congress. The negotiations between Mahatma Gandhi and the writer revealed that on the one side, the Gandhi Wing would not follow the lead of the writer and that, on the other, the writer would not agree to be a puppet President. There was, consequently, no other alternative but to resign the Presidentship.

Bose and Gandhi

I remember vividly the scene of that afternoon. On arriving at Mani Bhawan, the usual residence of the Mahatma in Bombay, I was ushered into a room covered with Indian carpets. Almost in the centre, facing the door, sat the Mahatma surrounded by some of his closest followers. All were clad in home-made Khadi. As I entered the room, I felt somewhat out of place in my foreign costume and could not help apologising for it. The Mahatma received me with his characteristic smile and soon put me at ease and the conversation started at once. I desired to obtain a clear understanding of the details—the successive stages—of his plan, leading on step by step to the ultimate seizure of head question upon question and the

Mahatma replied with his habitual patience. There were three points which needed elucidation. Firstly, how were the different activities conducted by the Congress going to culminate in the last stage of the campaign, namely the non-payment of taxes? Secondly, how could mere non-payment of taxes or civil disobedience force the Government to retire from the filed and leave with our freedom? Thirdly, how could the Mahatma promise "Swaraj" (that is, Home Rule) within one year-as he had been doing ever since the Nagpur Congress?

His reply to the first question satisfied me. The response to his appeal for ten million members and ten million rupees having been found to be satisfactory, he had proceeded to the next item in his plan—namely, the boycott of foreign cloth and the propagation of home-made Khadi. During the next few months, his efforts would be concentrated on the Khadi campaign. And he expected that the Government would take the initiative in attacking the Congress, the moment it realised that the peaceful constructive activities of the Congress were proving to be successful. When the Government did so, the time would come for disobeying governmental degree and marching to prison. The prisons would before long be filled to overflowing and then would come the last stage of the campaign—namely, the non-payment of taxes.

The Mahatma's replies to the other two questions were not convincing. I asked him if he expected that the boycott movement would create so much distress in Lancashire that pressure would be brought to bear on Parliament and the Cabinet to make peace with India, But the Mahatma gave me to understand that he did not consider that to be the means whereby the Government would be forced to come with terms with the Congress. What his real expectation was, I was unable to understand. Either he did not want to give out all his secrets prematurely or he did not have clear conception of the tactics whereby the hands of the Government could be forced. (Footnote: Looking back on the incident today, it strikes me that possibly the Mahatma expected a 'change of heart' on the part of the British Government, leading to an acceptance of India's national demands.) Altogether, his reply to the second question was disappointing and his reply to the third was no better. What was to him a question of faith—namely, that Swaraj would be won within one year—was by no means clear to me and personally speaking, I was prepared to work for a much longer period. However, I had not other course but to feel thankful for what I had been able to learn after an hour's conversation.

But though I tried to persuade myself at the same time that there must have been a lack of understanding on my part, my reason told me clearly, again and again, that there was a deplorable lack of clarity in the plan in which the Mahatma had formulated and that he himself did not have a clear idea of the successive stages of the campaign which would bring India to her cherished goal of freedom.

Depressed and disappointed as I was, what was I to do? The Mahatma advised me to report myself to Deshabandhu CR Das on reaching Calcutta.

Bose on Clash with Gandhi

Extracted from The Indian Struggle by Subhash Chandra Bose published by Research Publishing & Printing Foundation, Kolkata, India. In December, 1937, the writer (Netaji) paid another visit to his favourite health-resort, Badgastein, in Austria, and from there he visited England. While in England, in January, 1938, he received news that he had been unanimously elected President of the Congress. During the course of this visit, he met members of the British Cabinet, like Lord Halifax and Lord Zetland, as well as prominent members of the Labour and Liberal parties who then professed sympathy for India, *e.g.* Mr Attlee, Mr Arthur Greenwood, Mr Bevin, Sir Stafford Cripps, Mr Harold Laski, Lord Allen, etc.

As Congress President, the writer did his best to stiffen the opposition of the Congress Party to any compromise with Britain and this caused annoyance in Gandhian circles who were then looking forward to an understanding with the British Government. Later in the year 1938, he launched the National Planning Committee for drawing up a comprehensive plan of industrialisation and of national development. This caused further annoyance to Mahatma Gandhi who was opposed to industrialisation. After the Munich Pact, In September, 1938, the writer began an open propaganda throughout India in order to prepare the Indian people for a national struggle, which should synchronise with the coming war in Europe. This move, through popular among the people in general, was resented by the Gandhites who did not want to be disturbed in their ministerial and parliamentary work and who were at that time opposed to any national struggle.

The breach between the writer and the Gandhi Wing was now wide, though not visible to the public. At the Presidential election in January, 1939, he was therefore vigorously opposed by the Gandhi Wing as well as by Pandit Nehru. Nevertheless, he was victorious with a comfortable majority. This was the first time since 1923-24 that the Mahatma suffered a public defeat and in his weekly paper, Harijan, he openly acknowledged this defeat. The election had served to show the wide and influential following that the writer had, throughout the country, in open opposition to both Gandhi and Nehru. In March, 1939, at the annual session of the Congress, the writer who presided made a clear proposal that the Indian National Congress should immediately send an ultimatum to the British government demanding Independence within six months and should simultaneously prepare for a national struggle. This proposal was opposed by the Gandhi Wing and by Nehru and was thrown out. This situation arose in which though the writer was the President of the Congress, his lead was not accepted by that body. Moreover, it was seen that on every conceivable occasion, the Gandhi Wing was opposing the President with a view to making it impossible for him to function. A complete deadlock within the Congress was the result. There were two ways of removing this deadlock—either the Gandhi Wing should give up its obstructionist policy, or the President should submit to the Gandhi Wing.

With a view to finding a possible compromise, direct negotiations between Mahatma Gandhi and the writer took place, but they proved to be abortive. Under the Constitution of the Congress, the President was entitled to appoint the Executive (Working Committee) for the coming year, but it was clear that the Gandhi Wing would continue to obstruct, if the Executive was not appointed according to its choice. And the position of the Gandhi Wing within the Congress was such that determined obstruction on its part would render its virtually impossible for the President to function in an independent manner.

The Gandhi Wing was determined neither to accept the lead of the writer, nor to allow him control the machinery of the Congress, and it would tolerate him only as a puppet President. The Gandhi Wing had, moreover, this tactical advantage that it was the organised party within the Congress, acting under a centralised leadership. The Left Wing or the radical elements in the Congress who were responsible for the writer's re-election as President in January, 1939, were numerically in a majority—but they were at a disadvantage, because they were not organised under one leadership, as the Gandhi was. There was, till then, no party or group commanding the confidence of the entire Left Wing. Though at that time the Congress Socialist Party was the most important party in the Left Wing, its influence was limited. Moreover, when the fight between the Gandhi Wing and the writer began, even the Congress Socialist Party began to vacillate. Thus, in the absence of an organised and disciplined Left Wing, it was impossible for the writer to fight the Gandhi Wing. Consequently, India's primary political need in 1939 was an organsied and disciplined Left Wing Party in the Congress.

The negotiations between Mahatma Gandhi and the writer revealed that on the one side, the Gandhi Wing would not follow the lead of the writer and that, on the other, the writer would not agree to be a puppet President. There was, consequently, no other alternative but to resign the Presidentship.

Netaji's Message to Gandhi

- Mahatmaji,
- Now that you health has somewhat improved, and you are able to attend to public business to some extent, I am taking the liberty of addressing a few words to you

with a view to acquainting you with the plans and the activities of patriotic Indians outside India.

- Before I do so, I would like to inform you of the feelings of deep anxiety which Indians throughout the World had for several days, after your sudden release form the custody on grounds of ill-health. After the sad demise of Srimati Kasturbaiji in British custody, it was but natural for your countrymen to be alarmed over the state of your health. It has, however, pleased Providence to restore you to comparative health, so that 388 millions of your countrymen may still have the benefit of your guidance and advice.
- I should next like to say some thing about the attitude of your countrymen outside India toward yourself. What I shall say in this connection is the bare truth and nothing but the truth.
- There are Indians outside India, as also at home, who are convinced that Indian Independence will be won only through the historic method of struggle. These men and women honestly feel that the British Government will never surrender to persuasion or moral pressure or nonviolent resistance. Nevertheless, for Indians outside India, differences in method are like domestic differences.
- Ever since you sponsored the Independence resolution at the Lahore Congress in December, 1929, all members of the Indian National Congress have had one common goal before them. For Indians outside India, you are the creator of the present awakening in our country. In all their propaganda before the world, they give you that position and the respect that is due to that position. For the world-public, we Indian nationalists are all one-having but one goal, one desire and one endeavour in life. In all the countries free from British influence that I have visited since I left India in 1941, you are held in the highest esteem, as no other Indian political leader has been, during the last century.

- Each nation has its own internal politics and its own attitude towards political problems. But that cannot affect a Nation's appreciation of a man who has served his people so well and has bravely fought a first-class modern power all his life. In fact, your worth and your achievements are appreciated a thousand times more in those countries that are opposed to the British Empire than in those countries that pretend to be friends of Freedom and Democracy. The high esteem in which you are held by the patriotic Indians outside India and by foreign friends of India's Freedom, was increased a hundred-fold when you bravely sponsored the 'quit India' resolution in August, 1942.
- From my experience of the British Government while I was inside India-from the secret information that I have gathered about Britain's policy while outside India-and from what I have seen regarding Britain's aims and intentions throughout the world, I am honestly convinced that the British Government will never recognise India's demand for Independence. Britain's one effort today is to exploit India to the fullest degree, in her endeavour to win this war. During the course of this war Britain has lost one part of her territory to her enemies and another part to her friends. Even if Allies could somehow win the war, it will be United States of America, and not Britain, that will be top dog in future and it will mean that Britain will become a protege of U.S.A.
- In such a situation the British will try to make good their present losses by exploiting India more ruthlessly than ever before. In order to do that, plans have been already hatched in London for crushing the nationalist movement in India, once for all. It is because I know of these plans from secret, but reliable sources, that I feel it my duty to bring it to your notice.
- It would be a fatal mistake on our part to make a distinction between British Government and the British people. No doubt there is a small group of idealists in Britain-as in the U.S.A.-who would like to see India

free. These idealists, who are treated by their own people as cranks, from a microscopic minority. So far as India is concerned, for all practical purposes the British Government and the British people mean one and the same thing.

- Regarding the war aims of the U.S.A., I may say that the ruling clique at Washington is now dreaming of world domination. This ruling clique and its intellectual exponents, talk openly of the 'American Century,' that is, that in the present century the U.S.A. will dominate the world. In this ruling clique, there are extremists who go so far as to call Britain the 49th State if the U.S.A.
- There is no Indian whether at home or abroad, who would not be happy if India's freedom could be won through the method that you have advocated all your life and without shedding human blood. But things being what they are, I am convinced that if we do desire freedom we must be prepared to wade through blood.
- If circumstances had made it possible for us to organise an armed struggle inside India, throughout our own efforts and resources, that would have been the best course for us. But, Mahatmaji, you know Indian conditions perhaps better than anybody else. So far as I am concerned after twenty years' experience of public service in India, I came to the conclusion that it was impossible to organise an armed resistance in the country with out the help from outside-help from countrymen abroad, as well as from some foreign power or powers.
- Prior to the outbreak of the present war, it was exceedingly difficult to get help from a foreign power, or from Indians abroad. But the outbreak of the present war threw open the possibility of obtaining aid-both political, and military-from the enemies of the British Empire. Before I could expect any help from them, however, I had first to find out what their attitude was towards India's demand for freedom. British propagandists for a number of years, had been telling

the world that the Axis Powers were the enemies of Freedom and, therefore, of India's freedom. Was that a fact? I asked myself. Consequently, I had to leave India in order to find the truth myself and as to whether the Axis Powers would be prepared to give us help and assistance in our fight for freedom.

- Before I finally made up my mind to leave home and homeland, I had to decide whether it was right for me to take help from abroad. I had previously studied the history of revolutions all over the world, in order to discover the methods which had enabled other nations to obtain freedom. But, I had not found a single instance in which an enslaved people had won freedom without foreign help of some sort. In 1940, I read my history once again, I came to the conclusion that history did not furnish a single instance where freedom had been won with out help of some sort from abroad. As for the moral question whether it was right to take help, I told myself that in public, as in private life one can always take help as a loan and repay that loan later on. Moreover, if a powerful Empire, like the British Empire, could go round the world with the begging bowl, what objection could there be to an enslaved and disarmed people like ourselves taking help as a loan from abroad.
- I cam assure you, Mahatmaji, that before I finally decided to set out on a hazardous mission, I spent days, weeks and months in carefully considering the pros and cons of the case. After having served my people so long, to the best of my ability, I could have no desire to be a traitor or to give anyone a justification for calling me a traitor.
- It was the easiest thing for me to remain at home and go on working as I had worked so long. It was also an easy thing for me to remain in an Indian prison while the War lasted. Personally, I had nothing to loose by doing so. Thanks to the generosity and to the affection of my countrymen, I had obtained the highest honour which it was possible for any public worker in India to

achieve. I had also built up a party consisting of staunch and loyal colleagues who had implicit confidence in me.

- By going abroad on a perilous quest, I was risking-not only my life and my whole future career-but what was more, the future of my party. If I had the slightest hope that without action from abroad we could win freedom, I would never have left India during a crisis. If I had any hope that within our life time we would get another chance-another golden opportunity-for winning freedom, as during the present war, I doubt if I would have set from home. But I was convinced of two things; firstly, that such a golden opportunity would not come within another century-and secondly, that without action from abroad, we would not be able to win freedom, merely through our own efforts at home. That is why I resolved to take the plunge.
- Providence has been kind to me. In spite of manifold difficulties, all my plans have succeeded so far. After I got out of India, my first endeavour was to organise my countrymen, where I happened to meet them. I am glad to say that everywhere I found them to be wide awake and anxious to do everything possible for winning freedom for India. I then approached the Governments that were at war with our enemy, in order to find out what their attitude was towards India. I found out that contrary to what British propagandists had been telling us for a number of years-the Axis Powers were now, openly, the friends of India's freedom. I also discovered that they were prepared to give such help as we desired, and as was within their own power.
- I know the propaganda that our enemy has been carrying on against me. But I am sure that my countrymen, who knew me so well, will never be taken in. One who had stood for national self-respect and honour all his life and has suffered considerably in vindicating it, would be the last person in this world to give into any other foreign power. Moreover, I have nothing to gain personally at the hands of a foreign power. Having

received the highest honour, possible for an Indian at the hands of my own countrymen, what is there for me to receive from a foreign power? Only that man can be a puppet who has either no sense of honour and self-respect or desires to built up a position for himself, through the influence of others.

- Not even my worst enemy can even dare to say that I am capable of selling national honour and self-respect. And not even my worst enemy can dare to assert that I was nobody in my own country and that I needed foreign help to secure a position for myself. In leaving India, I had to risk everything that I had, including my life. But, I had to take that risk, because only by doing so could I help the achievement of India's freedom.
- There remains but one question for me to answer with regard to the Axis powers. Can it be possible that I have been deceived by them?
- I believe it will be universally admitted that the cleverest and the most cunning politicians are to be found amongst the Britishers. One who has worked with and fought British politicians all his life, can not be deceived by any other politicians in the world. If British politicians have failed to coax or coerce me, no other politician can succeed in doing so. And if the British Government, at whose hands I have suffered long imprisonment, persecution and physical assault, has been able to demoralize me, no other power can hope to do so.
- Moreover, as you personally are aware, I have been a close student of international affairs. I have had personal contacts with international figures before the outbreak of this war. I am, therefore, no novice, who could be duped by a shrewd and cunning politician. Last but not the least, before forming an opinion about the attitude of the Axis powers, I established close personal contact with important leaders and personalities in the Axis countries, who are responsible for their national affairs.
- Consequently, I make bold to say that my countrymen can have the fullest confidence in my judgement of

international affairs. My countrymen abroad will testify to the fact that since I left India, I have never done anything which could compromise in the least, either the honour or the self respect or the interest of my country. On the contrary, whatever I have done has been for the benefit of my nation for enhancing India's prestige before the world and for advancing the cause of India's freedom.

- Mahatmaji, since the beginning of the War in East Asia, our enemies have been carrying on a raging and tearing campaign against Japan. I shall, therefore, say something about Japan-particularly because at the present moment, I am working in the closest cooperation with the Government, Army and people of Japan.
- There was a time when Japan had an alliance with our enemy. I did not come to Japan, so long as there was an Anglo-Japanese alliance. I did not come to Japan, so long as normal diplomatic relations obtained between the two countries. It was only after Japan took what I consider to be the most momentous step in her history-namely declaration of war on Britain and America-that I decided to visit Japan of my own free will.
- Like so many of my countrymen, I read anti-Japanese propaganda material for a number of years. Like so many of my countrymen, I did not understand why Japan went to war with China in 1937. And like so many of my countrymen, my sympathies in 1937 and 1938 were with Chungking. You may remember that as President of the Congress, I was responsible for sending out a medical mission to Chungking in December 1938. But, what I realised after my visit to Japan and what many people at home do not yet realise, is that since the outbreak of the War in East Asia, Japan's attitude towards the world in general, and towards Asiatic nations in particular has been completely revolutionised.
- It is a change that has overtaken not merely the Government, but also the people of Japan. A new consciousness-what I may best describe as an Asiatic consciousness-has seized the souls of the people of Japan.

- That change explains Japan's present attitude towards the Philippines, Burma and India. That is what explains Japan's new policy in China.
- After my visit to Japan and after establishing close contact with the present day leaders of that country, I was fully satisfied that Japan's present policy towards Asia was no bluff but was rooted in sincerity.
- This is not the first instance in history when an entire nation has been seized with a new consciousness. We have seen instances of it before in France during the French revolution and in Russia during the Bolshevik revolution. After my second visit to Japan in November 1943, I visited the Philippines, met Filipino leaders there and saw things for myself. I have also been in Burma for a fairly long time and I have been able to see things with my own eyes after the declaration of independence. And I have been to China to find out if Japan's new policy was real, or if it was fake. The latest agreement between Japan and the National Government of China has given the Chinese people practically all that they had been demanding. Japan, under that agreement, has even agreed to withdraw her troops from China on the termination of hostilities.
- What then is Chunking-China fighting for? Can one believe that Britain and America are helping Chungking-China out of purely altruistic motives? Will not Britain and America demand their pound of flesh in return for the help that they are now giving to Chungking to make her continue the fight against Japan? I clearly see that Chungking is being mortgaged to Britain and America, because of past hatred and antagonism towards Japan.
- So long as Japan did not initiate her present policy towards China, there might have been some justification or excuse for a Chinese to seek British and American aid for fighting Japan. But now that an entirely new chapter in Sino-Japanese relations has begun, there is not the slightest excuse for Chungking to continue her meaningless struggle against Japan. That is not good for Chinese people; it is certainly not good for Asia.

- In April, 1942, you said that if you were free to do so, you would work for an understanding between China and Japan. That was an utterance of rare statesmanship. It is India's slavery that is at the bottom, responsible for the chaos in China. It is because of the British hold over India that the Anglo-Americans could bluff Chungking into hoping that sufficient help could be brought to Chungking to continue the war against Japan. You were absolutely right in thinking, Mahatmaji that a free India would work for peace between Japan and China. I go so far to say that the freedom of India will automatically bring about an honourable understanding between Chungking and Japan, by opening the eyes of Chungking to the folly that she is now committing.
- Since I came to East Asia and visited China, I have been able to study the Chinese question more deeply. I find that there is a dictatorship ruling in Chungking. I have no objection personally to dictatorship, if it is for righteous cause. But the dictatorship that rules at Chungking is clearly under foreign American influence. Unfortunately, the Anglo-Americans have been able to deceive the ruling clique at Chungking into thinking that if Japan could be somehow defeated, then China would become the dominant power in Asia.
- It is through this false hope of becoming the dominant power inn Asia, if Japan could be somehow defeated, that the ruling clique at Chungking has entered into an unholy alliance with the ruling clique at White House and at Whitehall. I know something of the propagandist activities of the Chungking Government in India and of its efforts to play upon the emotions of the Indian people and win their sympathy. But I can honestly say that Chunking, which has been mortgaged to Wall Street and Lombard Street, does not deserve the sympathy of the Indian people any longer, especially after Japan has initiated her new policy towards China.
- Mahatmaji, you know better than anybody else how deeply suspicious the Indian people are for mere

promises. I would be the last man to be influenced by Japan if her declarations of policy had been mere promises. But I have seen with my own eyes, how in the mildest of the World War, Japan has put through revolutionary changes in countries like the Philippines, Burma and National china. Japan is true to her word and her actions are in full conformity with her declarations.

- Coming to India, I must say that Japan has proved her sincerity by her deeds. There was a time when people used to say that Japan had selfish intentions regarding India. If she had them, why should she recognize the Provisional government of Free India? Why should she decide to hand over Andaman and Nicobar Islands to the Provisional Government of Free India? Why should there now be an Indian Chief Commissioner of the Andaman and Nicobar Islands stationed at Port Blair? Last but not the least, why should Japan unconditionally help the Indian people in East Asia in their struggle for their Independence?
- There are Indians all over East Asia and they have every opportunity of seeing Japan at close quarters. Why should three million Indians distributed all over East Asia, adapt a policy of the closest cooperation with Japan, if they had not been convinced of her bonafides and her sincerity? You can coerce one man or coax him into doing what you want him to do. But no one can coerce three million Indians distributed all over East Asia.
- If Indians in East Asia had taken help from Japan without putting forward their own efforts and without making the maximum sacrifice, they would have been guilty of wrongdoing. But, as an Indian, I am happy and proud to be able to say that my countrymen in East Asia are putting forward the maximum efforts to mobilise men, money and materials for the struggle of India's freedom.

- I have had experienced at home in collecting funds and materials and in recruiting men for national service for a period of twenty years. In the light of this experience, I can properly assess the worth and value of the sacrifice that, our countrymen in East Asia are now making. Their effort is magnificent. It is because they are putting forward a magnificent effort themselves and are prepared to make the maximum sacrifice that I see no objection to taking help from Japan for such necessary articles as Arms, Ammunition, etc., that we ourselves cannot produce.
- Mahatmaji, I should now like to say something about the Provisional Government that we have set up here. The Provisional Government of Azad Hind (or Fee India) has been recognised by Japan, Germany and seven other friendly powers and this has given Indians a new status and a new prestige in the eyes of the whole world. The Provisional Government has, as its one objective, the liberation of India from the British yoke, through an armed struggle. Once our enemies are expelled from India and peace and order is established, the mission of the Provisional Government will be over. It will then be for the Indian people themselves to determine the form of Government that they choose and also to decide as to who should take charge of that Government.
- I can assure you, Mahatmaji, that I and all those who are working with me, regard themselves as the servants of the Indian people. The only reward that we desire for our efforts, for our suffering and for our sacrifice is the freedom of our Motherland. There are many among us who would like to retire from the political field, once India is free. The remainder will be content to take up any position in Free India, however humble it may be. The spirit that animates all of us today is that it is more honourable to be even a sweeper in Free India, than to have the highest position under British rule. We all know that there are hundreds of thousands of able men and women at home to whom India's destiny could be entrusted, once freedom is achieved.

- How much help we shall need from Japan till the last Britisher is expelled from the soil of India, will depend on the amount of cooperation that we shall receive from inside India. Japan herself does not desire to thrust her assistance upon us. Japan will be happy if the Indian people could liberate themselves through their own exertions. It is we who have asked for assistance from Japan after declaring war on Britain and America, because our enemy has been seeking help from other powers. However, I have every hope that the help we shall received from our countrymen at home will be so great that we shall need the minimum help from Japan.
- Nobody would be more happy than ourselves, if by any chance our country men at home should succeed in liberating themselves through their own efforts, or if by any chance, the British Government accepts your 'Quit India' Resolution and gives effect to it. We are, however, proceeding on the assumption that neither of the above is possible and that an armed struggle is inevitable.
- Mahatmaji, there is one other matter to which I shall refer before I close and that is about the ultimate outcome of this war. I know very well the kind of propaganda that our enemies have been carrying on in order to create the impression that they are confident of victory. But I hope that my countrymen will not be duped thereby, and will not think of compromising with Britain on the issue of independence under the mistaken notion that the Anglo-Americans will win this war.
- Having travelled around the world under wartime conditions with my eyes open, having seen the internal weakness of the enemy on the Indo-Burma frontier and inside India, and having taken stock of our own strength and resources, I am absolutely confident of our final victory.
- I am not so foolish to minimise, in the least the strength of the enemy. I know that we have a long and hard struggle in front of us. I am aware that on the soil of India, Britain will fight bravely and fight hard in a

desperate attempt to save her Empire. But I also know that, however long and hard the struggle may be, it can have but one outcome-namely, our victory.

- India's last war of Independence has begun. Troops of the Azad Hind Fauj are now fighting bravely on the soil of India and in spite of all difficulty and hardship; they are pushing forward, slowly but steadily. This armed struggle will go on,.until the last Britisher is thrown out of India and until out Tricolour National Flag proudly floats over the Viceroy's house in New Delhi.
- Father of our nation! In this holy war for India's liberation, we ask for your blessings and good wishes.

JAI HIND.

SWARAJ OR GANDHI RAJ

Dr. George Da Silva, a veteran Congressman and president of the Mahakoshal Forward Bloc, wrote the following in March 1941.

The correspondence that passed between Mahatma Gandhi and Desgaurub (Pride of the Nation) Subhash Chandra Bose which has been released to the press by Sj (Mr) Mukundalal Sircar, is most amazing and at the same time, most edifying as it bears direct relation to our political stalemate and deadlock. The Mahatma has rejected the offer of cooperation humbly submitted by Subhash merely on the grounds of fundamental difference leaving the public in the dark as to the nature of it. This summary refusal without the least consideration of its different aspect at this juncture may well be described as another of Mahatma's Himalayan blunder. Subhash has been and will be in the Congress and this fundamental difference which smacks of Tripuri and Rajkot bungle and its after developments leave no doubt that it is of vindictive nature. If this difference between the two Congressmen could not even be transitorily adjusted at this hours of India's repudiation, what hope is there and could be there of any settlement an even semblance of unity which is dear to the Mahatma's heart between the Congress leadership and other parties?

It is in the knowledge of every one that the differences between the Mahatma and other parties could not be of less fundamental or easier solution. Are not the talks, the pourparlers and the conferences that have taken place and are being arranged, a mere camouflage to hood-wink the credulous and the ignorant and to best serve his own purpose of securing the following and impress the Government of his magical influence. Mahatma's recent statements to the Secretary of the All-India Students' Federation, that students should not involve themselves in power-politics and his further remark to the Secretary of the Nagpur Provincial Congress Committee that fair weather politicians should automatically leave the field, though beautifully vague are clear indication of his dictatorial tendencies.

In whichever way the Mahatma may rationlise, he may indulge in sublimation and whatever terrestrial and celestial merit of his theory of nonviolence may possess, the rejection of Subhas's offer is a pointer that the Mahatma's genius for remorseless and cold fanaticism is a cloak for real Politik. With this background and previous history, does it lie in the mouth of the Mahatma's followers that the other parties distrust him and doubt his bonafides?

Are not his proposal of Constituent Assembly, the provision of fundamental rights of citizens and safeguarding of religion and culture which are so much boasted are a mere eyewash? For, where is the guarantee that the country will not be ruled by fancies and fads and by crooks and cranks? There could not be a greater indictment of the Mahatma's policy and the demand for National Government than that made by Dr. Sumant Mehta, an eminent and veteran politician of Gujarat, when he said in one of his talks here that if the British Government grant the Mahatma's request, it will not be Swaraj but Gandhi Raj.

Day in and day out it has been dinned into our ears that we are fighting for our freedom. The perennial track to the jail has commenced and is in the progress This time to vindicate our freedom of speech but not unfortunately for independence. This expression has become a mere slogan and shibboleth without essential significance which ought to be attached to it.

For, freedom means self-expression and the secret of freedom is courage and ability to utilize the opportunity that comes our way. One cannot help crying over the split-milk for the Congress command has lost many good occasions by their obsession to brig about the desired unity in the past and there is every possibility that they will miss the present one.

The war situation is an opportunity which should have been used to stop the rudder less drift in our political destiny and for the salvation of the country but the lack of courage on part of our eminent public men, politicians and publicists to criticise the outworn and outlive leadership which is leading the country to a catastrophe. The Mahatma is said to be best friend of the British in India. He may not be an enemy of the country, yet, it is the duty of the public, specially of those who think for themselves to see that the Mahatma is not permitted to ride his hobby-horse when the country is about to be on fire.

BIBLIOGRAPHY

Arun, Pseud.: *Testament of Subhas Bose*, Delhi, Rajkamal Pub., 1946.

Bose, Mihir: *The Lost Hero: A Biography of Subhas Chandra Bose*, London, Quartet Books, 1982.

Bose, S. C., *The Indian Struggle, 1920-1942,* Bombay, Asia Publishing House, 1964.

Bose, Sisir K., and A. Werth and S.A. Ayer: *A Beacon Across Asia: A Biography of Subhas Chandra Bose*, New Delhi, Orient Longman, 1973.

Chakrabarty, B.: *Subhas Chandra Bose and Middle Class Radicalism: A Study in Indian Nationalism, 1928-1940*, London / New York, I. B. Taurus, 1990.

Chaudhuri, Kali P.: *Netaji and India,* Shillong, Kali Prasanna Chaudhuri, 1956.

Das, Hari Hara: *Subhas Chandra Bose and the Indian National Movement*, New Delhi, Sterling Publishers, 1983.

Ganpuley, N.G.: *Netaji in Germany: A Little-known Chapter*, Bombay, Bharatiya Vidya Bhavan, 1959.

Ghosh, K. K.: *The Indian National Army: Second Front of the Indian Independence Movement*, Meerut, Meenakshi Prakashan, 1969.

Hari Hara Das: *Subhas Chandra Bose and the Indian National Movement,* New Delhi, 1983.

Hayashida, T.: *Netaji Subhas Chandra Bose: His Great Struggle and Martyrdom*, Bombay, Allied Publishers, 1970.

Kitty Kurti: *Subhas Chandra Bose As I Knew Him,* Calcutta, Firma K.L. Mukhopadhyay, 1966.

Kurti, Kitty: *Subhas Chandra Bose As I Knew Him*, Calcutta, Firma K.L. Mukhopadhyay, 1966.

Mihir Bose: *The Lost Hero: A Biography of Subhas Chandra Bose*, London/Melbourne/New York, Quartet Books, 1982

Nair, A. M.: *An Indian Freedom Fighter in Japan*, Bombay, Orient Longman, 1983.

Noorani, A.G. : *Indian Political Trials : 1775-1947*, New Delhi, Oxford University Press, 2005.

Ram, S. and R. Kumar : *Encyclopaedia of Indian Freedom Struggle*, Commonwealth Pub., New Delhi, 2008.

Roy, Dilip Kumar: *The Subhash I Knew*, Bombay, Nalanda Publications, 1946.

Sopan, Pseud: *Netaji Subhas Chandra Bose. His Life and Work*, Bombay, Azad Bhandar, 1946.

Tagore, Rabindranath : *The Art of Tagore*, New Delhi, Rupa and Co., 2004.

Thomas, Vettickal : *Gandhian Sarvodaya : Realizing a Realistic Utopia*, New Delhi, Gyan Publishing House, 2002.

Thomas, Weber : *Gandhi, Gandhism and the Gandhians*, New Delhi, Roli Books, 2006.

Toye, Hugh: *The Springing Tiger: A Study of a Revolutionary*, London, Cassell, 1959.

Tripathi, Sridhar : *Gandhi's Philosophy of Education*, New Delhi, Anmol, 2007.

Verma, B.R. and S.R. Bakshi : *Gandhian Satyagraha and His Technique (1920-1928)*, New Delhi, Commonwealth, 2005.

INDEX

❑❑❑

Defective

Author's name on the spine is obscure.

Shuh
1/9/09